ETHICS OF DEALING
WITH PERSONS
WITH SEVERE HANDICAPS

ETHICS OF DEALING WITH PERSONS WITH SEVERE HANDICAPS
TOWARD A RESEARCH AGENDA

edited by

Paul R. Dokecki, Ph.D.

*John F. Kennedy Center for Research on
Education and Human Development
George Peabody College
Vanderbilt University
Nashville, Tennessee*

and

Richard M. Zaner, Ph.D.

*Department of Medicine
School of Medicine
Vanderbilt University
Nashville, Tennessee*

·P A U L·H·
BROOKES
PUBLISHING CO.

Baltimore · London

Paul H. Brookes Publishing Co.
Post Office Box 10624
Baltimore, MD 21285-0624

Copyright © 1986 by Paul H. Brookes Publishing Co., Inc.
All rights reserved.

Typeset by The Composing Room, Grand Rapids, Michigan.
Manufactured in the United States of America by
The Maple Press Company, York, Pennsylvania.

Library of Congress Cataloging-in-Publication Data
Ethics of dealing with persons with severe handicaps.

Based on a conference organized by the John F. Kennedy Center for
Research on Education and Human Development and Vanderbilt University's Center for Clinical and Research Ethics, held in spring 1985.

Includes bibliographies and index.
1. Mental retardation—Moral and ethical aspects—Congresses.   2.
Mental retardation—Social aspects—Congresses.   I. Dokecki, Paul
R.   II. Zaner, Richard M.   III. John F. Kennedy Center for Research
on Education and Human Development.   IV. Vanderbilt Univer-
sity.   Center for Clinical and Research Ethics.   [DNLM: 1. Decision
Making—congresses.   2. Ethics, Medical—congresses.   3. Mental
Retardation—congresses.   WM 300 E845 1985]
RC570.E85   1986   362.3   86-9648
ISBN 0-933716-65-6 (pbk.)

CONTENTS

CONTRIBUTORS

Harriet Able, Ph.D.
Research Associate
John F. Kennedy Center
Peabody College
Vanderbilt University
Nashville, TN 37203

Duane Alexander, M.D.
Director
National Institute of Child Health and
  Human Development
Building 31, Room 2A04
9000 Rockville Pike
Bethesda, MD 20892

Keith Allred, M.S.
Doctoral Student
Department of Special Education
Peabody College
Vanderbilt University
Nashville, TN 37203

Linda H. Backus, M.S.
Doctoral Candidate
Department of Special Education
University of Kansas
Lawrence, KS 66045

Donald M. Baer, Ph.D.
Roy A. Roberts Distinguished Professor
  of Human Development and Family
  Life and Psychology
1034 Haworth Hall
Department of Human Development
  and Family Life
University of Kansas
Lawrence, KS 66045

Patricia A. Barber, M.A.
Doctoral Candidate
Department of Special Education
University of Kansas
Lawrence, KS 66045

Bonnie Beck, M.S.
Doctoral Student
Department of Psychology
Peabody College
Vanderbilt University
Nashville, TN 37203

Shirley K. Behr, M.A.P.A.
Doctoral Candidate
Department of Special Education
University of Kansas
Lawrence, KS 66045

Martha Blue-Banning, M.Ed.
420 Fortson Drive
Athens, GA 30606

Elizabeth M. Boggs, Ph.D.
Henderson Road
R.D. 2, Box 439
Hampton, NJ 08827

Paul R. Dokecki, Ph.D.
Professor of Psychology and Special
  Education
and
Associate Director, John F. Kennedy
  Center
Box 6
Peabody College
Vanderbilt University
Nashville, TN 37203

William Donovan, Jr., M.Ed.
Doctoral Student
Department of Special Education
Peabody College
Vanderbilt University
Nashville, TN 37203

Craig R. Fiedler, Ph.D.
Department of Special Education
University of New Hampshire
Durham, NH 03828

Susan W. Gray, Ph.D.
Professor of Psychology Emerita
Box 151
Peabody College
Vanderbilt University
Nashville, TN 37203

Doug Guess, Ed.D.
Department of Special Education
Haworth Hall
University of Kansas
Lawrence, KS 66045

Stanley Hauerwas, Ph.D.
Professor of Theological Ethics
The Divinity School
Duke University
Durham, NC 27706

H. Carl Haywood, Ph.D.
Professor of Psychology and of
    Neurology
Box 9
Peabody College
Vanderbilt University
Nashville, TN 37203

Craig Anne Heflinger, M.A.
Doctoral Student
Department of Psychology
Peabody College
Vanderbilt University
Nashville, TN 37203

Edwin Helmstetter, Ph.D.
Department of Special Education
Washington State University
Pullman, WA 99164-2110

Kathleen V. Hoover-Dempsey, Ph.D.
Associate Professor of Psychology and
    Education
Box 319
Peabody College
Vanderbilt University
Nashville, TN 37203

Susan C. Hupp, Ph.D.
Assistant Professor of Educational
    Psychology
University of Minnesota
178 Pillsbury Drive, S.E.
Minneapolis, MN 55455

Georgia M. Kerns, M.Ed.
Doctoral Candidate
Department of Special Education
University of Kansas
Lawrence, KS 66045

John Lachs, Ph.D.
Professor of Philosophy
Box 12
Station B
Vanderbilt University
Nashville, TN 37235

Arthur C. Lowitzer, M.A.
Doctoral Student
Department of Special Education
Peabody College
Vanderbilt University
Nashville, TN 37203

William E. MacLean, Jr., Ph.D.
Assistant Professor of Psychology
Box 158
Peabody College
Vanderbilt University
Nashville, TN 37203

Robert M. Moroney, Ph.D.
Professor of Social Work
School of Social Work
Arizona State University
Tempe, AZ 85287

James M. Perrin, M.D.
Chief, Ambulatory Care and General
    Pediatrics
Children's Service
Massachusetts General Hospital
Boston, MA 02114

Charles E. Scott, Ph.D.
Professor of Philosophy
Box 1692
Station B
Vanderbilt University
Nashville, TN 37235

M. Shelton Smith, M.S.
Doctoral Student
Department of Psychology
Peabody College
Vanderbilt University
Nashville, TN 37203

Jean Ann Summers, B.G.S.
Acting Director
Kansas University Affiliated Facility
Bureau of Child Research
University of Kansas
Lawrence, KS 66045

Ann P. Turnbull, Ed.D.
Acting Associate Director
Bureau of Child Research
and
Professor, Department of Special
  Education
223 Haworth
University of Kansas
Lawrence, KS 66045

**H. Rutherford Turnbull, III, LL.B.,
LL.M.**
Professor of Special Education and Law
Haworth Hall
University of Kansas
Lawrence, KS 66045

Robert M. Veatch, Ph.D.
Professor of Medical Ethics
Kennedy Institute of Ethics
Georgetown University
Washington, DC 20057

Richard M. Zaner, Ph.D.
Ann Geddes Stahlman Professor of
  Medical Ethics
Department of Medicine
School of Medicine
Vanderbilt University
Nashville, TN 37232

PREFACE

THIS BOOK GREW from a conference on the ethics of intervention decision making for persons with severe mental retardation, held in the spring of 1985 at the John F. Kennedy Center for Research on Education and Human Development, a component of George Peabody College of Vanderbilt University. The conference served to rededicate the Kennedy Center—one of the 12 national mental retardation research centers—to the memory of President Kennedy's activities on behalf of persons with mental retardation. On October 11, 1961, Kennedy stated that "the manner in which our Nation cares for its citizens . . . is more than an index to its concern for the less fortunate. Both wisdom and humanity dictate a deep interest in the physically handicapped, the mentally ill, and the mentally retarded" (President's Panel, 1962, p. 196). President Kennedy's words and subsequent efforts illustrate the highest level of ethical commitment to fellow human beings.

Alfred A. Baumeister, director of the Kennedy Center, became interested in the ethical dimensions of mental retardation as a result of testifying before the U.S. Congress on behalf of the mental retardation research program of the National Institute of Child Health and Human Development (NICHD). He was struck by how often congressional comments and questions on apparently scientific-technical matters turned toward matters of value and ethical choice. He began to wonder whether research and scholarly inquiry had, or might come to have, something meaningful to contribute to the ethical debate. Over the last several years, Baumeister has eagerly helped to promote Kennedy Center work on the ethics of mental retardation. The 1985 conference and this book are among the fruits of his labors.

ETHICS AND MENTAL RETARDATION IN THE MODERN CONTEXT

John Dewey (1939) observed that human value issues become salient when we find ourselves in "conditions that are impending, obstructive, and that introduce conflict and need" (p. 54). Such turbulent conditions certainly pertain today in mental retardation. Issues regarding treatment of persons with mental retardation are emerging as among the most value-laden and contentious ones in American society. We are often reminded, as in President Kennedy's words just quoted, that an important criterion for judging the quality of a society is how its dependent and less fortunate people are treated.

But as in all other matters, Americans are not all of one voice on these issues. Whether (and how) persons with mental retardation should be treated, for what purposes, and at what costs are concerns that are discussed in the media, debated by legislators and government officials, and the subject of precedent-setting court cases.

Elizabeth M. Boggs, who helped us plan our conference, in the keynote chapter of this book, cites Paul Ramsey's (1971/1977) observation: "In any period when there is a moral consensus, ethics mainly gives backing to the consensus and few are needed for that important function. . . . Upon the absence of a moral consensus, [however], everyone needs to be an ethicist to the extent of his capacity for reflection and his desire to be and to know that he is a responsible person" (1971, p. 15). Epigrammatically, Ramsey can be translated as saying that in our socially turbulent modern context, just as war is too important to leave to the generals, ethics is too important to leave to the ethicists. In that spirit, we have brought together nationally recognized ethicists and others not primarily associated with the field of ethics but who have wide-ranging interests in mental retardation and related topics. We have tried to create an inquiring community to explore ethics and mental retardation from a variety of complementary perspectives.

We intend this book to be an instrument for placing the ethics of mental retardation squarely on the research agenda of many scholarly disciplines and for beginning to outline specific items on that agenda. Social and behavioral scientists, in particular, may need convincing that their disciplines have something to offer in the domain of ethics. It is one thing to engage in practice and research in an ethically responsible manner, perhaps guided by disciplinary ethical standards. It is quite another, however, to conduct research and scholarly inquiry with the specific intent of enriching the quality of ethical debate on vexing societal issues. But ethically relevant inquiry is precisely what we urge.

TOWARD A RESEARCH AGENDA

Boggs helps set the call for rational and evidence-based ethical discourse in mental retardation in a broad societal context. While not wishing to slight methodological issues, many of which will bedevil ethics researchers, she points out that "the most intractible dilemmas that will confront the investigators will be those involving conflict of values." For example, she asks: "Is it true that we can have liberty or equality but not both in full measure at the same time?" She urges scholars to gear their work to issues in the "middle of life," where real people encounter mental retardation's vexing everyday ethical dilemmas, rather than to people and topics "at the edges."

In Chapter 2, Paul R. Dokecki and his colleagues (Harriet Able, Keith Allred, Bonnie Beck, William Donovan, Jr., Craig Anne Heflinger, Arthur

Lowitzer, and Shelton Smith) develop a rationale for the possibility and desirability of rational and evidence-based ethical discourse in mental retardation. Their argument is nontraditional, counter to our prevailing emotivist culture and positivist-empiricist methodological world view. To help advance ethics research, they also report the results of three research activities: 1) a survey of leaders of major national organizations that deal with persons with mental retardation, in order to identify the most important current and emerging ethical views in the field; 2) a review of the literature in order to identify the ethical issues in mental retardation being addressed by the scholarly community; and 3) an analysis of the recommendations for future research made by leading scientists in mental retardation as part of NICHD's forward planning effort.

NICHD is the federal agency primarily responsible for funding research on mental retardation. In Chapter 3 of this volume, Duane Alexander, NICHD director, reports on the findings in mental retardation research by the National Commission for the Protection of Human Subjects of Biomedical and Behavioral Research. Although no final governmental action has been taken on this aspect of the commission's report, Alexander's chapter helps focus "attention as never before on the ethical issues and problems in conducting research on persons with mental retardation," and provides "useful guidance for IRBs [institutional review boards] to take into account when reviewing different types of research involving persons with different degrees of mental impairment, to determine acceptable risk and appropriate protection in the decision-making process."

In Chapter 4, Stanley Hauerwas explores the ethical complexities of the seemingly straightforward concept of the prevention of mental retardation. Through a penetrating analysis of the phenomenon of suffering, Hauerwas helps us see how we are all involved in mental retardation by virtue of our common humanity. Moreover, we begin to glimpse the contribution persons with mental retardation make to the human community since "prophetlike, the retarded only remind us of the insecurity hidden in our false sense of self-possession." Prevention, then, although it may be a worthy public goal from certain perspectives, must be seen as sometimes motivated by our own self-interest rather than sole concern for what persons with mental retardation suffer. Hauerwas would have us be free "from the false and vicious circle of having to appear strong before others' weakness" so that we may be "able to join with the retarded in the common project of sharing our needs and satisfactions."

Richard M. Zaner and the respondent to his chapter, John Lachs, next address Baby Doe and related issues, perhaps the best known and most debated set of ethical concerns in mental retardation today. Zaner asks: "What . . . are the prospects for and obstacles to ethically relevant research into intervention decisions on behalf of imperiled infants and fetuses?" He analyzes several cases in light of the newest public policies in this area. His identification of inconsistencies and remaining issues and Lachs's forthright addressing of the implications of the quality of life concept present pointed challenges to researchers and policy makers alike.

Susan W. Gray, a pioneer in early childhood intervention research whose work served as the inspiration for Project Head Start, has been concerned with the ethics of intervention research since the early 1960s. Although she has not worked in the area of severe handicaps, her widely acclaimed experience with economically disadvantaged young children and their families helps, as she states in Chapter 6 of this book, to "shed some sidelights on some of the ethical issues that arise in intervention research with children with severe retardation and their families." The respondent, Susan C. Hupp, extends Gray's observations through a consideration of ethics in the contexts first of intervention conceived of as a system and second of the intervention goal of providing "greater options for children with handicaps and their families."

Gray's work was a major influence in stimulating special educators to engage in early intervention with children with severe handicaps, especially through the agency of the family. An early inheritor of that legacy was Ann P. Turnbull. She and her colleagues in Chapter 7 (Martha Blue-Banning, Shirley Behr, and Georgia Kerns) take the initial steps in conducting a value and ethical examination of family research and intervention. Claiming that researchers seem to have a negative bias toward families of children with handicaps, the authors cite parents who ask: "Who are these researchers and why are they saying these things about us?" Turnbull et al. pose an ethical challenge to the research community by asking: "Where is the research on positive contributions?" The respondent, James M. Perrin, reiterates this concern for a more positive approach to understanding special children by extending the analysis to chronically ill children and their families.

Donald M. Baer, in Chapter 8, takes up an ethical issue that has emerged in federal court cases involving the rights of institutionalized persons with severe mental retardation. Although judges have consistently affirmed the public's responsibility to provide educational treatment in institutions, the limits of educability and of educational interventions have been hotly debated. Baer, who has served as an expert witness on this issue in several landmark court cases, argues for proceeding as a matter of policy, "as if all people are capable of learning under instruction, no matter how severe their retardation." The chapter's respondent, H. Carl Haywood[1], has also frequently

---

[1]Haywood, a past editor of the *American Journal of Mental Deficiency,* is uncomfortable with the linguistic convention adopted in this book to refer to people identified as disabled. The convention entails using the phrases "persons with severe handicaps" and "persons with mental retardation" in preference to "severely handicapped persons" and "mentally retarded persons." Apart from a certain awkwardness in the "persons with" construction, and granting the good motives of those who suggest "persons with" as an attempt to reduce the stigma and negative connotations often associated with the labeling process, Haywood argues that "persons with" is

served as an expert witness, and he attempts to temper somewhat Baer's position. Taken together, the chapter and response on the "issue of educability" delineate terms for further ethical debate and pose questions for additional empirical research.

Another legally contentious ethical matter concerns aversive procedures. In Chapter 9, H. Rutherford Turnbull, III, past president of the American Association on Mental Deficiency, and Doug Guess and their colleagues (Linda H. Backus, Patricia A. Barber, Craig R. Fiedler, Edwin Helmstetter, and Jean Ann Summers) use the case of aversive procedures to help develop and illustrate the application of a general approach for analyzing the moral aspects of special education and behavioral interventions. Drawing on several disciplinary perspectives and lines of ethical argument, Turnbull and Guess et al. attempt to recognize and deal with the complex realities of behavioral interventions, including existing empirical evidence, in order to enrich ethical discourse and improve the quality of intervention decisions. The respondent, William E. MacLean, Jr., further emphasizes the role of society in intervention, addressing the importance of efficacy in the ethics of intervention, and discussing legal and moral criteria for assessing interventions.

Robert Moroney, author of Chapter 10, and the respondent, Kathleen V. Hoover-Dempsey, pursue a value-based analysis of social policy for persons with severe handicaps, emphasizing family care. Moroney highlights the inadequacy of contemporary social policies, based as they are on the principle of economic rationality. Arguing for the principles of meaningful choice, reciprocity, and interdependency, Moroney identifies the critical value and ethical dimensions operating at the highest level of intervention decision making, that of public policy. Together, Moroney and Hoover-Dempsey raise important questions for researchers interested in the policy process, especially regarding the well-being of families.

Concern with intervention decisions in mental retardation almost invariably leads us to consider the role and functions of guardians, those empowered to make decisions for persons with severe retardation. Robert M. Veatch, in Chapter 11, presents a systematic ethical analysis of guardianship and makes a critical distinction between bonded and nonbonded guardians relative to the degree of discretion these different surrogates have in decision making. Operating much in the spirit of Boggs's call for ethical analysis in the "middle of life" rather than "at the edges," Veatch clearly tells us both what

---

misleading. "Persons with," Haywood asserts, tends to suggest that severe handicaps and mental retardation are conditions, deficits, or illnesses that persons "catch" or have inflicted upon them, and that those so inflicted should receive treatment that will restore them to a nonexistent prior "normal" state. The phrases "severely handicapped persons" and "mentally retarded persons," in contrast to their alternatives, are more graceful, are at least as socially responsible, and are more true to a view of disability as a social judgment made about certain people because of their discordance with environmental demands. Words are important, but Haywood is more than quibbling with words. Writers, editors, and readers should seriously consider the points he raises.

we know with confidence and what remains for ethics researchers to investigate about guardianship. Respondent Charles E. Scott helps us understand the assumptions and underlying structure of Veatch's argument so that we can more clearly envision the implications of adopting his perspective.

In summary, the authors contributing chapters and responses to this book raise many of the ethical issues encountered in making decisions for persons with severe handicaps over the life span. Their writings present a challenge to professional people and citizens alike to develop informed judgments about these crucial issues. The editors especially urge researchers and scholars to respond to this challenge by deploying their disciplinary methods in service of ethically relevant inquiry.

REFERENCES

Dewey, J. (1939). *Theory of valuation*. Chicago: University of Chicago Press.

President's Panel on Mental Retardation. (1962). *A proposed program for national action to combat mental retardation*. Washington, DC: Superintendent of Documents.

Ramsey, P. (1977). The nature of medical ethics. In S. J. Reiser, A. J. Dyck, & W. J. Curran (Eds.), *Ethics in medicine: Historical perspectives and contemporary concerns* (pp. 123–128). Cambridge, MA: MIT Press. (Reprinted from Veatch, R., Gaylin, W., & Morgan, C. [Eds.]. [1971]. *The teaching of medical ethics* [pp. 14–28]. Hastings-on-the Hudson, NY: Hastings Center.)

ACKNOWLEDGMENTS

WE ARE GRATEFUL to the many people and organizations that helped make possible the conference that spawned this book. Together with the John F. Kennedy Center for Research on Education and Human Development, Vanderbilt University's Center for Clinical and Research Ethics shared the primary responsibility for planning and operating the conference. Funds came from the Kennedy Center, the Center for the Study of Families and Children of the Vanderbilt Institute for Public Policy Studies, and the Vanderbilt University Research Council. Other sponsoring organizations included Vanderbilt's Center for Mental Health and Mental Retardation Policy Research, the Tennessee Department of Mental Health and Mental Retardation, and the National Institute of Child Health and Human Development (NICHD). The conference program committee included Harriet Able, Keith Allred, Bonnie Beck, William Donovan, Jr., Dianne Eberhard, Craig Anne Heflinger, Arthur Lowitzer, Jan Rosemergy, Shelton Smith, and Dona Tapp, all of Vanderbilt University; and Peter Vietze and Theodore Tjossem of the NICHD.

Special thanks are owed Dianne Eberhard. She played an indispensible administrative role in the conference and an equally valuable editorial role in preparing the manuscript.

ETHICS OF DEALING
WITH PERSONS
WITH SEVERE HANDICAPS

Chapter 1

ETHICS IN
THE MIDDLE OF LIFE
AN INTRODUCTORY OVERVIEW

Elizabeth M. Boggs

ETHICS IS A classical field of study, a branch of philosophy that, with logic and aesthetics, deals with one of what are often perceived to be the basic universal capacities of human beings: cognition, emotion, conscience— thinking, feeling, willing. Among academic disciplines, ethics is usually classed among the humanities. Its most consistent disciplinary neighbors are religion and law. In recent years, however, at least some people working in the field have claimed that ethics is a science. Ramsey (1971/1977), for example, calls ethics "the science of right and wrong conduct." This proposition seeks justification in the claim of ethics to be *systematic* and *rational.* There are some parallels between ethics and the conventional or natural sciences that may be worth exploring, particularly for a readership drawn from investigators or practitioners of the behavioral or biological sciences.

Calling ethics a science does not define it, of course. "Popularly, ethics seems to mean any body of prescriptions and prohibitions, do's and don'ts, that people consider to carry uncommon weight in their lives. When lives are deeply involved in certain activities, ethics can refer to the rules that guide those activities" (Jonsen & Hellegers, 1974, p. 3/1977). In addition to the normative content implied by popular definition, modern writers consider the scope of the discipline to include the study of processes by which moral questions are examined and resolved, and the ways in which the conclusions are put into practice whether at the individual or societal level (Dyck, 1973/1977). Jonsen and Hellegers (1974/1977) group these concerns under the heading of three theories, the theory of virtue, the theory of duties or action, and the theory of the common good. These theories respectively address: 1) the characteristics of the morally good man, 2) the nature of actions, their purposes and consequences, and the conditions of freedom and voluntariness under which they may be undertaken, and 3) the nature of a good society created by and forming the context for "good men acting rightly." All these concepts are relevant to the subject of this book.

Indeed the first one, the criteria for the virtuous man, must be raised with respect to the status of a person with mental impairment as a member of the moral community. This issue has received little attention in the past half century, although Macklin and Gaylin (1981) have treated it passim. Freedom and voluntariness are at the heart of current concerns for persons with disabilities, especially mental disabilities. As for the good society, can good men act rightly when ignorant of the nature of variability in their fellow men? One writer, for example, refers to "the fact of approximate equality," saying that although men differ from each other in intellectual capacity, none is so powerful as to be able to dominate another for more than a short period of time (Hart, 1965/1977). People with severe physical or mental disabilities and their advocates cannot accept Hart's premises. They are all too aware that historically, and even today, many disabled people have suffered severe and sustained repression and subjugation both in and out of institutions. Ethicists must join attorneys in confronting any presumption of "approximate equality" in personal power.

MORAL CONSENSUS

When ethicists speak of "moral principles" as being normative, they recognize that systems of ethics can be subject to reformulation from time to time. It appears that we are now living in such a time, a period of questioning and renewal in the discipline and in its impact on the general public as well as on men and women who belong to the helping professions. This renewal necessarily involves many people not trained in ethics as a specialty, a concession compatible with current consumerism. As Paul Ramsey (1971/1977) put it: "In any period when there is a moral consensus, ethics mainly gives backing to the consensus and few are needed for that important function. . . . upon the absence of a moral consensus [however], everyone needs to be an ethicist to the extent of his capacity for reflection and his desire to be and to know that he is a responsible person" (p. 15). "Everybody," however, may not have the same understanding of the task or willingness to participate in it.

Ramsey (1971/1977) further points out that when a breakdown in moral consensus occurs, it is usually signaled at the empirical level, at the point of application of an underlying hypothesis. "In fact ethical inquiry and discourse begin only when we discover we are in disagreement about what we ought to do. Then we are forced back upon our premises, and we must seek together in the human community . . . to find agreement at a deeper level.

We must ask about what makes anything right. We need to find out if we can agree [on fundamentals] . . . before returning to the specific case where we first disagreed'' (p. 15). Thus, during periods of consensus, only a few career ethicists may be needed as keepers of the faith, while little dramatic work is being done. It is when ethical dilemmas come to light that the pace of ethical debate quickens, becomes more strident, gets more public attention, and draws more "extras" onto the scene.

Ethical dilemmas are discovered empirically when someone attempts to apply what has been assumed to be a moral principle to a real life situation and finds an incompatibility, a *gegenbeispiel*. This is an example of application of a scientific method: develop an hypothesis or proposed principle, then postulate that it stands until it is found inconsistent with experience, or until a competing theory proves to be at least equally successful in explaining what is observed or in solving real-life problems. In applied physics, the test problem may be building a safe and usable bridge; in applied ethics it may be designing a legal system that "works" and enjoys popular support, thus passing the normative test, at least for the time being.

Ethical dilemmas when examined may be found to originate in substance (e.g., in the moral hypothesis that X is good) or in method (e.g., in the way in which the prescription for action was derived from the stated principle). Important as right method will be in moving us toward an "ethically relevant" research agenda, the most intractible dilemmas that will confront the investigators will be those involving conflicts of values.

Ramsey's (1978) well-known book, *Ethics at the Edges of Life,* comprises two parts: "At the first" and "At the last." Issues surrounding birth and death can be profiled more sharply, not only because of the heightened emotions associated with these events, but also because some variables become relatively unimportant as we move to these limits, thus simplifying ethical analysis. In contrast, life as it is experienced by individuals with severe disabilities in the middle of life, away from these edges, is likely to involve the interaction of many variables. They must deal with most of the factors others face and, in addition, those peculiar to their particular impairments. To be of help to service providers who seek to be ethical in their dealings, ethicists must be prepared to move toward the middle.

A SECULAR PERSPECTIVE

We are all familiar with the concept of ebb and flow in human affairs over time and especially in political, social, and philosophical thinking. Futurists see this as a qualitatively predictable phenomenon and have studied how movements originate, gain momentum, crest in wave form, and subside, only to be overtaken by a new surge, different but nevertheless similar in some respects (Cetron & Clayton, 1977). Such a cycle whose content comes close to our concerns has been described by Gaylin, Glasser, Marcus, and Rothman (1978), who document the recent displacement of many of the assumptions of the so-called Progressive Era, assumptions that prevailed during the first two-thirds of this century. "Put most succinctly," says Rothman, "the commitment to paternalistic state intervention in the name of equality is giving way to a commitment to restrict intervention in the name of liberty. . . . there now exists a widespread and acute suspicion of doing good among widely divergent groups on all points of the political spectrum" (pp. 73–74, 82). What used to be seen as "humanitarian" is now suspect, if not presumptively bad, because it smacks of coercion of the individual by the state, a hazard to which Americans are especially attuned by their history, as Glasser points out (Gaylin et al., 1978, p. 99). Is it true that we can have liberty or equality but not both in full measure at the same time?

In a recent editorial in *Science* entitled "The Undesirability Principle," Koshland (1985) draws an analogy using the rule of physics known as the uncertainty principle. This rule states that "the product of the uncertainties in two related quantities—the momentum of a particle and its position in space—is equal to or greater than a constant. This means that any choice that investigators make to increase the certainty in one variable is automatically paid for by increased uncertainty in the other variable" (p. 9). Koshland goes on to enunciate "the undesirability principle" by stating that "the product of the costs of two or more conflicting courses of action is a constant. Society, therefore, can obtain one goal to whatever degree of desirability it wishes provided that it is willing to pay the price in loss of desirability in other goals" (p. 9).

These rules may be represented schematically by graphing the function $XY = K$. This formula defines a curve that divides two-dimensional space into two simple parts, one in which the product XY is greater than K and one in which it is less. The latter is out of bounds under the rule. It is represented by the shaded area in Figure 1. The boundary itself defines the best accessible conditions. Along that curve the closer to zero we bring X, the more Y increases, and vice versa. Although all points on the curve have the same K, there may be an optimum position, a place characterized by some additional favorable factor, a trade-off. This may well be where the combined cost $(X + Y)$ is lowest. We tolerate a certain level of atmospheric pollution in order to maintain some level of convenience in transportation, for example.

This concept is not unfamiliar in ethics; indeed, it can be applied to the process of balancing liberty and equality in the cycle described by Gaylin et al. (1978) and the debates on paternalism versus autonomy elaborated by Gaylin and Macklin (1982) and others (Beauchamp, 1977; Fotion, 1979; Gert & Culver, 1979; Husak, 1981; Wikler, 1979).

Our intuitive approach to this model may be assisted by reorienting Figure 1 to the position shown in Figure 2, making it symmetrical around

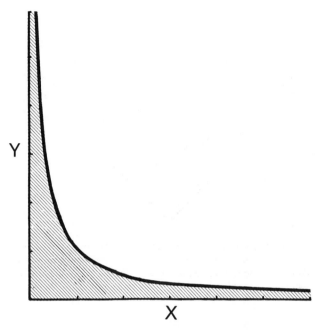

Figure 1. Koshland's "undesirability principle." The product, XY, of the respective costs (X, Y) of two competing social goals remains constant (XY = K). Subject to this principle, the point at which the combined cost X + Y is least is that at which X and Y are equal to each other; at that point, their sum is equal to twice the square root of K. This may be considered the optimum configuration consistent with the "undesirability principle."

what is usually perceived as the vertical axis. We all know that if one were to drop a small marble into this trough or cradle at either the left or right side it would slide down to the bottom, then climb a considerable way up the opposite side, and finally return to repeat the process, just as over time society moves to seek equity or liberty with more or less zeal.

In the physical metaphor, the marble eventually subsides and comes to rest at the bottom. With only a small kick provided at the top of each cycle, however, it would remain in oscillation indefinitely. The speed and height of the particle's motion are controlled by the energy applied, originally and through the kick. Social movements may get their kicks from a variety of external sources.

It may be hard for many people to accept the undesirability principle and to recognize that in real life, in the middle of life, there is no such thing as total freedom, complete equality, or absolute rights. My rights are circumscribed by your rights. My circumstances cannot be precisely equal to yours, since I cannot occupy the same place at the same time as you. Moreover, it may be that a condition approximating equality for all actually does not

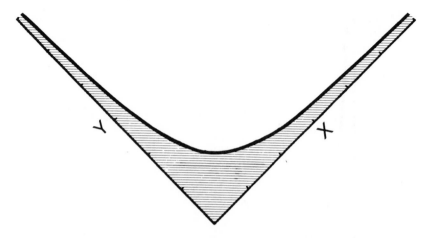

Figure 2. A reorientation of the curve in Figure 1, to put the point of minimum cost at what is readily perceived as the "low" point of the graphical representation. Other dynamic social forces tend to keep the actual combined cost at higher points, where X exceeds Y or vice versa, while remaining in conformity with the "undesirability principle."

maximize the benefits that we seek under the banner of equality. If you have more and I have less, is it then proper in the pursuit of equity to deny you the more, even though so doing does not increase my holdings? The fact that you have lost a leg or a piece of your brain does not require that I and others accept the same impairment. Rawls's much acclaimed *Theory of Justice* addresses this point:

> First Principle
> Each person is to have an equal right to the most extensive total system of equal basic liberties compatible with a similar system of liberty for all.
> Second Principle
> Social and economic inequalities are to be arranged so that they are both:
> (a) to the greatest benefit of the least advantaged, consistent with the just savings principle, and
> (b) attached to offices and positions open to all under conditions of fair equality of opportunity. (1971, p. 320)

In this statement the "just savings principle" refers to the obligation of each generation to make some provision for its successors.

Clearly one area of exploration that is of interest to readers of this book is the way Rawls's second principle plays out when the "least advantaged" are disadvantaged by handicap more than by economic circumstances. Surely one conclusion must support a priority given to primary prevention of mental retardation and other chronic disabilities, as well as to "early intervention" as secondary prevention. Some priority must be given to preventing disabilities originating in childhood, as a way of improving de facto equality and contributing to "just savings" for future generations. This dilemma is usually seen as a resource allocation problem, but it is also an example of the need to examine the issues in the middle of life, giving weight to both of the competing equities. To quote Breul and Diner (1980) in the area of social work: "Short of a utopia in which there is no human suffering or deprivation, persons concerned with social welfare will have to remain interested in both remedying the causes of social problems and in treating those who suffer from them. By understanding this issue in historical perspective, individual social workers will be better equipped to work out the relationships of their particular activities to the broader objectives of their profession" (p. 4).

In connection with efforts to prevent disability, it is important to make clear that people are not to be identified with or by their disabilities and that to give priority to the prevention of disabilities is not to denigrate persons who have them. This position is currently supported by persons who have disabilities, including those who recognize that their own disabilities are in all probability permanent (National Council on the Handicapped, 1986, pp. 30–31; United Nations, 1975). (But see Stanley Hauerwas's chapter in this volume.)

PEOPLE FIRST

WE ARE PEOPLE FIRST: Our handicaps are secondary (Parker, 1982) is the title of a book put together by a group of adults, most of whom were once residents of institutions for "the retarded." They too have joined the ranks of persons with disabilities who seek to speak for themselves (Carrillo, Corbett, & Lewis, 1982; Williams & Schoultz, 1982). The perception that people with mental retardation are first of all persons and citizens should inform our approaches to ethical issues that may arise in service contexts in which these persons may be found. It will prove economical to do so because most such issues have their counterparts in relation to persons who do not have retardation, issues that have already been explored. Therefore, it seems reasonable to adopt a method of analysis that asks first, "What does this problem have in common with problems affecting other (nondisabled) individuals?" This approach is consistent with the "normalization principle," a doctrine that calls for "making available" as far as possible "normal conditions of life" to persons who happen to have retardation (Nirje, 1969, 1980).

The residual part of the answer to the preceding question (how is the problem different?) is usually found to be much more focused in scope. In fact, it usually comes down to the question of personal autonomy, capacity, or competence with its associated question as to when and how to assure a correct method of surrogate decision making. And here again there has been the tendency to discuss stereotypical rather than real people, people at the edges rather than at the middle of life.

AUTONOMY FOR PEOPLE WITH RETARDATION

Some significant impairment of adaptive behavior, of discretion, of social competence, of comprehension of own self-interest is by definition characteristic of persons classified as mentally retarded, and with respect to interventions involving persons with severe retardation, there can be no equivocating that this aspect of impairment cannot be ignored. The temptation is to go to the other edge and use a paradigm of presumed total incompetence. Although it is more than 20 years since publication of *Report of the Task Force on the Law* by President Kennedy's Panel on Mental Retardation (1962), and although much has been written by many attorneys about partial competence and decision-specific competence, this subject has been skirted by most psychologists and dealt with superficially at best by most ethicists.

In studies in which attempts have been made to take professional service providers and ethicists a step further together, the subject area is likely to be narrowly targeted in a way that puts the matter under discussion once more on the edge. An example of treatment ''at the edges'' is found in a recent issue of the *Hastings Center Report,* in which Drane (1985) attempts to match the competence or incompetence of various classes of persons (to give medical consents) to the degree of gravity and complexity of the decision. For medical decisions that are ''not dangerous and are objectively in the patient's best interest,'' Drane finds ''retarded (educable)'' to be competent, but ''severe retardation'' typical of incompetence (p. 19). In another example, Macklin and Gaylin (1981) devoted an entire book to the question of whether sterilization is an issue with special relevance to mental retardation. Indeed, numerous authors have written about the ''at the edges'' issue of sterilization of women with retardation (see also National Institute on Mental Retardation, 1979), but much less has been written about the more central issue of marriage, for example. Marriage is one area where much more normative information, more field research, is needed. Janet Mattinson's (1970) book *Marriage and Mental Handicap* should not continue to stand in splendid isolation. The methods developed by Robert Edgerton and his colleagues (Edgerton, 1984) can be shared with ethicists and used by social psychologists to enter into the midst of life as it is lived by persons who are perceived by others as mentally retarded. To moralize on this issue without living with or talking with people personally affected is a sophisticated form of paternalism.

Unfortunately, the *Consent Manual* (Turnbull, 1977), developed by an interdisciplinary team for the American Association on Mental Deficiency, is seldom found in ethicists' libraries. On the other side, few professionals in the mental retardation field are familiar with Gaylin and Macklin's insightful comments on decision making by and for persons with retardation, contained in their recent book *Who Speaks for the Child* (1982).

There must be recognition by both ethicists and service providers that autonomy, competence, and paternalism are not subjects to be considered only when informed consent is on the table, but rather that the right approach—an individualized approach—to these issues is central to the quality of life and the prospects for psychological growth of each individual. This subject has been given detailed attention in the manual prepared by the Task Force on Least Restriction of the American Association on Mental Deficiency (Turnbull, 1981, Chapter 4). Basic to the problem is an understanding that in order to achieve competence, a person (child or adult) with mental retardation must know that he or she has choices and that what he or she decides will make a difference. Constant failure is clearly damaging to anyone and especially to a child, but unremitting success is not conducive to learning either, although in the early part of this century that theory was put into practice. Edward Ransome Johnstone (1918), a pioneer educator of that era, admonished teachers with: "You must therefore avoid letting them know that they fail. Your duty is to make them feel that they are succeeding. . . . You must always praise" (p. 25).

This swing from one side of the cradle (Figure 2) to the other, from being too demanding in the early days and, when that failed, being too protective, was addressed more realistically much later by Cobb (1966), who made clear that children must experience both success and failure and know that at least some of the time what they do can control outcomes in a consistent way. This principle goes beyond mere behavior management of persons as pigeons, to the basic experience of self-determination.

MOVING TOWARD THE MIDDLE

No one is advocating stasis, yet it is characteristic of the marble in the cradle that the wider it swings, the faster it moves through the midpoint, and the more time it spends away from the center. Ethicists, like traditional scientists, spend time examining phenomena near their edges because the structure of analysis can be simplified. It is useful to start from the edges and introduce changes incrementally, as perturbations. But ethical analyses at this level, while useful to academics, are of little help in real life to would-be virtuous persons seeking realizable ends under just conditions in a better society.

The following are suggested topics that can appropriately be included in a research agenda relevant to the ethics of dealing with persons with severe handicaps who find themselves in the middle of life.

1. *What are the boundaries of psychological intervention?* In the late 1950s when the Wisconsin legislature authorized the establishment of the Cen-

tral Wisconsin Colony in Madison (now the Central Wisconsin Center for the Developmentally Disabled), it mandated that a research program be instituted there, where mutual advantage to the residents and to the investigators could be realized. In 1962, shortly after the colony opened, its superintendent, Harvey Stevens, saw that he and his staff had to address a number of ethical issues. He convened a small interdisciplinary conference, which included representatives from medicine, psychology, ethics, and administration, as well as a parent with a background in research. The discussions influenced Stevens in his role as first president of the International Association for the Scientific Study of Mental Deficiency (Stevens, 1968). What to one observer was the most striking characteristic of this meeting, in addition to its intensity and sophistication, was the difficulty all the participants experienced in moving from the precise examples that could be adduced from the biomedical side to the less well-defined issues involving psychological interventions. This problem persists to this day.

Although we may have developed some protocols for handling operant conditioning techniques with formal recognition of subjects' rights, the underlying edge problem is that the edge at which intervention becomes defined is itself so ill defined. In medicine, the line marking the invasion of the physical person is usually clear. If performed without the consent of the subject, such invasion is defined in law as battery. In contrast, the invasion of the psychological person is not well defined, and an individual's defenses against such invasion are poorly delineated in law. Yet by its very nature, mental retardation invites psychological interventions; if one is to discuss when such interventions are ethical, one must begin by defining when they occur, or perhaps to what degree they occur; the question may be not whether they are intrusive but how intrusiveness is to be measured and how it is to be balanced against other presumably "good" things.

2. *What are the parameters of competence?* The nature of competence in persons with impairments has not been explored in sufficient depth. In addition, we have tended to deal only marginally with the effects of making simplistic presumptive rules at one edge or the other of the spectrum of paternalism. For example, some attorneys prefer to deny to a woman with a retardation any choice (direct or by surrogate decision) on certain reproductive matters, rather than run some risk of a "wrong" choice. The presumption is in favor of nonintervention, whatever that may bode.

3. *What should be the criteria for decisions when a surrogate must participate?* This question needs to be explored from the perspective of the affected person himself or herself. One cannot assume the "reasonable man test" for a person who happens to have limited reasoning capacity.

Neither should one be satisfied with the "best interest" test. The best example of an attempt to apply the "in the shoes of" test is probably the case of Joseph Saikewicz (Annas, 1978; Ramsey, 1978, pp. 300–317). Unfortunately, discussions of this case in the ethics literature have tended to focus on the procedural issues and the decision of the court to assert its primacy over the medical decision makers, rather than on the significance of the case as a defense of decision making individualized to reflect as well as possible what the person in question would have chosen had he been given the capacity and opportunity.

The ability to get inside the skin and the head of another person, especially one who has grown up with mental retardation, is not widely shared. How would such a person choose if he or she could? Perhaps for general insight the novelist does better than the scientist. In *Flowers for Algernon*, Daniel Keyes (1966) provides some insights based on imagination. *Flowers* is a science fictional autobiography in the form of a diary kept by Charly, a fellow with moderate mental retardation. Charly is chosen to receive an experimental drug that dramatically and progressively increases his intelligence to the point where he is telling the research psychologist what to expect in the way of results. This change is artfully portrayed by the increasing sophistication of the prose style in which the diary is written. At the outset, the diction and syntax are primitive. Nevertheless, using his limited vocabulary, Charly can convey poignantly how he feels overcome by humiliation when anxiety-provoking situations cause him to wet his pants despite himself, and how the inevitability of punishment for these episodes at the hands of his mother only escalates the anxiety next time around.

4. *Have parents been denied their appropriate roles?* As part of what is recognized as a current swing in the direction of antipaternalism, the role of parents has been circumscribed by courts and professionals in recent years, based on a presumption of potential conflict of interest. Setting aside for the moment the rights of parents and their own need for some redress of the intrinsic loss of autonomy that they experience merely by having the additional responsibility of a handicapped child, one can ask whether such circumscription is in the interests of any child, even one who has retardation. The observations of Goldstein, Freud, and Solnit (1979) deserve careful study in this context:

In the eyes of the law, to be a *child* is to be at risk, dependent, and without capacity or authority to decide free of parental control what is "best" for oneself. To be an *adult* is in law to be perceived as free to take risks, with the independent capacity and authority to decide what is "best" for oneself without regard for parental wishes. To be an *adult who is a parent* is therefore to be presumed by law to have the capacity, authority, and responsibility to determine and to do what is "good" for one's children, what is "best" for the entire family. (p. 7)

For these authors *the child has a right to autonomous parents.*

5. *When is enough enough?* For a professional to take unilateral control of treatment under the rationale of paternalism is to commit himself or herself to an extended therapeutic regimen. A commitment to the developmental model could be interpreted to require an unending quest; the client, student, or patient will always have the potential for further improvement. The professional who suggests discontinuing habilitation risks the moral disdain of his or her peers. But does the client have anything to say about it, and if so, when?

Light can be shed on this question by the opinions of persons with physical disabilities. Members of the disability rights movement are increasingly articulating a posture calling for a cease and desist order on therapy after a certain point, with a concomitant responsibility on the part of society to provide some accommodations for those who lack certain common capacities—for example, to walk, to see, to hear. Some go so far as to reject both the medical model and the economic model and embrace the sociopolitical model, which asserts that persons with physical impairments are handicapped primarily because society subjectively perceives them so and objectively fails to accommodate to the variation in human characteristics that they present (Gliedman & Roth, 1980; Hahn & Longmore, 1985).

The journal *Exceptional Parent* occasionally carries articles by or about young persons who have grown up with a disability and are tired of being "fixed." In a case history recently cited by Schleifer (1984) a 13-year-old with cerebral palsy is quoted as saying, "Everybody seems to want me to have this operation, but I don't want it. . . . My mother . . . always tells me that I have to like myself the way I am, and if I don't like myself the way I am then who will? Well, if I am supposed to like myself the way I am, why is everybody always trying to change me and why do they want me to have this operation?" Beyond the questions of informed consent and autonomy that this case can raise, is another ethical question not limited to persons with developmental disabilities: What is the balance between the individual's duty to improve himself or herself and to overcome a disability, defect, or bad habit that he or she may have acquired unintentionally, and the duty of society to accommodate that person? Conversely, given that houses and cars and bathrooms and telephones are designed ergonomically for average users, why should not all public utilities be designed to accommodate the full spectrum of human variety?

6. *What determines membership in the moral community?* Tredgold's (1908/1952) classic treatises on mental deficiency in the early 1900s devoted much attention to "moral defectives." In recent years the problems of persons with mental retardation who break the law have con-

tinued to be studied but without Tredgold's crusading spirit. None of this addresses the issues of the moral development of nondelinquent children or how an adolescent or adult with a mental handicap may arrive at an understanding of right and wrong other than by rote. The NICHD has been supporting inquiry into the moral development of normal children. An extension to children with atypical development in other areas would certainly be timely.

The foregoing topics can be seen as strung together in a double helix composed of autonomy and paternalism. They can be combined in the light of the undesirability principle to delineate optimum three-dimensional, real-life practices, not merely on the edges of life but in its midst.

REFERENCES

Annas, G.J. (1978, February). The incompetent's right to die: The case of Joseph Saikewicz. In *Hastings Center Report, 8*(1), 21–23.

Beauchamp, T.L. (1977, January). Paternalism and biobehavioral control. *Monist, 60,* 62–80.

Breul, F.R., & Diner, S.J. (Eds.). (1980). *Compassion and responsibility: Readings in the history of social welfare policy in the United States.* Chicago: University of Chicago Press.

Carrillo, A.C., Corbett, K., & Lewis, V. (1982). *No more stares.* Berkeley, CA: Disability Rights Education and Defense Fund.

Cetron, M.J., & Clayton, A. (1977). Investigating potential value changes. In H.A. Linstone & W.H.C. Simmonds. (Eds.). *Futures research: New directions* (pp. 214–229). Reading, MA: Addison-Wesley Publishing Co.

Cobb, H.V. (1966). The attitude of the retarded person towards himself. *Proceedings of the Third Conference of the International League of Societies for the Mentally Handicapped* (pp. 62–76). Brussels: The League of Societies for the Mentally Handicapped.

Drane, J.F. (1985, April). The many faces of competency. *Hastings Center Report, 15*(2), 17–26.

Dyck, A.J. (1977). Ethics and medicine. In S.J. Reiser, A.J. Dyck, & W.J. Curran (Eds.), *Ethics in medicine: Historical perspectives and contemporary concerns* (pp. 114–122). Cambridge, MA: MIT Press. (Reprinted from *Linacre Quarterly,* August 1973, pp. 182–200.)

Edgerton, R.B. (Ed.). (1984). Lives in process: Mildly retarded adults in a large city. *Monographs of the American Association on Mental Deficiency,* No. 6.

Fotion, N. (1979). Paternalism. *Ethics, 89*(2), 191–198.

Gaylin, W., Glasser, I., Marcus, S., & Rothman, D.J. (1978). *Doing good: The limits of benevolence.* New York: Pantheon Books.

Gaylin, W., & Macklin, R. (Eds.). (1982). *Who speaks for the child: The problems of proxy consent.* New York: Plenum Publishing Corp.

Gert, B., & Culver, C.M. (1979). The justification of paternalism. *Ethics, 89*(2), 199–210.

Gliedman, J., & Roth, W. (1980). *The unexpected minority: Handicapped children in America.* New York: Harcourt Brace Jovanovich.

Goldstein, J., Freud, A., & Solnit, A. (1979). *Before the best interests of the child.* New York: Free Press.

Hahn, H., & Longmore, P.K. (1985). *The emergence of the study of disability and society at the University of Southern California.* Unpublished manuscript.

Hart, H.L.A. (1977). Laws and morals. In S.J. Reiser, A.J. Dyck, & W.J. Curran (Eds.), *Ethics in medicine: Historical perspectives and contemporary concerns* (pp. 104–113). Cambridge, MA: MIT Press. (Reprinted from Hart, H.L.A. [1965]. *The concept of law* [pp. 181–207]. Oxford: Oxford University Press.)

Husak, D.N. (1981). Paternalism and autonomy. *Philosophy and Public Affairs, 10*(1), 27–46.

Johnstone, E.R. (1918, April). Discipline. In State of New Jersey, Department of Public Instruction, *The teaching of children mentally three years or more below the normal* (pp. 25–28). Trenton, NJ: State Gazette Publishing Co.

Jonsen, A.R., & Hellegers, A.E. (1977). Conceptual foundations for an ethics of medical care. In S.J. Reiser, A.J. Dyck, & W.J. Curran (Eds.), *Ethics in medicine: Historical perspectives and contemporary concerns* (pp. 129–136). Cambridge, MA: MIT Press, (Reprinted from Tancredi, L.A. [Ed.]. [1974]. *Ethics of health care* [pp. 3–20]. Washington, DC: National Academy of Sciences.)

Keyes, D. (1966). *Flowers for Algernon.* New York: Harcourt, Brace & World.

Koshland, Jr., D.A. (1985). The undesirability principle. *Science, 229*(4708), 9.

Macklin, R., & Gaylin, W. (Eds.). (1981). *Mental retardation and sterilization: A problem of competency and paternalism.* New York: Plenum Publishing Corp.

Mattinson, J. (1970). *Marriage and mental handicap.* Pittsburgh: University of Pittsburgh Press.

National Council on the Handicapped. (1986). *Toward independency: A report to the President and the Congress, 1986.* Washington, DC: U.S. Government Printing Office.

National Institute on Mental Retardation. (1979). Sterilization and mental handicap. *Proceedings of a symposium by the National Institute on Mental Retardation and the Ontario Association for the Mentally Retarded.* Toronto: Author.

Nirje, B. (1969). The normalization principle and its human management implications. In R. Kugel & W. Wolfensberger (Eds.), *Changing patterns in residential services for the mentally retarded* (pp. 179–195). Washington, DC: President's Committee on Mental Retardation.

Nirje, B. (1980). The normalization principle. In R.J. Flynn & K.E. Nitsch (Eds.), *Normalization, social integration, and community services* (pp. 31–49). Baltimore: University Park Press.

Parker, J.P. (1982). *We are people first—Our handicaps are secondary.* Portland, OR: EDNICK.

President's Panel on Mental Retardation. (1962). *Report of the Task Force on the Law.* Washington, DC: Author.

Ramsey, P. (1977). The nature of medical ethics. In S.J. Reiser, A.J. Dyck, & W.J. Curran (Eds.), *Ethics in medicine: Historical perspectives and contemporary concerns* (pp. 123–128). Cambridge, MA: MIT Press. (Reprinted from Veatch, R., Gaylin, W., & Morgan, C. [Eds.]. [1971]. *The teaching of medical ethics* [pp. 14–28]. Hastings-on-the-Hudson, NY: Hastings Center.)

Ramsey, P. (1978). *Ethics at the edge of life.* New Haven, CT: Yale University Press.

Rawls, J. (1971). *A theory of justice.* Cambridge, MA: Belknap Press.

Schleifer, M.J. (1984, October). Surgery for the adolescent: The impact on the family. *Exceptional Parent, 14*(7), 19, 20, 22–24.

Stevens, H. (1968). Mental deficiency in an international perspective. (Presidential address). In B.W. Richards (Ed.), *Proceedings of the First Congress of the Interna-*

tional Association for the Scientific Study of Mental Deficiency, Montpelier, 1967 (pp. xxxi–xii). Surrey, England: Michael Jackson Co.

Tredgold, A.F. (1952). *A textbook of mental deficiency.* London: Balliere, Tindall & Cox. (Original work published 1908).

Turnbull, H.R., III. (Ed.). (1977). *Consent manual.* Washington, DC: American Association on Mental Deficiency.

Turnbull, H.R., III. (Ed.). (1981). *The least restrictive alternative: Principles and practices.* Washington, DC: Task Force on Least Restriction, Legislative and Social Issues Committee, American Association on Mental Deficiency.

United Nations. (1975). *Declaration on the rights of persons with disabilities.* New York: Author.

Wikler, D. (1979). Paternalism and the mildly retarded. *Philosophy and Public Affairs, 8*(4), 377–392.

Williams, P., & Schoultz, B. (1982). *We can speak for ourselves.* London: Souvenir Press.

Chapter 2

SCHOLARS AND ETHICS

TOWARD AN ETHICALLY
RELEVANT AGENDA FOR
SCHOLARLY INQUIRY
IN MENTAL RETARDATION

Paul R. Dokecki, Harriet Able,
Keith Allred, Bonnie Beck, William Donovan, Jr.,
Craig Anne Heflinger, Arthur Lowitzer, and Shelton Smith

IN DECIDING WHETHER or not and how to intervene with persons with severe retardation, we encounter one of psychology's important findings: *Human development is uneven.* For example, Piaget used the term *décalage* to refer to a child having developed, in the main, to a given stage—say the stage of concrete operations—while functioning at less mature preoperational levels in selected psychological realms. We do not apply the concept of uneven development primarily to the persons with severe retardation who are the subjects of intervention decisions. Rather, the more important application of the concept is to society and its intervention decision makers. Biomedical and psychoeducational technologies have developed much beyond our understanding of the ethical dimensions of their use. We *can* do more than we know what we *ought* to do. It is as if we have developed to the point of being in a dense and dark technological forest without so much as an ethical flashlight. This uneven development of our society's mode of dealing with persons with severe retardation is not something we will grow out of naturally. What role, then, can scholars play in helping us catch up ethically?

INDIVIDUAL EMOTIVISM VERSUS COMMUNITY INQUIRY

The fundamental assumption here is that rational argument and evidence can enrich ethical discourse and help improve the quality of intervention deci-

sions. This assumption challenges the prevailing beliefs of what Alasdair
MacIntyre (1981) called our emotivist culture. Emotivism was defined by
MacIntyre as "the doctrine that all evaluative judgments and more specifically all moral judgments are *nothing but* expressions of attitude or feeling
[and] . . . are neither true nor false" (pp. 11–12). Emotivism entails the
view that rational methods are incapable of securing agreement about moral
judgments. Since science is a rational enterprise, it is not surprising that
scientists have been reluctant to apply their methods to ethical matters.

But a distinction must be made. A number of scholars, both philosophers
and social scientists, have identified latent value elements inherent in the
scientific enterprise in the process of criticizing the failures of mainstream
social science. In this tradition are recent volumes, such as *Social Science as
Moral Inquiry* (Haan, Bellah, Rabinow, & Sullivan, 1983); *Beyond Method*
(Morgan, 1983); Richard Bernstein's *Praxis and Action* (1971), *The Restructuring of Social and Political Theory* (1978), and *Beyond Objectivism and
Relativism* (1983); and Hilary Putnam's *Meaning and the Moral Sciences*
(1978) and *Reason, Truth, and History* (1981). These books are about science
as it *might* and *should* address values and ethics. They do not report the use of
scientific methods that *do* address ethical matters through creating empirical
knowledge that would enter into ethical discourse. The legacy of emotivism
stands in the way of this latter scholarly endeavor, while providing the target
for some of the criticism addressed in the former body of scholarly work.

The tension between the currently dominant position of emotivism, a
highly individualistic position, and alternative positions such as ours has deep
roots in human personality and culture. The issue is not just epistemological;
there are equally important existential dimensions. David Bakan is a psychologist who has helped to elucidate what is at stake. He has argued (1966) that
agency (the individualistic principle) and *communion* (the community principle) are dialectically related principles operating within each individual and
throughout human history. Each person, says Bakan, and each society arrives
at its own agency-communion blend or balance. Modern times have become
increasingly characterized by the triumph of agency over communion. The
major intervention task of our times, for Bakan, is to mitigate agency with
communion. This is so because societal gains from the ascendency of individualistic agency are reaching a point of diminishing returns, and the human
requirement for community has been increasingly unmet in the modern era, to
the detriment of human development.

In the realm of ethics, MacIntyre (1966) recognized a similar tension in
discussing emotivism and its rivals. On the emotivist view, facts and values
are always separate, and

> the only authority which moral views possess is that which we as individual
> agents give them. This view is the final conceptualization of . . . individual-
> ism: . . . the individual becomes his own final authority in the most extreme

possible sense. On the alternative view, to understand our central evaluative and moral concepts is to recognize that there are certain criteria we cannot but acknowledge. The authority of those standards is one that we have to recognize, but of which we are in no way the originators. (p. 264)

This alternative to individualistic emotivism implies the importance of a moral community embodying moral and evaluative concepts that have meaning beyond the autonomous individual person.

MacIntyre's analysis highlights the epistemological or methodological implications of emotivism and its emphasis on the autonomous individual as the sole authority for ethical judgments. But the matter goes beyond epistemology to everyday life where ethical decisions are made. For example, the image of the autonomous individual is a vivid one in current biomedical ethics. Robert Veatch (1984) points out that in the early 1970s, patients were attempting to free themselves from the ''tyranny of technology'' (p. 38). This struggle was embodied in the challenge posed by the principle of autonomy to the traditional principle of Hypocratic paternalism, which had the physician do whatever was believed to be in the best interests of the patient. Great benefits ensue when autonomy is given moral priority, as enumerated by Callahan (1984, p. 40): ''The rights of individuals and of their personal dignity; the execution of a powerful bulwark against moral and political despotism; a becoming humility about the sources or certainty of moral classes and demands; and a foundation for the protection of unpopular people and causes against majoritarian domination.'' For these and other reasons, Veatch claims that ''the case is overwhelming that autonomy takes moral precedence over paternalism. Respecting the patient's autonomy always takes precedence over benefiting the patient against the patient's autonomous will'' (p. 38). But Veatch sees this as ''a temporary triumph of autonomy'' (p. 40), since autonomy is a principle with implications limited to the special situation where its competitor is the principle of paternalism.

Callahan (1984) elucidates autonomy's limited implications by pointing to a number of its socially corrosive uses in everyday life. These community-threatening uses include the prevailing beliefs that: 1) each person is a moral agent sealed off from others, 2) all social relationships are contractual and voluntary, 3) respect for my autonomy is all that others owe me and I them, and 4) morality is at base relativistic and subjective. (This last point raises the epistemological issue once again.) Since the principle of individual autonomy produces many benefits, ''to be meddled with only at our peril'' (p. 40), Callahan does not propose getting rid of autonomy. Rather, he argues that

autonomy should be a moral good, not a moral obsession. It is *a* value, not *the* value. If, as too easily happens, it pushes other values aside, and if (all the worse) it rests on the conviction that there can be no common understanding of morality, only private likely stories, then it has lost the saving tension it competitively needs with other moral goods. Among them are piety toward tested and long-standing moral traditions, a search for morality in the company of others, community as an ideal and interdependence as perceived reality, and an embracing of autonomy as a necessary but not a sufficient condition for a moral life. (p. 42)

Here Callahan was following Bakan's dictum to mitigate agency with communion, to understand that the individual is a member of a community, a moral community.

Within moral community (exemplified historically in Aristotle's Athens), MacIntyre (1966) argued that

> when I say, "You ought to do this," or when I say, "This is good," I want to protest that I say more and other than, "You or anyone else—do this!" . . . For if that is what I mean, that is what I could and would say. If that is what I *do* say, then certainly what I say will have no authority but that which I confer upon it by uttering it. My attitudes and my imperatives have authority for me just because they are mine. But when I invoke words such as *ought* and *good* I at least seek to appeal to a standard which has other and more authority. If I use these words to you, I seek to appeal to you in the name of those standards and not my own name. . . . You cannot use the moral vocabulary and consistently deny the force of *ought,* and you cannot remain within the social commerce of the community, and abandon the moral vocabulary. (pp. 264–265)

In his widely acclaimed *After Virtue,* MacIntyre (1981) outlined the clash between the modern majority view of individualistic emotivism—symbolized by Nietzsche's position that an individual's will to power is the basis for morality, that the person who carries the biggest stick wins the day for his or her subjective moral position—and the decidedly minority view of ethics within a coherent moral community, symbolized by Aristotle's position that a moral community can use reason, based on external ethical standards, to establish a moral position. Although much influenced by MacIntyre, especially by his convincing arguments about the ethically corrosive features of emotivism, our analysis in this chapter departs from him in certain respects.

The first section of this chapter has identified troubling unevenness in human societal development vis-à-vis persons with severe retardation. Technological development has far outstripped ethical development. Society seems to have fallen victim to a highly individualist, subjectivist, and relativist view of morality, a view that gives virtually no place to rational and evidence-based discourse in the realm of ethics. It is little wonder, then, that social and behavioral scientists have contributed so little to the ethical understanding of mental retardation. In this chapter, however, we join with those who hold that rational ethical discourse is possible and that empirical evidence has a place in informing ethical choice. In subsequent sections, we report the results of three research activities conducted to help form an ethically relevant research agenda on the ethics of mental retardation: 1) a survey of leaders of major national organizations that deal with persons with retardation in order to identify the most important and emerging ethical views in the field; 2) a review of all of the articles since 1980 in selected groups of behavioral science journals and philosophical and ethical journals for the purpose of identifying the ethical issues in mental retardation being addressed by the scholarly community; and 3) an analysis of all the committee reports prepared by leading scientists in mental retardation for the forward planning effort of the National Institute of Child Health and Human Development (NICHD) in order to discern implicit and explicit ethical issues for the future. Before turning to these sources of data, it is necessary to develop a philosophical framework to organize our data and to help give form to the ethically relevant research agenda outlined at the conclusion of this chapter.

A FRAMEWORK FOR ETHICAL
REASONING INCORPORATING EMPIRICAL EVIDENCE

The philosophical position we tentatively adopt is Paul Taylor's (1961) informal logic and "good reasons" approach, as elaborated by Frank Fischer (1980), a position within the tradition of Wittgensteinian analytic moral philosophy. The work of Taylor and Fischer begins to provide an ethical flashlight powered by rational argument and evidence to inform decision making about persons with severe retardation in the dark technological forest. What we seek are not absolutely good or true reasons for deciding whether or not and how to intervene with persons with severe retardation; indeed, the Taylor/Fischer position is far from perfect. Rather, we seek reasons that are *good enough* to encourage rational and evidence-based discourse leading to intervention decisions.

In his book *Normative Discourse,* Paul Taylor (1961) explicated the informal logic of making normative statements. He asked, "What sorts of reasons are good reasons in justifying value judgments?" His purpose "was to bring out the over-all logical structure of the justification of value judgments" (p. 76). What might it mean to justify these ethical value judgments? According to Taylor (1961, p. 77):

> I distinguish four general phases in the overall process of justifying value judgments: verification, validation, vindication, and rational choice. We *verify* value judgments by appeal either to standards or to rules which we have adopted. We *validate* standards or rules (i.e., we justify our adopting certain standards or rules) by appeal to higher standards or rules. The adoption of standards or rules which themselves cannot be validated by appeal to any higher standards or rules results from our decision to accept a whole value system. We *vindicate* our accepting a whole value system by appeal to the way of life to which we are committed. Our commitment to a way of life can be justified in terms of a *rational choice* among different ways of life.

Taylor's is a hierarchic scheme of choices. For example, the act of providing a cognitive stimulation program for an infant with severe retardation might be judged to be valuable or ethical if it could be empirically

Table 1. Taylor's (1961) scheme of ethical justification

Levels of evaluative logic	Example criteria
Verification (of a standard)	Protecting the innocent (relative to other standards)
Validation (of a higher standard)	Being benevolent (relative to other, higher standards)
Vindication (of a whole value system)	Brotherly love (relative to other whole-value systems)
Rational choice (of a way of life)	Democracy within the Judeo-Christian tradition (relative to other ways of life)

verified as satisfying a standard, say, of *protecting the innocent.* This standard might be indexed by successfully providing the infant cognitive skills necessary for adapting to the world—as measured, say, by the Bayley Scales of Infant Development. As shown in Table 1, the standard of protecting the innocent, once verified, would be validated by showing that it is consistent with a higher standard, say, that of *being benevolent,* as manifested in certain situations. At the next level, being benevolent could be vindicated as contributing to a broadly operating whole-value system, say, that of *brotherly love.* This value system would be shown to be valuable or ethical if it could be argued that it is part of a rationally chosen way of life, say, that of *democracy within the Judeo-Christian tradition.* The attempt is to provide good reasons for the choice of the criterion or standard at each level relative to other possible choices.

Frank Fischer's (1980) *Politics, Values, and Public Policy: The Problem of Methodology* extended and elaborated Taylor in a useful and practical way. Fischer liberally interpreted Taylor's four levels of evaluative logic in the justification process by identifying roughly corresponding methods and modes of explanation. Table 2 shows that *evaluation research*—which ideally uses the controlled experiment—is employed in verification to determine cause-effect relations or empirical indices of economic efficiency relative to meeting a chosen standard. Fischer cited the Westinghouse Learning Corporation (1969) evaluation of Project Head Start as an example, and most research in psychology and education is at this first level. *Phenomenological analysis*—using philosophical and interpretive qualitative methods, such as in-depth interviewing, participant observation, ethnomethodology, and situational description—is used in validation, the second level, to interpret the situations in which the chosen standard is met as a manifestation of a higher chosen standard within a chosen whole value system. The qualitative evaluation approaches of Carini (1975) and Patton (1975) are examples. Morgan

Table 2.   Levels of evaluative logic viewed in terms of methods and modes of explanation

Levels of evaluative logic	Modes of explanation			
	Empirical causes	Situational interpretation	Causal relations	Speculative interpretation
Rational choice				Political philosophy
Vindication			Behavioral systems approach	
Validation		Phenomenological analysis		
Verification	Evaluation research			

Source: From Fischer, F. (1980). *Politics, values, and public policy: The problem of methodology,* p. 174. Boulder, CO: Westview Press. Copyright © 1980 by Westview Press, Boulder, CO; reprinted by permission.

(1983) also provided many additional examples of methods at this level and the vindication level as well. The *behavioral systems approach*—using organizational, community, and political systems analysis—is used in vindication to determine empirically how the whole chosen value system causally contributes to the achievement of values important in a chosen way of life. David McClelland's *The Achieving Society* (1961) is an example. *Political philosophy*—using speculation and interpretation of empirical knowledge of social systems—is used in rational choice, the fourth level, to compare various ways of life. The work of Dworkin (1977) and Habermas (1971), and Rawls's (1971) theory of justice are examples.

As can be seen in Table 3, the methods used within the levels of evaluative logic entail different inquiry emphases and modes of inference. At the first and third levels, verification, implemented through evaluation research, and vindication, implemented through the behavioral systems approach, emphasize the gathering of empirical data and formal inference based on these data. At the second and fourth levels, validation, implemented through phenomenological analysis, and rational choice, implemented through political philosophy, also deal with data and facts, but necessarily go beyond them by means of philosophical interpretation, speculation, and informal logic. (We provide examples of mental retardation research at each of these levels in the last section of this chapter.)

Related to our purpose, Fischer's scheme contributes "to the methodological debate that centers around the fact-value problem" and successfully confronts "the task of integrating empirical and normative perspectives" (p. 172). Our intent in presenting it is to offer a total outlook so that scholars

Table 3. Levels of evaluative logic as related to the social sciences

Levels of evaluative logic	Social science methodology	Role of empirical science	Mode of inference
Verification	Evaluation research	Emphasis on research design and controlled experimentation Reliability through statistical analysis Knowledge of secondary consequences	Causal explanation Knowledge of facts sufficient Formal inference
Validation	Phenomenological analysis	Descriptive facts of the situation Application of causal knowledge about consequences of following a rule	Interpretive understanding Knowledge of facts necessary but not sufficient Inference based on informal logic
Vindication	Behavioral systems approach	Descriptive knowledge of de facto individual and group values Empirical data about instrumental and contributive consequences	Causal explanation Knowledge of facts sufficient Formal inference
Rational choice	Political philosophy	Experiential knowledge about alternative ways of life Knowledge of human nature	Interpretive speculation Vision, imagination, and logical speculation Knowledge of facts necessary but not sufficient

Source: From Fischer, F. (1980). *Politics, values, and public policy: The problem of methodology,* p. 175. Boulder, CO: Westview Press. Copyright © 1980 by Westview Press, Boulder, CO; reprinted by permission.

from different disciplines and perspectives might select a piece of the action in the domain of ethically relevant research, while seeing how their particular work relates to the work of others in the overall domain. Although it is highly unlikely that many total justifications will be attempted or achieved, one example of a recent scholarly effort that did span all levels is *Strengthening*

Families, a book written by our group at Vanderbilt University on public policy for child care and parent education (Hobbs, Dokecki, Hoover-Dempsey, Moroney, Shayne, & Weeks, 1984).

As Fischer (1980) pointed out:

> It is possible to see that each type of knowledge associated with the four methodologies is only one level of a larger process constituting a full or complete evaluation. Evaluation research, phenomenological analyses, the behavior or naturalistic systems approach, and political philosophy are, in this regard, better understood as alternative perspectives on social phenomena rather than competing approaches to truth per se. Instead of competing methodologies, they can be viewed as coexisting perspectives on the same social reality, each with its own type of data and internal logic. (pp. 172–173)

Fischer was, in effect, arguing for methodological openmindedness. In a similar vein, Jonas Soltis (1984), echoing Dewey, argues that researchers in education should regard themselves "as members of an *associated community* and not merely as an aggregate of individuals or as warring camps, or as a pluralistic field of multiple unconnected research paradigms without common interests" (p. 9). Soltis concludes:

> Openmindedness is not empty mindedness, however, and it is not tolerance of all views good or bad. It is having a sincere concern for truth and a willingness to consider, test, argue, and revise on the basis of evidence our own and others' claims in a reasonable and fair manner. . . . This doesn't mean that we will always reach agreement, or even that we will always be able to understand and appreciate the arguments of others, or that we cannot be committed to a position of our own. Openmindedness only requires a sincere attempt to consider the merits of other views and their claims. It does not release us from exercising judgment. (p. 9)

The Taylor/Fischer framework is important because it argues for the possibility of rational discourse about ethical matters and it openmindedly encompasses the work of scholars from the social sciences and the humanities. With this framework in mind, we now identify the important ethical issues concerning persons with severe retardation, issues that might serve as a stimulus to the scholarly community.

ETHICAL ISSUES: VIEWS FROM THE FIELD

The media have covered ethical issues related to mental retardation extensively during the last several years, including reporting on a myriad of controversial cases involving persons with severe retardation of all ages. Advocacy, government, professional, and research organizations stand in the wings or are directly involved in most of these cases. The development of an ethically relevant research agenda requires an understanding of the role these organizations have played and will play regarding society's ethical choices on behalf of persons with severe retardation.

We conducted a telephone survey of 10 national organizations variously concerned with persons with severe retardation. The sample included: the American Academy of Pediatrics, the American Association on Mental Deficiency, the Association for Retarded Citizens/US, the Council for Exceptional Children, the Hastings Center, Georgetown University's Kennedy Institute of Ethics, the National Association of Developmental Disabilities Councils, the National Association of Superintendents of Public Residential Facilities for the Mentally Retarded, People First, and The Association for Persons with Severe Handicaps. A key person in each organization was asked to describe the principal ethical issues in mental retardation from his or her organization's special vantage point.

It comes as no surprise that the most commonly identified ethical issue was Baby Doe, the decisions whether to provide care for or withdraw care from newborns with handicaps. Who should make these decisions? What role should and must parents play? How much do we really know about medical and developmental prognosis? How, if at all, should quality of life enter the equation, and whose quality of life counts—the infant's or the family's? Shouldn't the availability to families of follow-up care and intervention programs of various kinds be considered, and how generally available are these services? Who should pay for these services: parents, parents' insurance, society-at-large? Does Baby Doe have less, equal, or more claim on scarce societal resources than a nonhandicapped infant? What is owed Baby Doe and his or her family in terms of social justice? It should be noted that respondents raised these last issues concerning fiscal responsibility and justice in relation to persons with severe retardation of all ages.

Respondents were also concerned about the *rights of persons with mental retardation*. What claim do they have on society? Does achievement of their rights always contribute to their health and welfare? What kind of services are they entitled to? Is it possible that granting them rights might infringe on the rights of others in society? Should the principle of autonomy or that of paternalism prevail in making intervention decisions? When is it ethically appropriate to use genetic therapy, sterilization, psychotropic drugs, or aversive therapy? How should the need for informed consent be guaranteed in the areas of treatment and research? What are the rights of persons with retardation concerning housing, employment, immunization and other forms of medical care, participation in athletics, and other forms of recreation? Do persons with retardation have rights to be sexually active, to marry, and to have children?

Some of these last questions about rights relate to the issue of the *integration of persons with retardation into the community*. Senator John H. Chafee has introduced a landmark deinstitutionalization bill (S2053) in the U.S. Congress that would dramatically increase community care of persons with retardation over the next several years, with a concomitant decrease in care provided by large residential institutions. Our survey respondents were concerned about enabling persons with severe retardation to have as full a life as possible. One identified obstacle to this goal is the public's attitudes toward persons with retardation, especially concerning their living in the community. In this matter, what is the acceptable trade-off between deinstitutionalization and possible danger to life and limb in the community? Moreover, will normalized services be adequate to the special needs of persons with retardation? What about the availability of family support services, such as respite care or day care? Finally, on the other side of the coin, how can we ensure an adequate environment and appropriate services for those people who continue to be institutionalized?

Respondents saw the areas of *education, training, and habilitation* as containing several ethical issues. For example, will Public Law 94-142 continue to be strictly enforced and high-quality special education and related services continue to be available? This is the "backlash" issue. And shouldn't training and habilitation be geared to meeting society's expectations for persons with retardation? Moreover, what constitutes *appropriate* expectations? Also, how vigorously should we pursue training those persons with retardation who seem refractory to intervention efforts?

Respondents identified an especially difficult and important issue: *Who should speak for persons with mental retardation?* Shouldn't such persons be enabled to speak for themselves whenever possible and be heeded when they do speak? What should be done when the best interests of persons with retardation and those of their parents conflict? Who is the proper surrogate decision maker for the person with retardation? The issue of professional paternalism pertains here as well.

Finally, respondents identified a cluster of *general societal concerns* with ethical implications. Why, for example, are not persons with handicaps seen very often on television? How can we overcome the false beliefs about the characteristics and capacities of persons with retardation, beliefs that often lead to discriminatory practices? What is the relationship between the beliefs and values of society's institutions and the decisions made on behalf of persons with retardation (e.g., the relationship between a hospital's value system and its medical care decisions)? And, finally, what is the appropriate role of the person with mental retardation in our culture?

This last set of issues suggests the overarching relevance of Joseph Margolis's (1984) recent observation that there is a dynamic relationship between our society's judgment of "the worth of a human life, however diminished its competence; and the limits of the resources of a society, however generous its intentions" (pp. 31–32). The issues identified by the respondent organizations ranged widely, from those at quite specific levels concerning basic standards, which might be addressed by the verification and validation processes, to issues of vindication at the level of the system and the fundamental choice of a way of life, as in this tension identified by Margolis. These issues provide ample stimulus for scholarly activity at all levels in the humanities and social sciences. In the next section, we identify the response of the scholarly community to the ethical concerns just presented.

ETHICAL ISSUES: VIEWS FROM THE SCHOLARLY COMMUNITY

In order to get a reasonably valid view of the response of the scholarly community to the web of ethical concerns in this area, we reviewed a group of major behavioral and social science journals in mental retardation and a group of prominent philosophical and ethical journals. Following is a representative overview, not an exhaustive account, of the literature.

The Behavioral Science Journals Survey

We reviewed seven behavioral and social science journals: *American Journal of Mental Deficiency, Analysis and Intervention in Developmental Disabilities, Education and Training of the Mentally Retarded, Exceptional Children, Journal of The Association for Persons with Severe Handicaps, Journal of the Division of Early Childhood,* and *Mental Retardation.* These journals mostly focus on children and youth and tend (except for *Mental Retardation*) to give priority to articles presenting empirical research. To be sure, an expanded view of scholarly concern about ethics would have emerged if we had reviewed the medical literature; but that was a task beyond the scope of this chapter.

Research group members reviewed every article in the selected journals since 1980 that specifically addressed an ethical issue either as the article topic, as a stimulus for or as part of the rationale for a study, or in drawing conclusions from the results of a study. We also sought instances where authors did not specifically identify any ethical issues, but where, in a reviewer's judgment, they might easily have done so. Finally, we determined for each article if there were any citations of the philosophical ethics literature. Space constraints permit only a cursory presentation of the results gleaned from the more than 1,000 articles we reviewed.

At the most general level, we found few articles in the empirical literature on mental retardation that addressed specific ethical issues. In fact, except for the journal *Mental Retardation,* the words *ethics* and *morality* were conspicuous by their virtual absence. Moreover, aside from a handful of citations to articles addressing ethical issues in medical journals, there was not a single reference to ethics journals (again, with the exception of a half dozen citations in *Mental Retardation*). A moderate number of articles were on topics with fairly immediate ethical import, although the ethical dimensions of the work were not directly acknowledged by the researchers.

More specifically, the journals in mental retardation dealt with the following topics that have relevance at some level to ethical matters: 1) institutionalization versus community integration of persons with retardation—especially constitutional rights, the need to train persons with retardation to function in normalized and mainstreamed settings, and the possible negative effects of public attitudes on integration efforts; 2) the roles and responsibilities of parents, professionals, persons with mental retardation, and other actors in making intervention decisions; 3) research ethics; 4) special interventions, including genetic screening, prenatal diagnosis, the education of children with herpes, and the hospice movement; 5) the educability of persons with severe retardation—the issue of how far we can and should go in implementing intervention programs, short of subjecting persons with retardation to undue and potentially inhumane stress; 6) the possible negative effects of labeling persons as retarded; 7) family factors in mental retardation—including the issues of the impact of a child with handicaps on a family, the need for social supports, and the special needs of low-income families; 8) the sexuality of persons with mental retardation—including the issues of sex education and sterilization, and concern about community attitudes; and 9) the rights of persons with mental retardation—including Baby Doe, the role of human rights committees, guardianship, the rights to education and medical treatment, issues regarding aversive therapy, the needs for early intervention and an extended school year for children with mental retardation, and funding issues in light of scarce resources. Also of interest were articles about the lessons to be derived from the Nazi experience, the abuse of children with mental retardation, the possible adverse effects of medication, and advocacy on behalf of persons with retardation—especially the degree of responsibility educators and other professional people have to be advocates.

The Philosophical Ethics Journals Survey

In the philosophical ethics area, we reviewed six journals: *Ethics, Hastings Center Report, Journal of Medical Ethics, Journal of Medicine and Philosophy, Perspectives in Biology and Medicine,* and *Philosopher's Index.*

A modest number of articles in the philosophical ethics literature addressed the situation of persons with severe retardation. By far the greatest number of these appeared in *Hastings Center Report.* Just as the social and behavioral science journals mostly failed to cite the ethics literature, so too the ethics journals ignored the empirical literature.

Ethics scholars most frequently (27 articles) explored Baby Doe and related intervention decisions concerning newborns with handicaps. Other topics addressed with moderate frequency included the cluster of issues involving genetic counseling, prenatal screening, abortion, and wrongful life. Then there were the issues of who should make decisions for persons with mental retardation, and the ethics of deinstitutionalization. Finally, there were scattered articles on research ethics, behavior modification, sterilization, and society's role and responsibilities in caring for persons with retardation.

With some sense of the scholarly contributions to the ethics of mental retardation from two different disciplinary perspectives, we can now move to nominate items for an ethically relevant research agenda.

TOWARD AN ETHICALLY RELEVANT RESEARCH AGENDA

The two bodies of literature we reviewed have been like two lightly loaded ships passing in the night. Two issues, among many, where interchange would be fruitful are Baby Doe and deinstitutionalization. Scholars could advance knowledge in these two areas by a coordinated treatment of empirical matters at the levels of verification and vindication and more interpretive and philosophic matters at the levels of validation and rational choice. These matters include assessing the effects, both positive and negative, of the presence of a person with handicaps on a family and the meaning derived by family members in the course of caring for their handicapped relative. The empirical and philosophical dimensions of the currently ambiguous concept of quality of life should be specified. Describing and ethically interpreting the variety of approaches to intervention decision making is an important topic, especially in light of the new U.S. Department of Health and Human Services Baby Doe regulations concerning hospital committees. Researchers should study the standards used to judge the value of interventions both psychometrically and ethically. Research could help develop and evaluate intervention guidelines for professional practice. Finally, research could help formulate public policy through, for example, analyzing the provisions of the earlier-mentioned Chafee bill as to the value and implementation issues it raises. Baby Doe and deinstitutionalization readily lend themselves to such combined empirical and humanistic analysis and could serve as models for many other similar scholarly efforts.

There is some cause to be encouraged by what scholars have done since 1980, perhaps more by what could be built on and extended than by what has already been accomplished. What of the future?

Researchers' Views of the Future

We were able to evaluate well what the empirical research community plans to do because of our fortune in obtaining the draft reports of the committees contributing to the NICHD Forward Plan in mental retardation. The committees were in the areas of: behavioral analysis research in mental retardation; developmental neurobiology, early diagnosis, and early intervention; epidemiology; family and community; genetics and cytogenetics; inborn errors of metabolism as applied to mental retardation; language and communication of persons with mental retardation; nutrition, teratology, and developmental pharmacology; obstetrics and perinatology; psychobiology; psychological processes; and socioecological processes.

We reviewed the reports in an attempt to find issues that each committee more or less directly identified as having ethical import. We also tried on our own to discern ethical issues that were not directly identified, issues implicit in what was proposed.

Although the committees were not asked by NICHD to address ethical issues, a few of the research topics cited by the committees had obvious relevance to the ethics of mental retardation. In the area of prevention, researchers observed that differing subcultural value systems make any general intervention approach problematic. Moreover, although one group identified the person with mental retardation's right to treatment, other groups identified the need to tailor interventions to the particular situation of each person with retardation. Involved here were several issues. First, there is the need to study the lives of persons with mental retardation in their totality before making quality of life judgments. Next was the recognition that a person with mental retardation might prefer a quality of life different from that prescribed by an intervention agent. Finally, there was the suggestion that, where possible, persons with mental retardation should participate in deciding matters significant to them.

Researchers furthermore questioned whether the goal of early intervention should be to prevent disability, to promote optimal development, or both. An additional concern was whether parents should be seen as clients or collaborators in early intervention programs. Particularly value-laden was the question of whether early intervention should be intended only for children at risk or for all children. In a related vein was the recommendation that research and intervention programs should include different types of families from all social levels. Researchers also recognized the need to integrate early intervention programs into a continuum of care, since the all-too-prevalent gap between the medical and psychoeducational delivery systems is problematic for families who have children with mental retardation.

Other ethical issues directly identified included the need to develop nonaversive interventions for self-injurious behavior and the need for research on psychotropic medication and its effects on cognitive functioning. The drugs issue is important because the use of drugs in reducing or controlling certain behaviors in many instances may not be worth the human and fiscal costs. Finally, researchers identified the need to maintain confidentiality of information about participants involved in research.

Generally, in the detailed committee reports we reviewed, there was an average of about one directly identified ethical issue per report, and most of those were in the behavioral rather than biomedical area. The importance of the identified issues cannot be denied; however, their small number is consistent with the lack of emphasis given ethical thinking in the empirical literature since 1980. But beyond these directly identified ethical issues, what were some of the ethically relevant issues identified by the committees?

Alasdair MacIntyre (personal communication, April 1985) suggested to us that we recognize certain empirical research topics to be ethical on their face, even though researchers may not directly acknowledge ethical relevance. Accordingly, a case could be made that *all* the mental retardation research supported by NICHD (and certain other agencies) has ethical import, since it is being supported by the agency because of its relevance to mental retardation as a nationally identified social problem. To a greater or lesser degree, each researcher's findings are available to be applied. Findings "ought" or "ought not" be applied, and the lives of individuals, families, and communities could thereby be affected for "good" or "ill," in ways deemed to be "right" or "wrong." In other words, the conduct of mental retardation research and the application of research findings occur in value-laden and ethically charged contexts.

The NICHD committee reports contain examples of value-laden research topics. Just a few such topics from the diverse areas of NICHD-supported research include: 1) improving the language and communication skills of persons with mental retardation; 2) developing drug therapies to ameliorate the negative aspects of mental retardation; 3) improving prenatal diagnostic procedures enabling the conduct of genetic counseling or gene therapy; 4) determining how molecular genetics and recombinant DNA findings can be used to prevent mental retardation; 5) improving the cognitive and adaptive behavioral competence of persons with mental retardation; 6) understanding the epidemiology of mental retardation, especially what broad environmental conditions contribute to delayed development; 7) developing our capacity to make more accurate medical and developmental prognostic judgments; 8) understanding the psychobiological transactions of a person's biological makeup and the environment; 9) developing obstetric and perinatal techniques to reduce the effects of early brain damage; 10) determining the intergenerational effects of social class on low birthweight and central nervous system defects; and 11) determining the relationship between motor and cognitive development for at-risk children. The list could be greatly expanded. The point we wish to make is that the ethical consciousness of researchers, of funding agencies, and of society-at-large must be raised by many means, including the use of the kind of rational and evidence-based ethical discourse we have advocated.

Much of the research supported by NICHD is relevant to the ethical justification level of verification through the use of science and experimental methods. A small percentage of the broader social and behavioral science work employs behavioral systems methods at the level of vindication. Largely missing from the NICHD funding perspective are: 1) more qualitative and interpretive research at the level of validation and 2) work that builds on what we know empirically relative to broad public policy issues using political philosophy at the level of rational choice. What might research look like at the levels beyond the usual one of verification, that is, those of validation, vindication, and rational choice?

Examples of validation-level research using what Fischer (1980) calls phenomenological analysis are the anthropological work of Edgerton (1984) and his colleagues at the University of California at Los Angeles and the work in progress by Harriet Able of our own research group in the John F. Kennedy Center for Research on Education and Human Development. Able (1985) is conducting in-depth interviews of parents, physicians, and nurses concerning experiences with infants with handicaps in neonatal intensive care units. The focus is on factors in the communication process leading up to the treatment/no treatment decision interpreted in the context of Habermas's ideal speech situation (McCarthy, 1978). System-level work related to the process of vindication is exemplified by Moroney's (1976) research on family policy issues in the care of persons with severe retardation and by the research of Bruininks, Meyers, Siegford, and Lakin (1981) in their on-going study of treatment modalities for persons with mental retardation across the country. At the level of rational choice, Bernard Farber's (1968) work on the social context of mental retardation can be cited. Farber analyzed mental retardation relative to the chosen economic way of life in the United States, namely, market capitalism.

A Reflection on the Field

The rich ethical agenda identified by organizations in the field of mental retardation (cited earlier in this chapter) has been only sketchily addressed by the scholarly community. There are undoubtedly many reasons for this, probably the most important being our emotivist culture with its individual, subjective, and relative view of ethics, as we have argued. Related to this broad cultural factor are more mundane reasons, such as the faculty reward systems in universities, social and behavioral science journal editorial policies, and the priorities of funding agencies. And funding priorities *do* have ethical implications. Choosing where to spend scarce research dollars is value laden, whether or not researchers and agency officials see it that way. In a mission-oriented agency such as NICHD, the ethics of resource allocation often becomes apparent in regard to the issue of relevance—the questions of which topics ought to be given priority (Should we emphasize the psychological and social or the biomedical?) and whether a more basic or a more applied research strategy should be adopted—pursuant to preventing and ameliorating mental retardation. Widespread public discussion and careful deliberation will be required to make ethically responsive choices on the issue of relevance.

The mental retardation research community should be encouraged to confront directly the ethical implications of this issue.

Research Ethics and Important Research

Returning to the actual conduct of research, 10 years ago, our Peabody College colleague and former Kennedy Center director, H. Carl Haywood, then editor of the *American Journal of Mental Deficiency,* wrote a paper still relevant today that is entitled, "The Ethics of Doing Research . . . and of Not Doing It" (Haywood, 1976).

The place where research and ethics most frequently connect in mental retardation, as in most areas of research, is in research ethics. Concerning the ethics of doing research, Haywood (1976, p. 313) maintained that "there is great national concern for the following issues: . . . protection from harm, both physical and psychological; protection from invasion of privacy; guarantee of choice (i.e., informed consent); and protection from exploitation (the "guinea pig" issue)." In addition to joining with Haywood in advocating that researchers pursue their work informed by these ethical considerations, we believe that Haywood's list constitutes a stimulus for behavioral science research on the topic of ethics itself. Researchers take many specific approaches in trying to follow these research ethics prescriptions. Some approaches to conducting research undoubtedly come closer than others to the letter and spirit of these prescriptions. This variance within the research arena itself constitutes a proper topic of investigation. We can improve research ethics in practice by gaining empirical knowledge of existing practices. Such research would be particularly useful to those conducting clinical trials and intervention research, especially where the risk-benefit ratio for participation is not altogether clear. An example is the national clinical trial being conducted with NICHD contract support on a dietary intervention to prevent maternal phenylketonuria (MPKU). Briefly, female infants detected and treated for PKU years ago have grown up more or less normally and are now having babies of their own. A very high percentage of these women are giving birth to infants with serious mental retardation different from PKU, conditions referred to generally as MPKU. The net effect is that we are currently seeing more retardation than was prevented by use of the PKU detection system and diet in the first place. The dietary treatment being tested with these PKU women to prevent MPKU is somewhat controversial as to its effectiveness, and, moreover, the researchers are in an ethically sensitive situation in obtaining informed consent. A clinical trial of this sort would afford an excellent occasion for behavioral science research on the process of obtaining informed consent. Results could help sensitize researchers to the subtleties of research ethics practice and help develop models for future clinical trials. Similar research might be conducted on psychoeducational interventions as well. Such studies would entail evaluation of ethical procedures primarily at the levels of verification and validation. In effect, researchers might begin to follow the dictum: Researcher research thyself.

Returning to Haywood's (1976) position, he elaborated the four previously mentioned fundamental areas of ethical concern in the context of ethical responsibilities of professionals working in mental retardation, especially professionals with behavioral science research competence. These responsibilities are as follows: "(a) find the best methods of treatment, education, habilitation, and care; (b) encourage research; (c) protect subjects from violation of the four fundamental areas of concern [previously mentioned]; and (d) protect subjects from wasted time, i.e., from use in frivolous or ill-conceived research on trivial issues" (p. 313). This list of ethical responsibilities suggests that those with research competence would be violating their ethics if they did *not* conduct research. This is not to suggest, however, that any and all research should be conducted at any cost. The title of a recent article by Seymour Sarason (1984) asked: "If It Can Be Studied or Developed, Should It Be?" Many would believe that this question should not even be asked, since freedom of inquiry is sacrosanct in our culture. Sarason, however, both asked the unaskable and gave what to many would be an unacceptable answer. Using a number of examples, including the mental-retardation-related topics of recombinant genes and ethnic and social differences in intelligence, Sarason argued that we should at least seriously consider the possibility of not researching certain topics. For Sarason, the criterion to be applied is whether or not research and technology would contribute to the psychological sense of community: "The attainment and maintenance of that sense, by individuals and collectivities, are the overarching criteria by which we should scrutinize, judge, and control any activity (by ourselves and others) that is intended to improve our lot" (p. 484). In a related view, the ethical responsibilities identified by Haywood (1976) suggest an ethical injunction against poor and trivial research and an ethical imperative to do high-quality and *important* research.

On the issue of importance, Haywood and Switzsky's more recent paper (1984) stresses the importance of the social ecological research perspective in pursuit of the optimal environment for persons with retardation. Such work must, of necessity, reach to the level of vindication and the use of behavioral systems approaches. Beyond empirical methods, social ecological research easily connects with more interpretive and philosophical work at the levels of validation and rational choice.

CONCLUSION

We conclude by returning to the metaphor used throughout this chapter. The multilevel approach to justifying ethical judgments and the accompanying research agenda we have argued for are intended to help even out our society's human development. The realm of value must catch up with the realm of fact, "ought" must be seen to be as important as "is," the dark technological forest must be illuminated by rational, evidence-based discourse.

Although most scholars in the humanities and the behavioral and social sciences have ignored the topic of ethics in mental retardation, the time is right for them to use their disciplinary tools and talents to help improve ethical discourse in this area. Ethics is not just a matter of emotion or personal preference. Reason and evidence can make a difference in ethical decision making. Developing an ethically relevant research agenda in mental retardation is a priority task so that scholars can help us make wise choices about some of the most difficult issues facing our society.

REFERENCES

Able, H. (1985). *Parent-professional communication relative to medical care decision making for seriously ill newborns.* Nashville, TN: Vanderbilt University.
Bakan, D. (1966). *The duality of human existence: Isolation and communion in Western man.* Boston: Beacon Press.
Bernstein, R.J. (1971). *Praxis and action: Contemporary philosophies of human activity.* Philadelphia: University of Pennsylvania Press.
Bernstein, R.J. (1978). *The restructuring of social and political theory.* Philadelphia: University of Pennsylvania Press.
Bernstein, R.J. (1983). *Beyond objectivism and relativism: Science, hermeneutics, and praxis.* Philadelphia: University of Pennsylvania Press.
Bruininks, R.H., Meyers, C.E., Siegford, B.B., & Lakin, K.C. (Eds.). (1981). *Deinstitutionalization and community adjustment of mentally retarded people.* Washington, DC: American Association on Mental Deficiency.
Callahan, D. (1984). Autonomy: A moral good, not a moral obsession. *Hastings Center Report, 14*(5), 40–42.
Carini, P.F. (1975). *Observation and description: An alternative methodology for the investigation of human phenomena.* Grand Forks: University of North Dakota Press.
Dworkin, R. (1977). *Taking rights seriously.* Cambridge, MA: Harvard University Press.
Edgerton, R. (1984). The participant-observer approach to research in mental retardation. *American Journal of Mental Deficiency, 88,* 498–505.
Farber, B. (1968). *Mental retardation: Its social context and social consequences.* Boston: Houghton Mifflin Co.
Fischer, F. (1980). *Politics, values, and public policy: The problem of methodology.* Boulder, CO: Westview Press.
Haan, N., Bellah, R.H., Rabinow, P., & Sullivan, W.M. (Eds.). (1983). *Social science as moral inquiry.* New York: Columbia University Press.
Habermas, J. (1971). *Knowledge and human interests.* Boston: Beacon Press.
Haywood, H.C. (1976). The ethics of doing research . . . and of not doing it. *American Journal of Mental Deficiency, 81,* 311–317.
Haywood, H.C., & Switsky, H.N. (1984). Perspectives on methodological and research issues concerning severely mentally retarded persons. In D. Bricker & J. Filler (Eds.), *Serving the severe mentally retarded: From research to practice.* Washington, DC: Council for Exceptional Children.

Hobbs, N., Dokecki, P.R., Hoover-Dempsey, K.V., Moroney, R.M., Shayne, M.W., & Weeks, K.H. (1984). *Strengthening families.* San Francisco: Jossey-Bass.
MacIntyre, A. (1966). *A short history of ethics.* New York: Macmillan Publishing Co.
MacIntyre, A. (1981). *After virtue.* Notre Dame, IN: University of Notre Dame Press.
Margolis, J. (1984). Applying moral theory to the retarded. In L. Kopelman & J.C. Moskop (Eds.), *Ethics and mental retardation* (pp. 19–36). Boston: Reidel Publishing Co.
McCarthy, T. (1978). *The critical theory of Jurgen Habermas.* Cambridge, MA: MIT Press.
McClelland, D.C. (1961). *The achieving society.* Princeton, NJ: D. Van Nostrand.
Morgan, G. (Ed.). (1983). *Beyond method: Strategies for social research.* Beverly Hills: Sage Publications.
Moroney, R.M. (1976). *The family and the state: Considerations for social policy.* London: Longmans.
Patton, M.Q. (1975). *Alternative evaluation research paradigm.* Grand Forks: University of North Dakota Press.
Putnam, H. (1978). *Meaning and the moral sciences.* London: Routledge & Kegan Paul.
Putnam, H. (1981). *Reason, truth, and history.* Cambridge: Cambridge University Press.
Rawls, J. (1971). *A theory of justice.* Cambridge, MA: Belknap Press.
Sarason, S.B. (1984). If it can be studied or developed, should it be? *American Psychologist, 39,* 477–485.
Soltis, J.F. (1984, December). On the nature of educational research. *Educational Researcher, 13,* 5–10.
Taylor, P.W. (1961). *Normative discourse.* Englewood Cliffs, NJ: Prentice-Hall.
Veatch, R.M. (1984). Autonomy's temporary triumph. *Hastings Center Report, 14*(5), 38–40.
Westinghouse Learning Corporation (1969, July 12). *The impact of Head Start: An evaluation of the effects of Head Start on children's cognitive and affective development.* Athens: Ohio University.

Chapter 3

DECISION MAKING FOR RESEARCH INVOLVING PERSONS WITH SEVERE MENTAL RETARDATION

GUIDANCE FROM THE NATIONAL COMMISSION FOR THE PROTECTION OF HUMAN SUBJECTS OF BIOMEDICAL AND BEHAVIORAL RESEARCH

Duane Alexander

TIME BRINGS CHANGES in all things, including the conduct of biomedical research. Today, except for occasional continued rumblings in the U.S. Congress about fetal research, and questions about life-extending treatments such as artificial hearts and organ transplants, there is a relative calm on the scene of protecting human subjects of research. Yet those who were active in clinical investigation in the early 1970s remember well the turmoil of those years, when the whole research enterprise was in some jeopardy because of a few sensationalized questionable violations of research ethics in protecting human subjects. The Tuskegee syphilis studies, the hepatitis studies in children with retardation at Willowbrook State School, the injection of cancer

The opinions expressed here are the author's and do not necessarily reflect the views of the National Institute of Child Health and Human Development. This chapter may be reproduced in whole or in part for the official use of the U.S. Government or any authorized agency thereof, or for the official use of state governments or any authorized agency thereof.

cells into incompetent adults at the New York Jewish Hospital, the sterilization of the retarded Relf sisters, use of a placebo in contraceptive trials, and
decapitation of aborted fetuses for research purposes in Finland were all front-
page news stories, and aroused serious public concern about medical research. In California, a court suit (*Nielsen v. Regents of the University of
California,* California Superior Court, San Francisco County, filed Sept. 11,
1973: case never heard) was filed to halt nontherapeutic research on children,
based on their inability to give informed consent. Fortunately, most research
was noncontroversial, the medical community presented its case convincingly
to the public, and a National Commission for the Protection of Human Subjects of Biomedical and Behavioral Research, established by Congress, produced thorough studies and reasonable recommendations that won acceptance
by the public, the research community, and the government, so that research
was again able to move forward. Nonetheless, just as it is sobering in these
days of commemorating the Allied victory in World War II to reflect on how
close we came to losing that conflict, it is important for those of us in research
to recall how close we came to having severe handicapping restrictions placed
on our research efforts, well-meaning though we may be. Just as eternal
vigilance is the price of liberty, eternal vigilance to assure that our conduct of
research is proper is the price of doing human research.

With this chapter having been originally presented at a conference dedicated to the memory of President John F. Kennedy, it is particularly appropriate
to cite the role of his brother, Senator Edward M. Kennedy, in establishing the just noted commission that played such an important part in restor-
ing public and government confidence in medical research and in charting
the ethically appropriate course for the regulation of such research. During the
1970s, Senator Kennedy was chairman of the Subcommittee on Health of the
U.S. Senate Committee on Labor and Public Welfare. In that capacity, he was
largely responsible for bringing to public attention some of the violations of the
protection of human subjects, but he saw to it that government action did not
stop there. It was his insistence on establishing the broad-based National
Commission for the Protection of Human Subjects of Biomedical and Behavioral Research to deal with these issues in a rational and deliberative way, rather
than allowing them to be responded to legislatively which could have led to the
prohibition of certain types of research, that was responsible for development
of research guidelines permitting research, while at the same time protecting
the subjects on whose participation that research depends. Kennedy played a
major role in guiding this legislation through Congress, in assuring that
sufficient funds were made available to the commission to carry out its
mandate, and in extending from two years to four years (1974 to 1978) the life
of the commission.

I was fortunate to be the physician on the staff of the National Commission. Included among its congressional charges was the development of

guidelines for research on the fetus, on children, and on those institutionalized with mental infirmities, as well as general guidelines for all research. The specific groups mentioned were singled out for attention because of their vulnerability, with a focus on whether they were able to provide informed consent.

THE QUESTION OF CONSENT

The basic reason research with infants, children, or persons with mental retardation is an issue surrounds the question of consent. Enunciation of the Nuremberg Code in 1948 in the United States formalized use of informed consent as a prerequisite for conduct of research on humans. It states: "The voluntary consent of the human subject is absolutely essential. This means that the person involved should have the legal capacity to give consent" (*U.S. v. Karl Brandt et al.,* 1947). The code makes no special reference to or provision for research on children or on persons with mental retardation, and technically would prohibit all research on these groups. However, the authors of the code claim there was no intent to do so, and state that children and persons with mental retardation were not included in the code because research involving them was not an issue in the trials. Subsequently, the Declaration of Helsinki in 1964 provided that consent of the legal guardian was satisfactory, even for nontherapeutic research, for subjects without the legal capacity to give consent themselves. This approach has generally been adopted in the United States and most other countries. Former U.S. Department of Health, Education & Welfare (DHEW) regulations provided that research on children or on persons with mental retardation could be conducted with the consent of the person's representative who is legally authorized to consent for research procedures, but existing law *makes* no provision for such a person in nontherapeutic research situations. Thus the dilemma of consent for research involving children and persons with mental retardation.

But why is consent for such research an issue at all? The answer to this question probably has its roots in differing philosophies of the nature of the human being and society. It is reflected in the differences and conflicts between the Aristotelian notion that a person's greatest good can be achieved only by joining together with others to contribute to the communal good, and the counter claims of later philosophers such as Hobbes and Locke who made rights of individuals paramount and gave autonomy and self-determination precedence over the communal good. It is not surprising, perhaps, that this basic philosophic conflict should be felt particularly strongly in this country, for in addition to being a melting pot of ideas and cultures, our very founding reflected an attempt to allow these divergent views to coexist. As Jefferson the philosopher put it, individuals band together and institute and establish governments, but not to pursue the common good; rather they do so to protect individual rights to life, liberty, and the pursuit of happiness. This basic conflict between individual rights and community interest is still with us and actually appears to be increasing as the population grows and opportunities for conflict increase. It is seen most obviously in such practices as invoking of eminent domain, in compulsory education and immunization, in compulsory motorcycle helmet laws, and in conscription for military service, but it is the underlying factor in the controversy over consent for research with children or persons with mental retardation as well.

Individual rights advocates hold that the right of infants, children, and persons with mental retardation to have their integrity and self-determination respected must be preserved, even at the cost of not acquiring information that would benefit others in their group and society as a whole. On the other side, community interest advocates hold that an individual has a duty to contribute to the common good and that children or persons with retardation may, therefore, within certain limits, be participants in research, even though they themselves cannot give consent, provided the research may contribute to the well-being of society without harming them.

The writings of present-day ethicists who have addressed the question of research on children and persons with mental retardation reflect the underlying dichotomy. The individual rights advocates are probably represented most clearly by theologian Paul Ramsey (1970), who perceives consent as a canon of loyalty between physician and subject that is an absolute requirement and the only justification for medical research. Therefore, those who cannot give mature and informed consent should not be subjects of medical experimentation unless it is for their own direct medical benefit. Ramsey calls experimenting on patients unable to give consent in ways unrelated to them as patients no less than "a sanitized form of barbarism," and totally rejects the notion of proxy consent except for direct benefit. To Ramsey, the notion of volunteering another for research is totally morally unacceptable, except in the face of epidemic conditions endangering also each individual. Even in experimentation involving no possible risk to the child or individual with retardation, Ramsey objects: There cannot even be unwarranted touching. "What is involved," he says, "is the right of each of us to determine for ourselves not just the extent to which we will share ourselves with others, but the timing and the nature of any such sharing" (p. 39). It is *no consent* rather than *no risk* that is the controlling factor for Ramsey.

Counter to Ramsey's views is the social good or community interest position, a view shared to some extent by ethicists Tristram Engelhardt (1978), Richard McCormick (1974), and Robert M. Veatch (1978). Although agreeing that consent is the key, McCormick, for example, claims that it is illogical to accept parental or guardian consent for therapeutic research but not for nontherapeutic research. Since parental consent is considered a reasonable assumption of the child's wishes or the wishes of the person with retardation in the therapeutic setting, may it not be so considered for nontherapeutic research as well? McCormick argues that in some situations it may be *assumed* that a child would consent if he or she were asked to, because there are certain "things that all of us, simply as members of the human community, *ought* to do for others" (p. 76). Included among these things is a certain level of involvement in nontherapeutic experimentation that may not be for our own benefit but is not harmful. To participate for the good of others, says McCormick, is good for the child, and therefore he or she *ought* to *choose* to do so, provided the research involves no discernable risk, undue discomfort, or inconvenience.

Thus, the lines are drawn. Placed in a historic context, we see that there is really nothing new under the sun, just a different form of expression of an age-old conflict. This is what Congress in 1973 asked the National Commission to attempt to resolve.

THE COMMISSION'S INFORMATION GATHERING ABOUT PERSONS WITH SEVERE MENTAL RETARDATION

The duties of the National Commission with regard to research involving institutionalized persons with mental infirmities were delineated as follows:

> The Commission shall identify the requirements for informed consent to participation in biomedical and behavioral research by . . . the institutionalized mentally infirm. The Commission shall investigate and study biomedical and behavioral research conducted or supported under programs administered by the Secretary [DHEW] and involving . . . the institutionalized mentally infirm to determine the nature of the consent obtained from such persons or other legal representatives before such persons were involved in such research; the adequacy of the information given them respecting the nature and purpose of the research, procedures to be used, risks and discomforts, anticipated benefits from the research, and other matters necessary for informed consent; and the competence and the freedom of the persons to make a choice for or against involvement in such research. On the basis of such investigation and study, the Commission shall make such recommendations to the Secretary as it determines appropriate to assure that biomedical and behavioral research conducted or supported under programs administered by him meets the requirements respecting informed consent identified by the Commission. (National Commission, 1978, pp. xv–xvi)

The charge to the commission focused on all those institutionalized with mental infirmities, only a small portion of whom have severe retardation. Thus the commission's recommendations dealt in large part with mentally ill subjects who have varying degrees of disability and may or may not lack legal competence to give informed consent. For the purposes here, then, it is necessary to review commission activities and recommendations as they focus specifically on those with severe retardation, who may or may not be institutionalized but always lack the capacity to give informed consent. For these subjects, institutionalization represents only a further complication in the decision-making process regarding their research participation.

As a basis for understanding the final recommendations of the commission, it is important to examine what was learned by members in the course of gathering information on the topic. Perhaps the outstanding characteristic of this commission was its insistence, under the guidance of its chairman, Kenneth Ryan, on gathering factual information and using that information as a basis for its decision making. Chairman Ryan said on a number of occasions that he was not sure if good facts made good ethics, but he did know that bad facts would make bad ethics. As a commission staff member and an observer, it was particularly impressive to me to note the frequent changes in opinion of individual commission members as they accumulated information on a topic.

In its work of compiling information on the nature of research conducted on persons with mental retardation, the commission was struck by the diversity of this research, which ranged from studies of basic physiology to social systems, from normal developmental processes to behaviors associated with mental retardation. They also noted that such research could involve interventions that could benefit the subjects directly, could contribute general knowledge about the class of subjects, or could even be unrelated to their condition of mental retardation. Research intended to benefit the subjects themselves included studies to improve medical or behavioral treatments or to develop new education and training methods, such as differential responsiveness to drug treatment, assessment of techniques to eliminate self-injurious behavior, or teaching of personal hygiene and social skills. Evaluation of these therapies ranged from systematic observation of behavior, to psychological testing, to medical tests such as collection of urine, blood, or spinal fluid samples.

Other research intended to produce knowledge about mental retardation in general included causative factors, but was not necessarily aimed at benefiting the individual patient. Similar procedures are involved as for therapeutic research, but the only immediate benefit to the subject may be additional attention or the personal interaction involved in the research. Other nontherapeutic research involves evaluation of alternatives to institutionalization such as outpatient care, community care, and other community support programs. Variations in within-institution care may also be studied, such as effects of differences in resident/staff ratios and staff-patient interaction. Such studies may or may not provide direct benefit by demonstrating harmful effects of institutionalization and encouraging improvements and alternatives. The commission's study of the range of research convinced members of the need for some hierarchy in decision making depending on the risks involved and whether the subject might benefit from the research.

The commission also evaluated the extent of research involving institutionalized persons with mental infirmities. It learned that most of the federally sponsored research related to mental retardation was conducted by 12 mental retardation research centers supported by the National Institute of Child Health and Human Development (NICHD), and in university-affiliated facilities for mental retardation. At that time, the entire federal expenditure on programs serving persons with retardation was $5 billion, of which 1½%, or $62 million, was spent on research. The commission was distressed to discover the small percentage of funding provided for research on mental retardation compared to the enormous cost for service programs. This fact helped to convince them that they must make efforts to increase research among this population rather than impede it.

The commission contracted to have an analysis conducted of the degree of risk to various categories of subjects presented by research in which they participated. The resulting data obtained from surveys of research involving institutionalized persons with mental infirmities characterized the research as particularly low in degree of risk and probable occurrence of any harm. More than one-third of the projects were categorized as completely without risk, and nearly one-half of the research on these projects was expected to benefit them individually. In studies not expected to benefit subjects, only 1% of studies were considered to have even a low or very low probability of a serious medical complication. Consent was obtained from a third party for such research in about one-third of the projects, but because the study population included clearly competent subjects as well as those with retardation, these data are not interpretable for the topic of research on persons with severe retardation.

The commission also undertook an extensive review of state laws pertaining to competency determinations, as well as the legal status of persons with mental disabilities to give consent for medical care and in managing their personal affairs. The commission found that most state statutes on competency make no provision for competency to consent for health care, but relate to management of property or business affairs. No states had direct provisions for consent for research. The commission also learned that most persons classified as mentally incompetent have not had an official guardian appointed by a court or a legal determination of their competency. Even placement in an institution did not carry with it an automatic determination of incompetence to consent. The commission's review of court cases relevant to the issue of consent for research by persons with retardation disclosed only a few relevant cases. The most applicable is *Wyatt v. Stickney* (1972) in Alabama. In that case, the court mandated that with regard to research:

> Patients shall have a right not to be subjected to experimental research without the express and informed consent of the patient if the patient is able to give such consent, and of his guardian or next of kin, after opportunities for consultation with independent specialists and with legal counsel. Such proposed research shall first have been reviewed and approved by the institution's Human Rights Committee before such consent shall be sought. Prior to such approval the

Committee shall determine that such research complies with the principles of the statement on the Use of Human Subjects for Research of the American Association on Mental Deficiency and with the principles for research involving human subjects required by the United States Department of Health, Education, and Welfare for projects supported by that agency. (p. 380)

In a companion decision the *Wyatt* court imposed the same restrictions as for research, including review by the Human Rights Committee and personal or third-party consent (depending on the capacity of the resident), before the use of behavior modification programs involving noxious or aversive stimuli. Thus, even when the intervention in question is designed to benefit an incompetent patient, added layers of protection such as institutional and court review, or total prohibition, may be imposed when the proposed procedure is risky, invasive, noxious, or permanent.

The status of the law with respect to interventions that do not benefit the incompetent person was also reviewed. The few cases dealing with this issue relate primarily to sterilization and organ transplantation. In the latter, the decision has hinged on whether the court could construe some benefit to the donor. Thus, in a Louisiana case, donation of a kidney from a child with retardation to his sister was not allowed despite parental consent because the court found no benefit to the subject with retardation, whereas a Kentucky court permitted a kidney transplant from a man with severe retardation to his brother on the basis that death of the brother would have been traumatic for the incompetent subject. In summary, the conditions under which a guardian could give consent to a nontherapeutic *medical* procedure on an individual with severe retardation are not clear, and the law gives *no* guidance on *behavioral* interventions. What *is* clear is that when nontherapeutic procedures are permitted, additional review may be required to evaluate the reasonableness of the guardian's consent. The commission also noted a developing doctrine called "substitute judgment." In this case, the issue revolves not around benefit to the subject, but a decision may be made according to an inference of the subject's past willingness to participate in such activities, or of what the substitute decision maker would presume the subject would do in such circumstances. Thus, a legal basis was developing for assuming consent on the part of a subject for nonbeneficial interventions.

One of the most educational experiences for commission members was their visit to the Eunice Kennedy Shriver Mental Retardation Research Center at the Fernald State School in Waltham, Massachusetts. There they saw the type of research being conducted among persons with severe mental retardation, they had a chance to interact with these persons, and they had the opportunity to talk with investigators about the research being conducted. Commission members were particularly impressed by three facts: 1) the number of individuals with retardation over age 21 who were in a consent limbo—they were clearly incompetent to make decisions, but no guardian had been appointed for them by a court and often there was not an involved parent; 2) there was no clear transitional line from innovative research or training to standard practice; and 3) most important, the patients they saw made them question when it was ethical *not* to conduct research when there is a clear need to improve the care and training of persons with retardation, not only to prevent mental retardation but to avoid placement in an institutional setting.

The commission's final activity before they began to debate was to hold a public hearing to obtain testimony from organizations and individuals on research involving persons with retardation. A number of those testifying warned that involving an adversarial procedure in such research would be contrary to medical ethics and would diminish accountability of professionals. Others suggested that individually nontherapeutic research on persons with retardation was acceptable, provided that: 1) such research was related to their condition and involved only minimal risk, 2) any objection from the subject would prohibit the research, and 3) permission from parents or guardians was obtained. Therapeutic research, advocates advised, could exceed minimal risk if benefits exceeded the risk, and even the subject's objection could be overridden in such cases. The Association for Retarded Citizens/United States suggested that research was acceptable only if it was directed toward retardation, was potentially therapeutic, posed no substantial danger to participants, and was reviewed and approved by a local committee. Lawyer Neil Chayet suggested the use of parent surrogates for projects of greater than minimal risk for patients who were not clearly competent. The surrogate could decide the appropriateness of research for a given subject and give "permission" for the conduct of research rather than "consent." The American Association on Mental Deficiency pointed out that excessive regulation of minimal risk research would be counterproductive, and that including institutionalized subjects who had mental retardation was valuable, was more efficient than recruiting subjects outside an institution, and should be considered acceptable if it also could be conducted acceptably on noninstitutionalized subjects. H. Carl Haywood, testifying for the Mental Retardation Division of the American Psychological Association, emphasized the benefits of research involving persons with retardation and urged the commission not to allow past abuses to jeopardize the entire research enterprise. He stated that placing unreasonable restrictions on the ability of scientists to carry out such research would infringe on the rights of persons with retardation by not allowing development of better treatments or services. Increased regulations would mean increased research costs and, in turn, less research. He suggested that institutional consent alone was never sufficient and that informed consent procedures be overseen by a local committee. Finally, one witness after another emphasized the importance of not excluding persons with mental retardation from research.

THE COMMISSION'S GUIDELINES AND RECOMMENDATIONS

With their information gathering complete, the commission began their debate and the attempt to develop recommendations for research within the framework of the three basic ethical principles they had identified that should underlie the conduct of all research involving human subjects: respect for persons, beneficence, and justice. At the outset, the commission noted that they had been particularly impressed by the lack of knowledge relating to the care and treatment of persons with mental retardation, and that in no other area of their mandate had the need for research been so clearly manifest. Improvements in the diagnosis and treatment of such persons were felt to be mandatory and were strongly dependent upon research. Because of the diversity both of research and of the population of institutionalized persons with mental infirmities, the commission developed recommendations that would provide flexibility and room for judgment by local institutional review boards.

The issues involved in the conduct of research among persons with mental retardation were viewed in terms of a conflict between the objective of developing better methods of diagnosis and treatment and the need to refrain from interventions that present unjustified risk or exploit vulnerable patients. The commission's deliberations focused on three issues: 1) whether research involving persons with retardation must always be relevant to their condition; 2) how to ensure these patients' individual autonomy to the extent possible while providing protection, and 3) how much risk is ethically permissible to ask persons with retardation to assume for the benefit of others. Each of these issues is discussed in the following paragraphs.

The commission's debate on relevance focused on whether persons with retardation should participate in research not relevant to their particular condition and whether institutionalized subjects should be included if noninstitutionalized subjects were available. Some members felt that institutionalization itself imposed additional burdens and that institutionalized persons were less likely to have caring persons to assist and protect them, so that even research related to their mental disability should be conducted only on noninstitutionalized persons. Other commission members felt that participation in research is not always a burden and may produce benefits just from being involved. The commission's resolution of these issues was to put the burden on each investigator who proposed to recruit subjects from an institution to justify the involvement of such subjects to an institutional review board, and to prohibit research not related to their condition for institutionalized subjects not capable of giving informed consent or assent even if the research involved only minimal risk.

On the issue of protecting autonomy, the commission spent many hours in debate because of the diverse capabilities of persons who are institutionalized with mental infirmities. Focusing on persons with severe retardation, however, the commission recommended that assent of such persons or their lack of objection would be sufficient authorization for them to participate in research that presented no more than minimal risk if that research was relevant to the subjects' condition. The commission also allowed participation in research involving potential benefit, or research without individual benefit but involving no more than a minor increment above minimal risk that was designed to yield important knowledge about the subject's condition, even in the absence of assent, provided that a patient's guardian gave permission. Debate also centered on whether an individual's objection to participation in research could be overridden. The commission concluded that the objection of such a person to participate in research should be binding unless the research involved an intervention that could directly benefit that person, the intervention was available only in the research context, and the subject's participation was authorized by a court.

The final question of amount of permissible risk from research divided the commission more than any other. Some felt that it is never justified to expose patients with retardation to more than minimal risk for the sole benefit of others. Others felt that the risk could be justified, but only if there was a remote possibility that the subjects themselves might eventually receive some benefit. Others felt that if the proposed subjects were the only ones suitable for the research, even the persons with severe retardation who were incapable of objecting might be included if the risk was not unreasonable. The commission finally concluded that while research of no more than minimal risk was generally permissible for such patients, research presenting more than minimal risk and no direct personal benefit was acceptable only under very limited conditions. These conditions include only a minor increment of risk over minimal, vital importance of the anticipated knowledge to be gathered for understanding the subject's condition or the possibility of some future direct benefit, supervision of the process of obtaining assent by an auditor, permission of a guardian or court, and prohibiting inclusion of such subjects over their objection.

With these general guidelines agreed upon, the commission proceeded to write its recommendations. First, they established general conditions for all research on the institutionalized persons with mental retardation. These conditions included requirements for a review and determination by an institutional review board that the research methods were appropriate and the investigators sufficiently competent to conduct the research, that appropriate nonhuman studies had been conducted before involving human subjects, that adequate justification for involving these particular subjects in the research was provided, that risks would be minimized by using procedures performed for diagnostic or treatment purposes whenever possible, that privacy and confidentiality would be maintained, that selection of subjects would be equitable, and that a person responsible for the health care of the subject would give permission to ask the subject to participate in research based upon a determination that the research would not interfere with the patient's health care. With these basic guidelines established, the commission then dealt with three categories of research—minimal risk, more than minimal risk but direct potential benefit, and more than minimal risk but no direct benefit—and established increasingly stringent requirements for the conduct of each (Table 1).

In minimal risk research, for subjects incapable of consenting, the commission proposed the additional requirements that the research be relevant to the subject's condition and that the subject assent or not object to participation. The commission was so anxious to avoid impeding this category of research that no guardian or third party permission was required. It also allowed overriding a subject's objection if the research provided direct benefit to the subject and a court specifically authorized that subject's participation.

For research posing greater than minimal risk but holding out the prospect of direct benefit, the commission proposed permitting the research if the institutional review board (IRB) determined that the risk was justified by the anticipated benefit, and, for patients incapable of assenting, a guardian gave permission *or* a court specifically authorized the subject's participation. For this category of research also, the commission provided for court authorization for participation in research over a subject's objection. The commission also suggested that an IRB might in some circumstances appoint a "consent

Table 1. Commission recommendations for research involving persons with severe mental retardation

Requirements	Minimal risk	More than minimal risk with benefit	More than minimal risk and no benefit
Relevant to mental retardation	Yes	Yes	Yes, and of vital importance or future direct benefit
Limit on risk	Minimal	No limit, but personal benefit must exceed risk	Minor increase over minimal; group benefit
Assent	Yes, or not object	Yes	Yes
Third party	Not involved	Guardian or court required if assent not possible, or for child	Guardian or court required if assent not possible, or for child
Override objection	Yes, if beneficial, by court only	Yes, if beneficial, by court only	No
Auditor	Optional	Optional but encouraged	Required

auditor'' to observe the consent or assent process to determine whether the subject assented or objected to participation and whether the permission of a guardian should be supplemented by court authorization.

For research presenting more than minimal risk and without the prospect of direct benefit to individual subjects, the commission proposed requiring that the risk be only a minor increase over minimal risk, and that the IRB determine that the anticipated knowledge gained would be of vital importance for understanding or ameliorating the type of disorder or condition of the subject or be reasonably expected to benefit the subject in the future. For this category of research on patients incapable of assenting, guardian permission was required and the subject could *not* be involved over his or her objection. Furthermore, in these cases, the IRB was *required* to appoint a consent auditor to determine whether the subject assented or objected to participation.

Finally, the commission provided what it termed a safety valve. Recognizing that it could not foresee all future circumstances, it recommended that research that did not meet any of these requirements could be conducted, provided that: 1) it presented an opportunity to understand, prevent, or ameliorate a serious problem affecting the health or welfare of persons with mental retardation, 2) a National Ethical Advisory Board and the head of the responsible federal agency determined that the conduct of the research would be in accord with the three basic ethical principles for research involving human subjects, and 3) adequate provisions for obtaining assent or guardian permission were made.

FATE OF THE COMMISSION'S WORK

With the commission's work completed, the ball moved to the court of the Department of Health, Education & Welfare. As they had with other commission recommendations, department officials initially drafted proposed regulations that basically implemented the recommendations. Before they were published as proposed rulemaking, however, changes were made that added far more stringent restrictions than the commission had proposed. Consequently, when published, the regulations generated a storm of protest, largely from the research community, but also from advocacy groups for persons with retardation, on the grounds that the proposals would severely hamper research. To make a long story short, the proposals remain just that six years later, and the Department of Health and Human Services regulations for protection of human subjects have special sections dealing with research on children, prisoners, fetuses, and pregnant women, but none on persons with mental illness or retardation. The only special guidance current regulations provide for this population is a directive to the IRB (Protection of Human Subjects, March 8, 1983) to determine that "where some or all of the subjects are likely to be vulnerable to coercion or undue influence, such as persons with acute or severe physical or mental illness, . . . appropriate additional safeguards have been included in the study to protect the rights and welfare of these subjects'' (Sec. 46.111 b).

With no final action taken on its recommendations, was the commission's work on this topic in vain? I think not. It focused attention as never before on the ethical issues and problems in conducting research on persons with mental retardation. It provided useful guidance for IRBs to take into account when reviewing different types of research involving persons with different degrees of mental impairment, to determine acceptable risk and appropriate protection in the decision-making process. It demonstrated that it is possible to strike a balance between the imperative for research and the need for protecting vulnerable subjects. And, of greatest importance, it made the case strongly that research on mental retardation is of the utmost necessity if we are to improve the status of this population. Persons with mental retardation are respected as persons, treated with beneficence, and provided justice not by leaving them alone, or even by giving them adequate care, but by attempting to improve their condition and that of future generations through research that includes their participation. The commission's message was clear: This research is important, and this is the way to do it appropriately; get to work and do it. Or as the humanitarian and idealist John F. Kennedy might have put it, ''What better way to love your neighbor than to try to find a way to heal him.''

REFERENCES

Englehardt, H.T. (1978). Basic ethical principles in the conduct of biomedical and behavioral research involving human subjects. In *The Belmont Report, 1*(8). DHEW Publication No. OS 78-0014. Washington, DC: U.S. Government Printing Office.

McCormick, R. (1974, Autumn). Proxy consent in the experimentation situation. *Perspectives in Biology and Medicine, 18*, 2–20.

McCormick, R. (1976). Experimentation on the fetus: Policy proposals. In *Research on the fetus: Appendix*. DHEW Publication No. OS 76-128. Washington, DC: U.S. Government Printing Office.

National Commission for the Protection of Human Subjects of Biomedical and Behavioral Research. (1978). *Report and recommendations: Research involving those institutionalized as mentally infirm*. DHEW Publication No. OS 78-0006. Washington, DC: U.S. Government Printing Office.

Protection of Human Subjects, 45 CFR 46.111 b (March 8, 1983).

Ramsey, P. (1970). *The patient as person*. New Haven: Yale University Press.

U.S. v. Karl Brandt et al. (1947). Trials of war criminals before Nuremberg Military Tribunals under Control Council Law No. 10, the medical case (Vol. 2.), pp. 181–183.

Veatch, R. (1978). Three theories of informed consent: Philosophical foundations and policy implications. In *The Belmont Report, 2*(26). DHEW Publication No. OS 78-0014. Washington, DC: U.S. Government Printing Office.

Wyatt v. Stickney, 344 F. Supp. 373, 380 (M.D. Ala., 1972).

Chapter 4

SUFFERING THE RETARDED
SHOULD WE
PREVENT RETARDATION?

Stanley Hauerwas

THE MOVIE BEGINS. A man and woman stand looking into a baby's crib. The baby is never shown. The room is dark and the countenance of the couple is yet darker. They have obviously been through a trauma and are still in shock. The joy and excitement associated with the birth of a child has been crushed from their lives. Their high expectations have been transformed to absolute despair.

They turn toward us and the man speaks: "Don't let this happen to you. Our child was born retarded. He will never play the way other children play. He will not be able to go to school with other children. He will never have an independent existence and will require us to care for him throughout his and our lifetime. Our lives have been ruined. It is too late for us but not for you."

The mother speaks: "Don't let what happened to us happen to you. Be tested early if you think you are pregnant. Maintain good prenatal care under the direction of a physician. Do not smoke, drink, or take any drugs except those absolutely necessary for your health. Please do not let this happen to you—prevent retardation."

A film much like this was sponsored a few years ago by the Association for Retarded Citizens/United States (ARC/US). No doubt the film was made with the best of intentions and concern. Surely we ought to prevent retardation. Certainly as many couples as can ought to be encouraged to maintain good prenatal care. Moreover, the Association for Retarded Citizens

This chapter is reprinted with permission, with minor modifications, from: Hauerwas, S. (1984). Suffering the retarded: Should we prevent retardation? In F. Dougherty (Ed.), *The deprived, the disabled, and the fullness of life* (pp. 67–105). Wilmington, DE: Michael Glazier, Inc.

is probably right to assume they will stand a better chance of getting research funds for the retarded if they can convince the public, and thus the government, that their long-term policy is to eliminate retardation, like the goal for cancer. For if retardation can be eliminated, then the amount of monies needed for constant care will be significantly reduced. Better a short-term large outlay now than a continuing cost.

Nevertheless, there seems to be something deeply wrong, something disturbing about this film and its message, "Prevent Retardation." Perhaps part of the difficulty involves the wrong analogy between preventing retardation and preventing cancer, polio, or heart diseases, because these latter diseases exist independent of the subjects who have them. The disease can be eliminated without eliminating the subject of the disease. But the same is not true of the retarded person portrayed in the film. To eliminate retardation means to eliminate the subject in cases such as this one.

Yet surely this point is not decisive. The film, after all, is not suggesting that we kill anyone who is now retarded. On the contrary, the film's producers have dedicated their lives to enhancing the lives of retarded citizens. They have led the war on unjust forms of discrimination against the retarded. They surely do not seek to make the lot of the retarded worse than it is already; rather they simply seek to prevent some from being unnecessarily born retarded. What could be wrong with that?

Still I think something is wrong with a general policy that seeks to prevent retardation. But to say what is wrong with such a policy involves some of the profoundest questions of human existence, including our relationship to God. In particular, assumptions about the nature and necessity of suffering, and our willingness to endure it in our own and other lives, will need to be addressed. For the very humanity that causes us to cry out against suffering, that motivates us to seek to eliminate retardation, is also the source of our potentially greatest inhumanity.

By trying to understand why this is the case, moreover, I hope to illumine how our moral and religious presuppositions shape our medical care. Too often medicine becomes the means by which we eliminate those who suffer in the name of humanity. Thus it has become common in our society to assume that certain children born with severe birth defects who also happen to be retarded should not be kept alive in order to spare them a lifetime of suffering. But why do we assume that it is the role of medicine to save us from suffering? By exploring whether we ought to try to eliminate the retarded I hope, therefore, to make candid a whole set of assumptions about suffering and medicine's role in its alleviation.

SETTING THE ISSUES

Before addressing these large issues, however, I think it wise to specify more exactly some of the problems raised by the film as well as some of the problems of the film. Obviously, the film seriously conflicts with the conviction of many who belong to and support the Association for Retarded Citizens. The film gives the impression that there is nothing more disastrous, nothing more destructive, than for a child to be born retarded; on the other hand, the film's sponsoring organization maintains that the retarded are not significantly different from the so called normal. Indeed, the ARC/U.S. believes that with appropriate training most retarded persons can become contributing members of a society even as complex as our own. Thus the negative impression of retardation the film conveys is not one that those sponsoring the film believe or think warranted. And it could have the unintended effect of reinforcing the largely negative assumptions about the retarded that are present in our society.

Perhaps equally troubling is the indiscriminate use of the notion of "retardation" in the film. Not only does the film fail to denote the wide variety of retardation—some much less serious than others—but even more troubling, it fails to make clear that our attribution of retardation may be due as much to our prejudices as to the assumed limits of the retarded. It has become increasingly recognized that disease description and remedies are relative to a society's values and needs. Thus retardation might not "exist" in a society that values cooperation more than competition and ambition.

The increasing realization that retardation is a social designation used too often to justify discrimination against the retarded, however, should not blind us to the fact that the retarded do have specifiable problems peculiar to them. When the societal components of the diagnosis "retarded" are stressed, we cannot fail to recognize that the retarded are different in specifiable ways and that their difference requires special forms of care.

Yet our approach to dealing with retardation is extremely important if we are to avoid two different perils. The first, drawing upon assumptions of societal prejudice embodied in all designations of retardation, seeks to aid the retarded by preventing discriminatory practices in a manner similar to the civil rights campaigns for blacks and women. In this view, because the retarded are said to have the same rights as anyone, all they require is to be treated "normally." Without denying that the retarded have "rights" or that much good has been done under the banner of "normalization," this way of putting the matter is misleading and risks making the retarded subject to even greater societal cruelty (see Hoffmaster, 1982). Would it not be unjust to treat the retarded "equally"? Instead, retardation ought to be so precisely understood that those who are thus handicapped can be accommodated according to their needs.

But that may be a reason for avoiding the word *retardation* altogether. As I have already noted, there are so many different ways of being retarded, there are so many different kinds of disabilities and corresponding forms of care required, that to isolate a group as "retarded" may be the source of much of the injustice we perpetrate on those whom we identify as "not normal."

The second peril is that of oppressive care, of care based on the assumption that the retarded are so disabled they must be protected from the danger and risks of life. Such a strategy subjects the retarded to a cruelty fueled by our sentimental concern to deal with their differences by treating them as something less than human agents. Too often such a strategy has resulted in isolating the retarded from the rest of society in the interest of "protecting" them from societal indifference. As a result they are trained to be retarded.

The challenge is to know how to characterize retardation and to know what difference it should make, without our very characterizations of that difference being used as an excuse to treat the retarded unjustly. In this respect, however, we see this is not just a problem for the retarded, but a basic problem of any society, since societies are only possible because we are all different—different in skills and different in needs (e.g., see Hauerwas, 1977). Societies must find ways to characterize and institutionalize those differences so that we see our differences as enhancing rather than diminishing each of our lives. From such a perspective the retarded are but a poignant test of a society's particular understanding of how our differences are relevant to the achievement of a common good.

The various issues I have raised can be illustrated by pointing to one final fallacy that the film underwrites. It gives the impression that retardation is primarily a genetic problem recognized at or soon after birth. But that is simply not the case. Half the people who bear the label "retarded" do so as the result of some circumstance after their conception or birth. Many are retarded due to environmental, nutritional, or accidental causes. To suggest, therefore, that we can eliminate retardation by better prenatal care, or more thorough genetic screening and counseling, is a mistake. Even if we were all required to have genetic checks before being allowed to marry we would still have some among us that we currently label as "retarded."

We must ask, What would a "prevent retardation" campaign mean for this group? If a society were even partially successful in "eliminating" retardation, how would it regard those who have become retarded? Once retardation was largely eliminated on grounds of being unacceptable for a human being, could the retarded who remain look forward to a society able to recognize the validity of their existence or willing to provide the difference in care they require? Of course it might be suggested that with fewer retarded there would be more resources to care for those remaining. That is no doubt true, but the question is whether there would exist the moral will to direct those resources in the direction of the retarded. At present, we possess more than enough resources to care for the retarded well. That we do not provide such care is not for lack of resources but lack of moral will and imagination. What will and imagination there are come from those who have found themselves unexpectedly committed to care for a retarded person through birth or relation. Remove that group of dedicated individuals, and I seriously doubt we will find any source in society that can provide the moral conviction necessary to sustain our alleged commitment to the retarded.

To reckon whether this is mere speculation, consider this thought experiment. We live in a time when it is possible through genetic screening to predict who has the greatest likelihood of having a retarded child, particularly if we marry someone of similar genetic characteristics. It has become general policy for most of the population to have such screening and to choose their marriage partner accordingly. Moreover, amniocentesis has become so routine that the early abortion of handicapped children has become the medical "therapy" of choice.

How would such a society regard and treat a couple who refused to be genetically screened, who refused amniocentesis, and who perhaps thus gave birth to a less than normal child? Would such a society be happy with the increased burden on its social and financial resources? Why should citizens support the birth and care of such a child when its existence could have easily been avoided? To care for such a child, to support such "irresponsible" parents, means only that the "truly" needy will unjustly be deprived of care in the interest of sustaining a child who will never contribute to societal good. That such an attitude seems not unreasonable to many people also suggests that in our current situation a campaign to "prevent retardation" might have negative implications for those who are retarded as well as for those who may have the misfortune to be born retarded or become retarded in the future.

SUFFERING AND THE RETARDED

But surely there is something wrong with the claim that since we can never ensure that no one will be born or become retarded, then we cannot try to prevent retardation at all. On such grounds it seems we cannot change our lives to ensure that few will be born retarded so that those who are retarded now and in the future will not be cruelly treated and may even receive better care. Such is certainly a vicious and unworthy position. We should surely rightly seek to avoid those forms of retardation that are avoidable.

It seems obvious that we should seek to prevent retardation. To challenge that assumption would be equivalent to questioning our belief that the world is round or that love is a good thing. But like so many of our obvious beliefs, if we ask why they seem so self-evident we often feel unable to supply an answer. Perhaps they seem obvious precisely because they do not require a reason for holding them.

I suspect that at least part of the reason it seems so clear that we ought to prevent retardation is the conviction that we ought to prevent suffering. No one should will that an animal should suffer gratuitously. No one should will that a child should endure an illness. No one should will that another person should suffer from hunger. No one should will that a child should be born retarded. That suffering should be avoided is a belief as deep as any we have. That someone born retarded suffers is obvious. Therefore if we believe we ought to prevent suffering, it seems we ought to prevent retardation.

Yet, like many other "obvious" beliefs, the assumption, if analyzed, that suffering should always be prevented becomes increasingly less certain or, at least, involves unanticipated complexity. Just because it implies eliminating subjects who happen to be retarded should at least suggest to us that something is wrong with our straightforward assumption that suffering should always be avoided or, if possible, eliminated. This is similar to some justifications of suicide—namely, in the interest of avoiding or ending suffering, a subject wills no longer to exist. Just because in suicide there is at least allegedly a decision by the victim does not alter the comparison with some programs to prevent retardation: both assume that certain forms of suffering are so dehumanizing it is better not to exist than to endure.

As I have indicated earlier, this assumption draws upon and is supported by some of our most profound moral convictions. Yet I hope to show that as a general rule our assumption that suffering should always be prevented is a serious and misleading oversimplification. To demonstrate why this is so a general analysis of suffering is required. We assume we know what suffering is because it is so common, but on analysis suffering turns out to be an extremely elusive subject. Only once that analysis has been done will we be in a position to ask if the retarded suffer from being retarded or whether the problem is the suffering we feel the retarded cause us.

The Kinds and Ways of Suffering

"To suffer" means to undergo, to be subject. But we undergo much we do not call suffering. Suffering names those aspects of our lives that we undergo and that have a particularly negative sense. We suffer when what we undergo blocks our positive desires and wants. Suffering also carries a sense of the surd: it denotes those frustrations for which we can give no satisfying explanation and that we cannot make serve some wider end. Suffering thus names a sense of brute power that does violence to our best-laid plans. It is not easily domesticated. There can be, therefore, no purely descriptive account of suffering, since every description necessarily entails some judgment about the value of certain states or purposes.

For this reason we often associate, if not identify, suffering with pain. But pain and suffering are clearly not equivalent. If we are in pain we may well be suffering, but not every pain is equivalent to suffering—thus some who feel great pain deny they are suffering (see Hauerwas, 1979). But it is even more likely that I may claim to be suffering yet be in no pain. Pain is neither a necessary nor sufficient condition for claims that we and others are suffering.

I certainly do not mean to deny a close connection between pain and suffering; rather, I only wish to challenge the assumption that they are equivalent. Exactly how to characterize the nature of pain and suffering, as well as their relation, is no easy matter. Certainly it will not do to try to map pain and suffering in terms of objective and subjective elements of our experiences. Even though pain may have physical correlatives that appear to make it more objective than suffering, pain nonetheless has a subjective side—what may be extremely painful for one may be less so for another. Moreover, suffering is by no means just the subjective side of pain, for we rightly believe we are able to attribute suffering to someone, though that person may not "feel" or think he or she is suffering. Such attributions are as tricky as they are dangerous.

In short, while pain may often be the occasion for suffering, it is by no means necessarily so. I may think of myself as in pain, but not suffering. I may think of myself as in great suffering, but not in great pain. That pain and suffering are often rightly associated surely is based on our presumption that each involves that which we undergo—what disrupts our projects or equilibrium—but what certainly does not entail the assumption that pain and suffering are equivalent.

But perhaps all this has put us on the wrong foot. To look for a common meaning of suffering (and pain) may be a mistake. Simply because we have the word *suffering* does not mean it possesses a constant meaning or referent. In this respect it is interesting to note that most of the literature on suffering, at least in a theological context, seldom begins by offering an analysis of suffering. Instead the reality of suffering is presupposed in order to get on to the larger and allegedly more important issue of how innocent suffering can be understood or justified in a world claimed to be created by a good God. Without denying that many useful things have been said about that issue, one cannot help but wonder if the cart has not been put before the horse, since it is by no means clear we possess an adequate understanding of suffering, much less "innocent suffering."

No doubt the intensity of our own suffering or of our sympathy for others' suffering has reinforced our assumptions that we have a firm grip on its meaning. But it is not clear, for example, that the kind of suffering occasioned by starvation is the same as that of cancer, though each is equally terrifying in its relentless but slow resolution in death. Indeed, even the assumption that such experiences impose on us a common outcome is not as straightforward as it appears. It is interesting that we also use "suffer" in an active sense of "bearing with," "permitting," or "enduring." While such expressions do not eclipse the passive sense associated with suffering, they at least connote that we do not associate suffering only with that for which we can do nothing.

Perhaps this is the clue we have been needing to understand better the nature of suffering. We must distinguish between those forms of suffering that happen to us and those we bring on ourselves as requisite to our purposes and goals. Some suffering that befalls us is integral to our goals, only we did not previously realize it. We tend to associate pain, however, with what happens to us, since it seems to involve that which always stands as a threat to our goals and projects rather than as some means to a further end. In like manner, we suffer from illness and accidents—thus our association of pain with sickness and physical trauma. Of course pain and illness are interrelated because most of the time when we are ill we hurt, but it is also true that conceptually pain and illness seem to stand on that side of suffering that is more a matter of fate than choice.

This distinction helps us to see the wider meaning of suffering. We not only suffer from diseases, accidents, tornadoes, earthquakes, droughts, floods—all those things over which it seems we have little control—but we also suffer from other people, from living here rather than there, from doing this kind of job—all matters we might avoid—because we see what we suffer as part of a larger scheme. This latter sense of "suffer," moreover, seems more subjective, since what may appear as a problem for one may seem as nothing but an opportunity for another. Not only is what we suffer relative to our projects, but how we suffer is relative to what we have to be or wish to be.

In this sense suffering shares many of the characteristics and puzzles associated with luck. Like suffering, luck seems to involve aspects of life over which we have no control, yet we think some forms of luck are "deserved" or "undeserved." The latter judgment seems to imply that someone has led a life for which he or she "tempted fate" and thus got what he or she deserved (e.g., see Nagel, 1979; Williams, 1976). We therefore seem to assume that certain kinds of suffering, like certain forms of luck, go with particular forms of life.

Without denying that the distinction between forms of suffering that happen to us and those that we instigate as requisite to our goals is important, we would be mistaken to press the distinction too hard. Once considered, it is by no means clear if the distinction is as evident or as helpful as it first appears. For example, we often discuss how at one time something that looked like it happened to us—something we suffered—turned out to be something we did, or at least chose not to avoid. Our increasing knowledge of the relation of illness to life-style is certainly enough to make us think twice before drawing a hard and fast distinction between what happens to us and what we do.

But the situation is even more complex. We often find that essential in our response to suffering is the ability to make what happens to me mine. Cancer patients often testify to some sense of relief when they find out they have cancer. The very ability to name what they have seems to give them a sense of control or possession that replaces the undifferentiated fear they had been feeling. Pain and suffering alienate us from ourselves. They make us what we do not know. The task is to find the means to make that which is happening to me mine—to interpret its presence, even if such an interpretation is negative, as something I can claim as integral to my identity. No doubt our power to transform events into decisions can be the source of great self-deception, but it is also the source of our moral identity.

I should emphasize that I am not suggesting that every form of pain or suffering can be or should be seen as some good or challenge. Extreme suffering can as easily destroy as enhance. Nor am I suggesting that we should be the kind of people who can transform any suffering into benefit. We rightly feel that some forms of suffering can only be acknowledged, not transformed. Indeed, at this point I am not making any normative recommendations about how we should respond to suffering; rather I am suggesting the distinction between the suffering that happens to us beyond our control and the suffering that we accept as part of our projects is not as clear as it may at first seem. More important is the question of what kind of people we ought to be so that certain forms of suffering are not denied but accepted as part and parcel of our existence as moral agents.

In spite of our inability to provide a single meaning to the notion of suffering or to distinguish clearly between different kinds of suffering, I think this analysis has important implications. It may well be that those forms of suffering we believe we should try to prevent or eliminate are those that we think impossible to integrate into our projects socially or individually. It is exactly those forms of suffering that seem to intrude uncontrollably into our lives that appear to be the most ready candidates for prevention. Thus our sense that we should try to prevent suffering turns out to mean that we should try to prevent those kinds of suffering that we do not believe can serve any human good.

Even this way of putting the matter may be misleading. Some may object that while it is certainly descriptively true that we find it hard to integrate certain kinds of suffering into our individual and social lives, that ought not be the case. The issue is not what we do, but rather who we ought to be to be able to accept all suffering as a necessary aspect of human existence. In viewing our life narrowly as a matter of purposes and accomplishments, we may miss our actual need for suffering, even apparently purposeless or counterpurposeful suffering. The issue is not whether retarded children can serve a human good, but whether we should be the kind of people—the kind of parents and community—who can receive, even welcome, such people into our midst in a manner that allows them to flourish.

It may be objected that even though this way of putting the issue seems to embody the highest moral ideals, in fact, it is deeply immoral because the suggestion that all forms of suffering are capable of being given human meaning is destructive of the human project. Certain kinds of suffering—Auschwitz, floods, wars—are so horrible we are able to preserve our humanity only by denying them human significance. No "meaning" can be derived from the Holocaust except that we must do everything we can to see that it does not happen again. Similarly, perhaps individuals can respond to natural disasters in a positive manner, but humanly we are right to view such destructions as a scourge we will neither accept nor try to explain in some positive sense.

Our refusal to accept certain kinds of suffering, or to try to interpret them as serving some human purpose, is essential for our moral health. Otherwise we would far too easily accept the causes of suffering rather than trying to eliminate or avoid them. Our primary business is not to accept suffering, but to escape it both for our sake and our neighbors'. Still in the very attempt to escape suffering, do we not lose something of our own humanity? We rightly try to avoid unnecessary suffering, but it also seems that we are never quite what we should be until we recognize the necessity and inevitability of suffering in our lives.

To be human is to suffer. That sounds wise. That sounds right, that is, true to the facts. But we should not be too quick to affirm it as a norm. Questions remain as to what kind of suffering should be accepted and how it should be integrated into our lives. Moreover, ahead of these questions is the even more challenging one of why suffering seems to be our fate. Even if I knew how to answer such questions I could not try to address them in the scope of this chapter. But perhaps I can do something better. I suspect that there can be no general answer to such questions that will not mislead as much as inform. By directing our attention toward the retarded perhaps we can better understand what and how suffering is never to be "accepted" and yet why it is unavoidable in our lives. In preparation for that discussion, however, I need to try to suggest why it is that suffering seems so unavoidable.

On Why We Suffer

To ask why we suffer makes the questioner appear either terribly foolish or extremely arrogant. It seems foolish to ask since in fact we *do* suffer, and no sufficient reason can be given to explain that fact. Indeed, if suffering were explained, it would be denied some of its power. The question seems arrogant because it seeks to put us in the position of eating from the tree of good and evil. Only God knows the answer to such questions. Our task is to learn not to ask them, but rather to try to make the best of the fact that suffering goes along with being finite and, perhaps, sinful beings.

Without denying that the question of why we suffer can be foolish and pretentious, I think it is worth asking since it has such an obvious answer: We suffer because we are incomplete beings who depend on one another for our existence. Indeed the matter can be put more strongly since we depend upon others not only for our survival but also for our identity. Suffering is built into our condition because it is literally true that we exist only to the extent that we sustain, or "suffer," the existence of others—including not just others like us but mountains, trees, animals, and so on.

This is exactly contrary to cherished assumptions. We believe that our identity derives from our independence, our self-possession. As Arthur McGill (1983) suggests, we think "a person is real so far as he can draw a line around certain items—his body, his thoughts, his house—and claim them as his own" (p. 89). Thus death becomes our ultimate enemy—the intimation involved in every form of suffering—because it is the ultimate threat to our identity. Again, as McGill suggests, that is why what we suffer so often seems to take demonic proportions: "our neediness seems to make us helpless to what we undergo. In this sense, our neediness represents a fundamental *flaw* in our identity, a basic inability to rest securely with those things which are one's own and which lie inside the line between oneself and the rest of reality. Need forces the self to become open to the not-self; it requires every man to come to terms with the threats of demonic power" (p. 90).

The irony is, however, that our neediness is also the source of our greatest strength, for our need requires the cooperation and love of others, from which derives our ability not only to live but to flourish. Our identity, far from deriving from our self-possession, or our self-control, comes from being depossessed of those powers that promise only illusory power. Believing otherwise, fearful of our sense of need, by our attempt to deny our reliance on others, we become all the more subject to those powers. As we shall see, this has particularly significant implications for our relations with the retarded, since we "naturally" disdain those who do not or cannot cover up their neediness. Prophetlike, the retarded only remind us of the insecurity hidden in our false sense of self-possession.

It may be objected that such an account of suffering is falsely subtle, since it is obvious why we suffer—bad things happen to us. We are injured in accidents, we lose everything in a flood, our community is destroyed by a tornado, we get cancer, a retarded child is born. These are not things that happen to us because of our needs, but rather they happen because they happen. Yet each does relate to concrete needs—the need for security and safety, the need for "everydayness," the need for health, the need for new life. If we try to deny any of these needs, as well as many others, we deny ourselves the necessary resources for well-lived lives and make ourselves all the more subject to demonic powers. This line of thought suggests one of the reasons the ARC/U.S. film appeals to parents, as all parents are frustrated by the presence of a retarded child. Most parents suffer willingly for their children if they think such suffering will make their children "better." The problem with the retarded is they seem to offer little hope of ever being decisively better. So we are tempted to eliminate retarded children because of our unwillingness to suffer for a child who will never get better. Of course, parents of retarded children soon learn, as finally all parents of normal children also learn, that they can rejoice in their children's "progress" even if such progress fails to correspond to their original ambitions for their children's "betterment."

I have not tried in this brief and inadequate account of why we suffer to offer anything like a theodicy. Indeed I remain skeptical of all attempts to provide some general account or explanation of evil or suffering. For example, it is by no means clear that evil and suffering raise the same questions, since certainly not every form of suffering is evil. Moreover, as I have suggested here, I do not think any explanation that removes the irrationality of certain forms of suffering can be right. Much in our lives should not be made "good" or explained.

All I have tried to do is to state the obvious—we suffer because we are inherently creatures of need. This does not explain, much less justify, our suffering or the evil we endure. But it does help us understand why the general policy to prevent suffering is at least odd. Our task is to prevent unnecessary suffering, but the hard question, as we have seen, is to know what constitutes unnecessary suffering. it is even more difficult when the question concerns another, as it does in the case of the retarded. It is that question to which I now turn.

DO THE RETARDED SUFFER FROM BEING RETARDED?

I suggested earlier that behind the claim we ought to prevent retardation lies the assumption that we ought to prevent suffering or, in particular, unnecessary suffering. By providing an analysis of suffering I have tried at least to raise some critical questions about that assumption. But another issue requires equal analysis: Are we right to assume that the retarded are suffering by being retarded? Certainly they suffer retardation, but do they suffer from being retarded?

No doubt, like everyone, the retarded suffer. Like us they have accidents. Like us they have colds, sores, and cancer. Like us they are subject to natural disasters. Like us they die. So there is no doubt the retarded suffer, but the question is whether they suffer from being retarded. We assume they suffer because of their retardation, just as we or others suffer from being born blind or deaf. Yet it is by no means clear that such cases are similar or even whether those born blind or deaf suffer from blindness or deafness. Is it possible that they are in fact taught by us that they are decisively disabled, and thus learn to suffer? If that is the case, then there is at least some difference between being blind and being retarded since the very nature of being retarded means there is a limit to our ability to make clear to the retarded the nature of their disadvantage and the extent of their suffering. Of course that may also be true of being blind or deaf, but not in the same way.

Do the retarded understand that they are retarded? Certainly most are able to see that they are different from many of us, but there is no reason to think they would on their own come to understand their condition as "retardation" or that they are in some decisive way suffering. They may even perceive that there are some things some people do easily that they can do only with great effort or not at all, but that in itself is not sufficient reason to attribute to them great suffering due to their being retarded. Of course it may be objected that if we are to care for them, if we are to help alleviate some of the results of their being retarded, we cannot help but try to make them understand their limits. We have to make them conscious of their retardation if we are to help them be free from some of the effects of their condition. But again, this is certainly not as clear as it first appears, for it by no means follows that by learning to confront their limits in order to better their life, the retarded necessarily understand they are thereby suffering from something called retardation, Down syndrome, or the like.

Yet we persist in the notion that the retarded are suffering, and suffering so much from being retarded that it would be better for them not to exist than to have to bear such disability. It is important that I not be misunderstood. I am not suggesting that retardation is a minor problem or that nothing should be done to try to prevent, alleviate, or lessen the effects of being retarded; I am trying, rather, to suggest that the widespread assumption that the retarded suffer from being retarded is by no means obvious.

Perhaps what we assume is not that the retarded suffer from being retarded but rather, because they are retarded, they will suffer from being in a world like ours. They will suffer from inadequate housing, inadequate medical care, inadequate schooling, lack of love and care. They will suffer from discrimination as well as cruel kidding and treatment from unfeeling peers. All this is certainly true, but it is not an argument for preventing retardation in the name of preventing suffering; rather it is an argument for changing the nature of the world in the interest of preventing such needless suffering we impose on the retarded.

It may be observed that we have very little hope that the world will or can be changed in this respect, but even if that is the case, it would be insufficient grounds for the general policy of eliminating the retarded. On such grounds anyone suffering from treatment that results in their suffering would be in jeopardy. If justice comes to mean the elimination of the victim of injustice rather than the cause of injustice, we stand the risk of creating admittedly a less troubled but deeply unjust world.

The need to subject this set of assumptions to rigorous analysis is particularly pressing in relation to the care of children born retarded or otherwise handicapped. A policy of nontreatment is often justified in the hope they will die and thus be spared a life of suffering. I by no means wish to argue that every child should receive the most energetic medical care to keep it alive, but if such care is withheld it cannot be simply to spare the child a life of suffering. On such grounds few children with any moderately serious chronic health problem would be cared for at birth. We all, healthy and nonhealthy, normal and abnormal, are destined for a life of suffering.

It may be objected that this is surely to miss the point behind the concern to spare certain children a life of suffering. The issue is the extent and intensity of the suffering. But again such a judgment is a projection of our assumptions about how we would feel if we were in their situation. But that is exactly what we are not. We do not know to what extent they may suffer from their disability. We do not know how much pain they will undergo, but we nonetheless act to justify our lack of care in the name of our humane concern about their destiny. We do so knowing even that our greatest nobility as humans often derives from individuals' struggles to make positive use of their limitations.

I am not suggesting that the care we give to severely disabled children (or adults) will always result in happy results for themselves or those around them. But to refrain from such care to spare them future suffering can be a formula for profound self-deception. Too often the suffering we wish to spare them is the result of our unwillingness to change our lives so that those disabled might have a better life. Or even more troubling, we refrain from life-giving care simply because we do not like to have those who are different from us to care for.

Our Suffering of the Retarded

Why, therefore, do we persist in assumptions that the retarded suffer from being retarded? At least something of an answer comes from a most unlikely source: Adam Smith's *Theory of Moral Sentiments*. In that book Smith (1976) endeavors to account for why, no matter how "selfish a man may be supposed, there are evidently some principles in his nature which interest him in the fortune of others, and render their happiness necessary to him, though he derives nothing from it except the pleasure of seeing it" (part 1, 1). Such a sentiment, Smith observes, is by no means confined to the virtuous, since even the most "burdened ruffian" at times may derive sorrow from the sorrow of others.

That we do so, according to Smith, is something of a puzzle. Since we have no "immediate experience of what other men feel, we can form no idea of the manner in which they are affected, but by conceiving what we ourselves should feel in the like situation. Though our brother is upon the rack, as long as we ourselves are at our ease, our senses will never inform us what he suffers. They never did, and never can, carry us beyond our own person, and it is by the imagination only that we can form any conception of what are his sensations" (part 1, 2).

It is through our imagination, therefore, that our fellow-feeling with the sorrow of others is generated. But our sympathy does not extend to every passion, for there are some passions that disgust us—thus the furious behavior of an angry man may actually make us more sympathetic with his enemies. That this is so makes us especially anxious to be people capable of eliciting sympathy from others. Thus "sympathy enlivens joy and alleviates grief. It enlivens joy by presenting another source of satisfaction; and it alleviates grief by insinuating unto the heart almost the only agreeable sensation which it is at that time capable of receiving" (part 1, 1). By knowing our sorrow is shared by another we seem to be less burdened with our distress. Moreover, we are pleased when we are able to sympathize with one that is suffering, but we even look forward more to enjoying another's good fortune.

Because we seek to sympathize as well as be the object of sympathy, Smith observes:

> Of all the calamities to which the condition of mortality exposes mankind, the loss of reason appears, to those who have the least spark of humanity, by far the most dreadful, and they behold that last stage of human "wretchedness" with deeper commiseration than any other. But the poor wretch, who is in it, laughs and sings perhaps, and is altogether insensible of his own misery. The anguish which humanity feels, therefore, at the sight of such an object, cannot be the reflection of any sentiment of the sufferer. The compassion of the spectator must arise altogether from the consideration of what he himself would feel if he was reduced to the same unhappy situation, and, what perhaps is impossible, was at the same time able to regard it with his present reason and judgment. (part 1, 11)

We thus persist in our assumption that the retarded suffer from being retarded not because we are unsympathetic with them but because we are not sure how to be sympathetic with them. We fear that the very imagination that is the source of our sympathy, on which our fellow feeling is founded, is not shared by them. To lack such an important resource, we suspect, means they are fatally flawed, for one thus lacks the ability to be the subject of sympathy. We seek to prevent retardation not because we are inhumane but because we fear the retarded lack the means of sympathy. Exactly because we are unsure they have the capacity to suffer as we suffer, we seek to avoid their presence in order to avoid the limits of our own sympathy.

As Smith observes, we have no way to know what the retarded suffer as retarded. All we know is how we imagine we would feel if we were retarded. We thus often think we would rather not exist at all than exist as one retarded. But as a result we miss exactly the point at issue. For the crucial point is that the retarded do not feel or understand their retardation as we do, or imagine we would, but rather as they do. We have no right or basis to attribute our assumed unhappiness or suffering to them.

Ironically, therefore, the policy of preventing suffering is one based on a failure of imagination. Unable to see like the retarded, to hear like the retarded, we attribute to them our suffering. We thus rob them of the opportunity to do what each of us must do—learn to hear and live with our individual sufferings.

Need, Loneliness, and the Retarded

In many respects, however, our inability to sympathize with the retarded—to see their life as they see it, to suffer their suffering—is but an aspect of a more general problem. As Smith observes, we do not readily expose our sufferings because none of us is anxious to identify with the sufferings of others. We try to present a pleasant appearance in order to elicit fellow-feeling with others. We fear to be sufferers, to be in pain, to be unpleasant, because we fear so desperately the loss of fellow-feeling on the part of others. We resent those who suffer without apology; we expect the sufferer at least to show shame in exchange for our sympathy.

As much as we fear suffering we fear more the loneliness that accompanies it. We try to deny our neediness as much, if not more so, to ourselves as to others. We seek to be strong. We seek to be self-possessed. We seek to deny that we depend on others for our existence. We will be self-reliant, and we resent and avoid those who do not seek to be like us—the strong. We will be friends to one another only so long as we promise not to impose seriously our sufferings on the others. Of course, we willingly enter into some of our friends' suffering—indeed to do so only reinforces our sense of strength—but we expect such suffering to be bounded by a more determinative strength.

That we avoid the sufferer is not because we are deeply unsympathetic or inhumane, but because of the very character of suffering. By its very nature suffering alienates us not only from one another but from ourselves, especially suffering that we undergo that is not easily integrated into our ongoing projects or hopes. To suffer is to have our identity threatened physically, psychologically, and morally. Thus our suffering even makes us unsure who we are.

It is not surprising, therefore, that we should have trouble with the suffering of others. None of us willingly seeks to enter into the loneliness of others. We fear such loneliness may result in loss of control of our own life. We feel we must be very strong to be able to help the weak and needy. We may be right, but about that we also may fail to be able to give the kind of help they really need. Too often we seek to do something rather than first simply learn how to be with, to be present to, the sufferer in his or her loneliness. We especially fear, if not dislike, those whose suffering is the kind for which we can do nothing.

The retarded, therefore, are particularly troubling for us. Even if they do not suffer by being retarded they are certainly people in need. Even worse they do not try to hide their needs. They are not self-sufficient, they are not self-possessed, they are in need. Even more they do not evidence the proper shame for being so. They simply assume that they are what they are, and they need to provide no justification for being such. It is almost as if they have been given a natural grace to be free from the regret most of us feel for our neediness.

That such is the case, however, does not mean that the retarded do not suffer from the general tendency to be self-sufficient. Like us, they are more than capable of engaging in the self-deceptive project of being their own person. Nor is such an attempt entirely wrong, for they, like us, rightly seek to develop skills that can help them help themselves as well as others. But yet we perceive them as essentially different from us, as beings whose condition has doomed them to a loneliness we fear worse than suffering itself, and, as a result, we seek to prevent retardation.

That we are led to such an extreme derives partly from our frustration at not being able to cure the retarded. We seek to help them overcome their disability, but we know that even our best efforts will not result in the retarded not being retarded. After all, what we finally seek is not simply to help the retarded better negotiate their disability but to be like us: not retarded. Our inability to accomplish that frustrates and angers us, and sometimes the retarded themselves become the object of our anger. We do not like to be reminded of the limits of our power, and we do not like those who remind us.

We fervidly seek to help the retarded, to do for the retarded, to make their lot less subject to suffering. No doubt much good derives from such efforts. But our frenzied activity can also be a failure to recognize that our attempts to help, our attempts "to do for" the retarded, must first be governed by our ability to do "with" the retarded. Only as we learn to be and do with the retarded do we learn that their retardation, our projection of their suffering, does not create an unbridgeable gap between them and us. We learn that they are not incapable of fellow-feeling with us, and just as important, that we are not incapable of fellow-feeling with them.

That such fellow-feeling is possible does not mean that they are "really just like us." They are not like us. They do not have the same joys we have, nor do they suffer just as we suffer. But in our joys and in our sufferings they recognize something of their joy and their suffering, and they offer to share their neediness with us. Such an offer enables us in quite surprising ways to discover that we have needs to share with them. We are thus freed from the false and vicious circle of having to appear strong before others' weakness and we are then able to join with the retarded in the common project of sharing our needs and satisfactions. As a result we discover we no longer fear them.

I am not suggesting that such sharing comes easily. Few of us are prepared to enter naturally into such a life. Indeed most of us, cherishing the illusion of our strength, must be drawn reluctantly to such a life. But miraculously many are so graced. Day in and day out, through life with their retarded child, brother, or friend they learn to see themselves through the eyes of the other who happens also to be retarded. Moreover, by learning not to fear the other's retardation, they learn not to fear their own neediness.

Thus, if we are to make a movie to help others avoid unnecessary risks that can result in retardation, let us not begin soon after the birth. To begin there is grossly unfair because it catches us before we are even sure what has happened to us. Let the film begin several years after the birth, after the parents of a child born retarded have discovered, like all parents must, that they are capable of dealing with this. It is not the child they would have willed, but then all children turn out to be different than our expectations. This child, to be sure, raises particular challenges, but let the film show the confidence of the couple that comes from facing those challenges. Unless suggestions for preventing retarded children are bounded by such confidence, we cannot help but make the life of the retarded that much more difficult. But even more destructive, such a campaign cannot help but make our own illusory fears of the retarded and our own needs that much more powerful.

REFERENCES

Hauerwas, S. (1977). Community and diversity: The tyranny of normality. *National Apostolate for the Mentally Retarded, 8,* 1–2.

Hauerwas, S. (1979). Reflections on suffering, death, and medicine. *Ethics in Science and Medicine, 6,* 229–237.

Hoffmaster, B. (1982). Caring for retarded persons: Ideals and practical choices. In S. Hauerwas (Ed.), *Responsibility for devalued persons: Ethical interactions between society, the family, and the retarded* (p. 28–41). Springfield, IL: Charles C Thomas.

McGill, A. (1983). *Suffering: A test case of theological method.* Philadelphia: Westminster Press.

Nagel, T. (1979). *Mortal questions.* Cambridge, England: Cambridge University Press.

Smith, A. (1976). *The theory of moral sentiments* (edited by D.D. Raphael and A.L. Macafie). Oxford: Oxford University Press.

Williams, B. (1976). Moral luck. *Proceedings of the Aristotelian Society,* supplementary vol. L, 115–135.

Chapter 5

SOUNDINGS FROM UNCERTAIN PLACES

DIFFICULT PREGNANCIES AND IMPERILED INFANTS

Richard M. Zaner

WHEN GENETIC OR CONGENITAL anomalies have been diag-nostically established for either a fetus or an infant, what ethically relevant considerations apply prior to, during, and in the aftermath of intervention decisions? Is research into these considerations possible, and if so, what type of research is most likely to be productive? What, in short, are the prospects for and obstacles to ethically relevant research into intervention decisions on behalf of imperiled infants and fetuses?

FRAMING THE ISSUES: OBSTACLES AND NEW DIMENSIONS

It is hardly news that intervention decisions regarding imperiled infants and fetuses are fraught with conflicting beliefs, are often charged with urgency, and have been topics of impassioned debate at every level of personal and social life for almost two decades. Time has not softened these disputes, nor has accord been reached through compromise. If anything, disagreement has become even more acrimonious: rival positions have hardened, antagonisms have deepened, and prospects for consensus have become ever more remote. Whether it is abortion, birth control, or "Baby Doe," few issues have spurred public attention in both the popular press and scholarly literature as have these. Moreover, the intensifying of litigation, and the onerous prospects of media publicity, render the clinical management of, much less serious re-search into, such situations difficult at best.

None of this makes ethically relevant research welcome. Not even the otherwise familiar masks of anonymity and confidentiality practiced by scholarly journals in the review process can nowadays escape the well-known problems of subject honesty or the threats of legal action—as I learned when I proposed a form of qualitative research focused on both parents and caregivers for imperiled infants in the newborn intensive care unit (NICU). Even though armed with a seven-page, single-spaced consent form including an immaculately thought out concept of how to safeguard identifying characteristics of places and people, it became clear that unless I could succeed in becoming a rather selective amnesiac, the subjects faced the perilous risk of criminal and civil liabilities should they agree to participate and their words somehow become known despite all efforts to protect their privacies. Not only the subjects, but the institution itself was advised by counsel that it faced the same alarming, albeit remote, risks, as well as the potential loss of federal funding through legal suit. My memory, I was advised, could itself be subpoenaed, and since I do not enjoy legally protected ''privilege'' like my physician colleagues, I could not guarantee confidentiality in this highly sensitive area.

That research proposal was offered when the first of three versions of ''Baby Doe'' regulations was developed, based on Section 504 of the 1973 Rehabilitation Act (*Federal Register,* 1983, 1984a). Eventually, each of the regulations was ruled unconstitutional. Since then, several new developments have signaled that these discussions have entered a critical new phase, with possibly even greater barriers to serious research.

On the one hand, with the amendment last year to the Child Abuse Prevention and Treatment Act (Public Law 98-457), signed by President Ronald Reagan in August,1984, the issues presented by ''Baby Does'' no longer fall under due process for nondiscrimination against persons with handicaps. Now, the withholding of treatment for imperiled infants is defined as a new category of child abuse and neglect—not only as potential civil torts, but as criminal acts.

On the other hand, while the Supreme Court's decisions on abortion (*Beal v. Doe,* 1977; *Doe v. Bolton,* 1973; *Harris v. McRae,* 1980; *Maher v. Roe,* 1977; *Poelker v. Doe,* 1977; *Roe v. Wade,* 1973) have set limitations on permissible abortion procedures, other developments in obstetrics and radiology have given discussions of difficult pregnancies a new dimension. With the development of increasingly effective and routinized *in utero* diagnostic capabilities—amniocentesis (Strong, 1983), chorion biopsy (Cadkin, Ginsberg, Pergament, & Verlinski, 1984; Rodeck & Morsman, 1984), alpha fetoprotein (AFP) testing for neural tube defects (Kolata, 1980; Sun, 1983), and diagnostic ultrasonography (Perone, Carpenter, & Robertson, 1984; Wright & Shaw, 1981)—the potential for legal vulnerability has dramatically increased, stemming from negligence, error from practice beyond one's skills, failure to use diagnostic procedures where indicated, and damage from the procedures themselves. It should be further emphasized that this increased use of *in utero* diagnostic techniques, and their enhanced accuracy, frequently come to loggerheads with prevailing abortion laws, reopening that already-exacerbated issue in new ways. As might also be expected, refinements and advances in antenatal diagnostic technologies will likely enable new *in utero* therapeutic procedures—for instance, to correct abnormalities such as hydrocephalus, hydronephrosis, bladder outlet obstruction, ascites and diaphragmatic hernia (Blane, Doff, Bowerman, & Barr, 1983; Cadkin et al., 1984; Clewell et al., 1982; Hobbins et al., 1984; Kramer, 1983; Michejda, Patronas, Di Chiro, & Hodgen, 1984; Rodeck & Morsman, 1984). As therapeutic success is achieved, it seems inevitable that post–24-week, that is, "viable," fetuses could well come within the reach of current "Baby Doe"–type regulations—both as regards requirements and exceptions to treatment (Englehardt, 1985).

It is thus not unreasonable to suggest that these discussions have taken on significantly new dimensions—which, as indicated, may well further complicate if not compromise "ethically relevant research" into intervention decisions. Several illustrations are helpful.

CASE 1: MULTIPLE CONGENITAL ANOMALIES IN A PREMATURE INFANT

Space does not allow a review of the case history prior to birth of this 27-week gestational age, 2,460 g male infant, admitted to the NICU of the regional tertiary acute-care medical center by referral from an outlying hospital. Born by cesarean section due to fetal distress (Apgars 2 and 6 after delivery) to a 17-year-old woman married to a 22-year-old man, the infant was initially admitted to the pediatric surgical unit for correction of an omphalocele (a midline abdominal wall defect resulting in the visceral organs lying exposed), and a diaphragmatic defect (partial absence on both sides). After surgery, which merely cosmetically closed the abdominal skin, since little else was able to be done at that time, the infant was then admitted to the NICU (at 3 weeks of age) for evaluation and treatment. Because of respiratory problems from birth, the infant had been on mechanical ventilation; this was continued to maintain stabilization in order to permit evaluation. Over a period of days, the following prominent problems were diagnosed: 1) midline abdominal wall defect, with partial absence of diaphragm; 2) multiple heart defects, including several reverse shuntings of blood flow, overriding aorta, and patent ductus arteriosis; 3) diffuse encephalopathy and abnormal seizure activity, either due to congenital problems or secondary to hypoxia during surgery (resuscitation was performed and surgery completed), with poor neurological outcome; 4) gastrointestinal feeding was not possible, owing to the midline defect;

therefore, the infant was placed on TPN ("tube" feeds), which could not be removed, with the result that caloric intake was inadequate; and 5) pulmonary status required mechanical ventilation at the highest settings (100% oxygen concentration with high pressures and rates), which had to be maintained for the entire course of treatment due to diaphragmatic defect, low blood pressure, and other problems.

The outlook for intact survival was soon judged to be almost nil, and for survival itself quite poor. Eventually, a DNR ("do not resuscitate") order was instituted: If a cardiac arrest occurred, no resuscitation would be attempted; no further blood-gas tests would be run; efforts to comfort would be used; and treatments for fever would only be symptomatic. The ventilator would be kept on at necessary settings, however, to maintain pulmonary function. The parents agreed with this decision.

Case Analysis

Although the U.S. Department of Health and Human Services (DHHS) had not yet published its final regulations providing the guidelines required by the 1984 Amendment to the Child Abuse Prevention and Treatment Act, a proposed rule had been published on December 10, 1984 (*Federal Register,* 1984b). The final rule, however, was subsequently developed, and has been published in the *Federal Register* (1985). The amendment itself had created a new category of child abuse and neglect concerned with "withholding" of treatment. This is defined as "the failure to respond to an infant's life-threatening conditions by providing treatment (including appropriate nutrition, hydration, and medication) which, in the treating physician's reasonable medical judgment, will be most likely to be effective in ameliorating or correcting all such conditions" (*Federal Register,* 1985, p. 14878). Certain exceptions to the requirement are given, but do not include exceptions to medication, hydration, and nutrition. These are when:

1. The infant is chronically and irreversibly comatose;
2. The provision of such treatment would merely prolong dying or not be effective in ameliorating or correcting all of the infant's life-threatening conditions, or would otherwise be futile in terms of the survival of the infant; or
3. The provision of such treatment would be virtually futile in terms of the survival of the infant, and the treatment itself under such circumstances would be inhumane. (*Federal Register,* 1985, p. 14878)

The attending neonatologist and primary care staff, knowing the new law, faced a number of difficult issues in this case. Among these were: first, neither the amendment language nor that of the proposed rule or final rule distinguish between two different resuscitation/maintenance purposes (which include the use of "life-supports"): a) to allow medical *evaluation,* and b) to provide *therapy* (either corrective or ameliorative). While the distinction may not always be critical, in cases like the present one it is vital. Evaluation—which may take days (to allow for neurological, ultrasonographic, cardiological, and other evaluations)—may disclose that initially noted anomalies (such as the omphalacele) are associated with underlying impairments (possible neurological problems), and additional anomalies may be noted (such as the heart defects), which themselves are life-threatening and even incompatible with intact survival or even survival. As these conditions are diagnosed, the possible use of medical or surgical procedures designed to be therapeutic may then become problematic. Even more, such measures as mechanical ventilation, initially used as an *evaluative* measure as distinct from *therapeutic* purposes, can present a harsh dilemma. If evaluation shows the kind of prognosis as was given this infant, should the ventilator or other measures designed to be therapeutic be kept in place or be removed? The problem becomes even more serious if the infant continues to require extremely high settings for a long period and weaning is not possible, since chronic lung disease (irreversible destruction of lung tissues) invariably sets in. Since no distinction between these two purposes is made, physicians and parents are left not knowing what to do.

Second, the issue just discussed is made more severe in another way: The exception language of the amendment (and both rules) mention "withholding" of treatments, but do not mention either their allowable "withdrawal" or "discontinuation." If "reasonable medical judgment" indicates, then, that treatments are "futile"—they can neither "correct" nor "ameliorate" all of the "life-threatening conditions"—they may be "withheld." But to which "treatments" does this refer—to those *already in place*, or to those that *might* be used but are *not yet in place?* Specifically, may the ventilator be *discontinued* from the infant; or, to the contrary, must it be kept in place, and only *contemplated* treatments "withheld"? The "do not resuscitate" order reflects this dilemma acutely, for at best only *partial* "withdrawal" was effected, plus the "withholding" of *additional* treatments (cardiac massage, drugs, mechanical resuscitative means).

In a third issue, the implication of this unclarity is made further problematic in a somewhat eerie way: If a treatment is "virtually futile in terms of the survival of the infant," then the *treatment itself* is "under such circumstances . . . inhumane." In an attempt to clarify the intent of Congress here, the proposed rule avers (reaffirmed in the final rule, *Federal Register,* 1985, p. 14892) that Congress sought "to recognize that, in some cases, the pain and suffering to the infant or other medical contraindications related to 'the treatment itself' clearly outweigh the very slight potential benefit of the treatment for an infant highly unlikely to survive" (*Federal Register,* 1984b, p. 48164). To close all doors to "quality of life" considerations, it is then stated that "Congress did not intend this provision to sanction consideration of the future 'quality of life' of an infant likely to survive if the treatment is provided or consideration of the anxiety of parents in connection with such an infant" (p. 48164; see also *Federal Register*, 1985, p. 14880). Presumably, the "pain and suffering" in question is meant to refer *strictly* to "the treatment itself" for an infant unlikely to survive, and *not* to the infant's potential "quality of life" or parental "anxiety."

If, however, mechanical ventilation, for instance, is "virtually futile"— indeed, is itself a factor in the continuing and irreversible destruction of lung tissue so long as weaning is impossible—then this "treatment itself" seems clearly "inhumane." If it is "inhumane," and a violation of the "dignity" of the dying infant, it is hardly a moral or even legal leap to the conclusion that continued ventilation could be judged immoral and even illegal—a criminal act against the dying infant. If, finally, "withholding" is distinct from "withdrawal," and only the former is intended by Congress and DHHS, then the dilemma is both striking and eerie: We are required to ventilate, which is itself "inhumane" and possibly criminal!

Fourth, in the case of the *exceptions*, the amendment does not mention parents, and the proposed rule accordingly did not either—whether as decision makers, participants in decisions, or even as having to be consulted by physicians exercising their "reasonable medical judgments." In the manuscript copy of its final rule, however, DHHS notes the considerable consternation this exclusion, or apparent exclusion, created. To clarify this crucial issue, DHHS states that "the decision to provide or withhold medically indicated treatment is, except in highly unusual circumstances, made by the parents or legal guardian." Indeed, the clarification continues, "Parents are the decision makers concerning treatment for their disabled infant, based on the advice and reasonable medical judgment of their physician (or physicians)." The final rule then emphasizes that both the Child Protection Service (CPS) of the particular state, and the Infant Care Review Committee (ICRC), are designed to assist children and their parents, and in no case to make decisions about the care of and treatment for the imperiled infant: "This is the parents' right and responsibility. . . . The parents' role as decision maker must be respected and supported unless they choose a course of action inconsistent with applicable standards established by law" (*Federal Register*, 1985, p. 14880).

Since this significant clarification was not at hand prior to the issuance of the final rule, however, physicians in our case faced a quandary, inasmuch as parents seemed to have no place in this kind of decision, and this was contrary to NICU practice. In one scenario consistent with the final rule, the difficulty seems easily surmountable, for if physicians advised treatment and parents wanted to "withhold," this would be clearly "inconsistent with applicable standards established by law." In such a case, it would be proper to notify the state CPS and institute appropriate legal proceedings to ensure that the infant was treated.

Suppose, however, that although physicians advised "withholding," the parents wanted to "have everything done" for their infant. While this is just as "inconsistent" with established law as is the first case, since both go against "reasonable medical judgment," would it be equally appropriate to notify CPS and institute legal proceedings to ensure that the parents' decision in this instance would not prevail?

What is troublesome here is DHHS's willingness to go along with parents' "right and responsibility" to make decisions, while at the same time stating that one class of decisions—"withholding" of treatment—is really *not* fully the parents' prerogative. To be sure, parents can make these decisions, but *only*, says the final rule, "based on the advice and reasonable medical judgment of their physician (or physicians)." And although it is clear that when parents and physicians disagree, and the issue is continued treatment, it is reasonable to expect CPS intervention and possible legal proceedings, it is by no means clear that such disagreement over the issue of nontreatment would similarly bring about CPS intervention and legal proceedings.

Preferable as the final rule seems to be here, the DHHS attempt at clarification seems to have left us with equally serious questions. The problem concerns how best to manage physician/parent disagreement, especially when the physician advises withholding and the parent wants continuation of all treatments. It would seem that in this case the parents might well get their way, while in the former case it is probable that the physician would prevail. That is, despite the importance of the final rule's clarification and reaffirmation of parental decision making, there may well be an underlying bias in it, one that tends toward treatment whenever there is disagreement, which may not at all be in the best interests of the infant itself.

In a fifth issue, although the language of the amendment does not mention quality of life considerations per se, the proposed and final rules do, and specifically state that these are not a legitimate part of "reasonable medical judgment." The final rule, indeed, asserts in several different places that "the Department's interpretative guidelines," which purport to be consistent with the amendment and congressional intent, do "not sanction decisions based on subjective opinions about the future 'quality of life' of a retarded or disabled person" (*Federal Register,* 1985, p. 14880).

The rejection of *quality of life* by DHHS seems to have arisen, in part at least, owing to persuasion from various child advocacy groups. For instance, the Association for Retarded Citizens/United States said in its comment on one version of the federal guidelines, that "no quality of life or other such considerations are acceptable to the ARC," and gave as its basic reason that "we come down strongly on the side of the child" as opposed to that of the parent (*Federal Register,* 1984a, p. 1629). J.G. Willke, M.D., president of the National Right to Life Committee, also strongly objected: "Fetal discrimination against Down's syndrome and other handicapped infants has been increasing for years in this country. This discrimination consists of denial of medical treatment, even food and water, which would be routinely provided to nonhandicapped infants. The ethic which promotes infanticide is related to the elitist 'quality of life' argument used to justify abortion-on-demand" (1982, cited in Smith, 1982, p. 6).

On the other hand, the Judicial Council of the American Medical Association (AMA) specifically combined the "medically beneficial standard" with "quality of life" considerations and "parental decision-making" unless there is convincing evidence to the contrary (Weir, 1983).

In this dispute, which is very much like that over whether parents should be primary decision makers, however, there is little if any analysis concerning just what is to be understood by *quality of life*. The term has been interpreted with great flexibility by various individuals and groups. But while this fact may have been the reason behind various rejections of the notion, that is hardly sufficient reason to reject it out of hand. In any case, neither the DHHS rejection nor the AMA's acceptance is critically justified, and neither faces the issue of how best to decide when parents and physicians disagree.

A sixth and final point is that in its proposed definition of "treatment," the proposed (and final) rule states that it includes "further evaluation by a physician whose expertise is appropriate to the condition(s) involved or further evaluation at a facility with specialized capabilities" (*Federal Register,* 1984b, p. 48163). The apparent intent of Congress was to emphasize that the "initial steps" of medical evaluation to determine appropriate treatments "often require specialized evaluation" such as is available mainly at regional NICU centers (*Federal Register,* 1985, p. 14890).

While much is left to the "reasonable medical judgments" of physicians practicing outside such centers, several problems occur in this definition. First, does the requirement for "special evaluation" imply that regional NICUs should expect an increase in such referrals, with the consequence that additional NICU staff, beds, or new "specialized" units should be constructed? At whose expense? Is there any way of knowing any of this in advance, so as to make such planning rational? Second, does the requirement signify that pediatricians who are not qualified with "special evaluation" skills may nevertheless become at least minimally qualified? For instance, the increased use of office-based ultrasonography has prompted the Section on Obstetric and Gynecologic Ultrasound (SOGU) of the American Institute of Ultrasound to begin developing guidelines defining minimum competence in its use, partly in response to the increased legal vulnerability this technology has brought in its wake (Perone et al., 1984). Will the same sort of attainment of "minimal competency" now be expected of office-based pediatricians? Is this a more rational approach to the potential problem of ensuring the availability of such "specialized evaluations"?

Potential Research Agendas

Reflection on these, and still other issues—raised within the clinical settings in which "Baby Does" are actually evaluated and treated—suggests a number of areas in serious need of research. They are the following:

1. In what ways is the distinction between "evaluation" and "therapy" actually utilized in clinical practice? Do office-based pediatricians or level I or II hospitals (those without specialized NICUs) make use of this distinction? How is the distinction used in different NICU units? Is treatment by office-based pediatricians the same as that in level I or II hospitals? In its definition of "treatment," DHHS mentions the requirement for "specialized evaluation." Is this different from "specialized therapy"?

2. How does "specialized evaluation" (at an NICU, for instance) relate to the issue of "withholding"? Physicians (including those in NICUs) frequently differentiate between "withholding" and "withdrawal" (or "discontinuation"). If "specialized evaluation" shows anomalies as serious as those in our case, which action may be taken? Moreover, it seems possible to detect even more subtle distinctions within NICU practice, between a kind of "partial withholding" (withholding only some measures that are otherwise possibly therapeutic) and "full withholding"; between "partial withdrawal" (discontinuing only some treatments) and "full withdrawal." For instance, in our case, it is clear that partial withdrawal was done, along with withholding of any future contemplated measures (including resuscitative means). This action, and other cases very much like it, force one to wonder about the *symbolic* value of the ventilator, and not simply its evaluative or therapeutic purposes. This is especially important, since mechanical ventilation does not seem reasonably included in "medication, nutrition, and hydration"—to which there are no exceptions—and yet seems to have something like their somewhat visceral and symbolic meaning, while the same is not true, apparently, of renal dialysis, taking blood gases to help establish electrolyte balances, or other measures.

    Finally, what is the relation between these and the various types of "codes" ("no code," "partial code," and "full code," for instance)? In order to permit rational decisions regarding permissible and impermissible actions under the Amendment, it is vital to understand this range of distinctions, especially as they are found actually in use in both routine and NICU settings.

3. The third exception requires a very difficult and vital kind of "weighing" when treatments are found to be "virtually futile." Just what factors are or should be included in this? How is "pain and suffering" from

the "treatment itself" or "other medical contraindications" to be weighed against the "very slight potential benefit"? What is the precise difference between the "pain and suffering" from a specific treatment and "quality of life" considerations, such that the one is permissible and the other is not? After all, if this "pain and suffering" from "the treatment itself" is "inhumane" for an infant who is "unlikely to survive" even with the treatment, does this not smuggle in "quality of life" considerations *for that length of time this infant will continue to live,* whether it be merely a matter of a few hours or even days? If this is true, then is it not also true that the "inhumanity" of the "treatment itself" in such a case is *not* a "medical judgment," at least not in the strict sense apparently intended by DHHS? For that matter, if (as seems patently obvious) "quality of life considerations" *are* very much a part of our judgments and plans for our *normal* children, and if the core intent of DHHS is to prevent the discriminatory treatment of "handicapped infants," or to ensure that they are treated no differently, then are not "quality of life considerations" very much a part of appropriate decision making for *both* "normal" and "abnormal" infants?

4. Although the final rule reaffirms the right and responsibility of parents to make even "withholding" decisions on behalf of their own infants ("on the basis of their physician's reasonable medical judgment"), neither this clarification nor the proposed rule's exclusion of parents from these decisions were based on *evidence*—at least none is cited. It is, however, perfectly obvious that not all people, parents included, are equally competent in their respective abilities, including the ability to make "withholding" decisions: some parents might well not be able to make this sort of decision, with or without their physician's or an ICRC's assistance, while others might be superb decision makers, with or without their physician's or an ICRC's assistance. The important point here is that DHHS apparently insists on considering parents *as a group,* as it does physicians. But *are* parents as a group, or physicians as a group, necessarily good or bad decision makers? Such a question is obviously absurd. Especially with respect to issues like that of "withholding," though it is true of decision making more generally, "groups as groups" simply do not "make decisions" at all; only *individuals* do.

Clearly, there is much room for significant research here: What factors are there that might tend to promote competency in decision making (especially regarding "withholding" or "continuation" decisions)? Are there ways through which parents can be helped to acquire these factors? Are physicians subject to stress and bias in these situations, such that their decision-making abilities might be compromised? Beyond such issues as these, however, is another, more basic one: what exactly *is* "competent decision making" in cases such as ours?

5. The notion of "quality of life" has for the most part been a merely speculative idea, subject to much flexibility and variability. Is there any way to give it more specific, shareable content? A good start might be to find out just what individual physicians and parents actually mean to include in the idea when they variously use it. This would seem to me an especially interesting project as regards the population targeted in this book, persons with severe retardation. For if "quality of life" is used, as seems often the case, to include possible mental retardation, then a number of serious issues are raised. For instance, what does an NICU physician understand about mental retardation or normal development? What do parents with infants in an NICU know about mental retardation or normal development, and to what extent (if any) do they actually think about such issues during their infant's hospitalization?

    It must also be wondered whether DHHS's equation of "quality of life" with "subjective opinion" is at all legitimate. After all, the equation itself clearly begs the question: Whether such "quality of life" considerations are *one and all* merely "subjective" (i.e., apparently, arbitrary) is obviously a matter of study and analysis, and thus cannot be simply presupposed. While it may well be proper to exclude the demonstrably arbitrary and idiosyncratic, this hardly justifies the presumption that every quality of life judgment is the same. Nor does it follow from the mere fact of a wide diversity of ideas about an infant's future quality of life that all such ideas are therefore inadmissible. DHHS's exclusion, then, seems not only a *petitio principii,* but a most dangerous one at that, since it effectively writes into federal law what seems little more than an unjustified *bias.*

    In any event, it seems important to know a good deal more about how parents and physicians actually include such considerations in their decision making, as well as what they seem to mean by *quality of life* for such infants. Whether what they individually think is justified or not is, of course, quite another issue.

6. Finally, possible differences between the practices of office-based pediatricians (and level I and II hospitals), and those with "special evaluative" knowledge and skills (and level III hospitals' NICU units), pose a number of issues for research, which will need to be far better understood as the Amendment's impact becomes more evident. Along with the issues already indicated, there are others. For instance, what are the exact nature, tasks, mandates, and authority of Infant Care Review Committees? Will it be necessary for *every* hospital to establish such a commit-

tee? Should the ICRCs in different hospitals have the same mandates? Indeed, which hospitals need such a committee?

CASE 2: DIAGNOSTIC DETECTION OF FETAL ANOMALIES

This case concerns a 16-year-old unmarried girl in her first pregnancy. After having some prenatal care in her hometown, including one ultrasound performed because a routine office visit showed an apparently enlarged quantity of amniotic fluid, the girl was referred to the regional tertiary, acute-care center for evaluation and follow-up. An ultrasound examination was performed (about 2–3 weeks after the first one) and suggested, though with some uncertainty, that the single fetus was 28 ±3 weeks gestation. The lower uterine segment and cervix appeared normal; the placenta was posterior and fundal with normal texture. Oligohydramnios was found; the more important finding was a large cystic structure occupying the pelvis and abdomen, and a "markedly distended urinary bladder," consistent with bilateral hydronephrosis and hydroureter. Renal parenchyma was noted to be decreased, with possible irreversible dysplasia already started. To the right and anterior of the distended bladder was a tubular cystic structure that was interpreted as a patent urachus (the fetal canal connecting the bladder with the median umbilical ligament). The fetal heart was located to the right of the midline (rechtocardia), and a small left plural effusion was noted. The stomach appeared to be displaced by the abdominal mass, but was located in the left abdomen beneath the left hemidiaphragm. The brain showed mild ventricular dilatation, especially of the left lateral ventricle, which was interpreted as mild hydrocephalus, possibly progressive, with etiology unknown. Biparietal diameter was also noted to be inconsistent with gestational age, coinciding with that of a fetus 32 ± 2 weeks. Femur length and abdominal circumference were normal for 28 ± 3 weeks. The fetus was noted to be male.

These conditions were found by the multidisciplinary maternal/fetal team to be most consistent with posterior-urethral valves with bilateral hydronephrosis (distention of kidneys with urine, due to ureter obstructions and accompanying beginning atrophy of renal parenchyma) and hydroureter (distention of the ureter with urine, due to obstruction). There was also thought to be either a gastrointestinal tract obstruction or possibly an abnormality in swallowing (which, if later confirmed, would suggest a possible neurologic defect).

Faced with the problem of determining alternative management plans for this minor girl and her parents (the minor boyfriend had disclaimed further involvement), the maternal/fetal team drew up the following management alternatives:

1. Termination of pregnancy—regarded as not a feasible option due to:
   a) gestational age greater than 24 weeks, b) fetal viability, and c) absence

of threat to life or health of the mother ("psychological health" risk being problematic under prevailing state law).

2. Amniocentesis for lung maturity studies and chromosomal studies for possible genetic defect—regarded as possible plan in view of uncertain family history, but this option was rejected owing to: a) probable low results, and b) relative risks involved with amniocentesis, which outweighed the benefits at this gestational age.

3. Labor induction now with either vaginal or cesarean section delivery as indicated—this was rejected, as: a) delivery at 28 weeks gestation would most likely result in significant morbidity (and possible mortality) due to prematurity, and b) morbidity and mortality risks of cesarean section, which are greater than allowing the pregnancy to continue.

4. Fetal therapeutic intervention—a ventriculoamniotic shunt could be surgically implanted to effect drainage of accumulated fluid in the fetus's kidneys and ureters. This was regarded as not indicated for this fetus at this time because of: a) presence of multiple fetal anomalies (increased mortality risks, and the procedure did not fit the protocol of the team, which required a single anomaly), b) risks of intraamniotic shunting outweighed the benefits to be gained in view of the amount of viable renal parenchyma present at the time, and c) fetal gestational age (intrauterine shunting has been most effective at less than 19 weeks gestation).

5. Weekly ultrasound studies and obstetrical reviews—this option was recommended by the team, along with full disclosure to the mother and her parents of the options and the team's reasoning and recommendations. Weekly ultrasound studies were deemed appropriate for the detection of any further renal atrophy or ventricular dilatation; weekly obstetrical reviews were seen as necessary to monitor cervical status, and fetal and maternal statuses. Concerning possible induction of labor, the team felt that attainment of 31–32 weeks gestation would result in a decision for delivery as opposed to shunting, as the risks of prematurity at this age are significantly decreased and neonatal shunting would then be possible, with fewer risks than intrauterine shunting.

Several times, the girl and her parents had expressed a strong desire for resolving the issue by abortion. It was pointed out to them, however, that "abortion" is not necessarily a *destructive* intervention, since a fetus can be *removed* and still be alive. Since, according to state law, the girl's fetus was considered "viable," the only permissible intervention would be termination of pregnancy and removal of the likely alive fetus, with subsequent necessary neonatal care. It was necessary to emphasize, nevertheless, that fetal removal was not medically indicated at this time due to gestational age and the decreased risks to the fetus from removal at a later age (31–32 weeks). Knowing now that this fetus was afflicted with multiple anomalies—primarily oligohydramnios, bilateral hydronephrosis, obstructed ureters, rechtocardia, and possible renal dysplasia, pulmonary hypoplasia, and neuropathy—this recommendation was unacceptable to the girl and her parents, and they decided to seek evaluation at a diagnostic center in another state, rather than have the girl continue the pregnancy for even 3 or 4 more weeks.

Case Analysis

First, as reported by Blane et al. (1983) and Kramer (1983), prenatal ultrasonography can now safely and noninvasively permit the accurate diagnosis of many congenital anomalies, including oligohydramnios, hydronephrosis, and obstructed ureters. Identification of "up to 90% of the kidneys by 17–20 weeks gestation and 95% by 22 weeks" is common. If unrelieved, hydronephrosis may produce progressive renal damage and eventual failure. If detected early enough (17–20 weeks), fetal surgery to shunt fluids to the amniotic fluid can benefit the fetus, but only in cases of bilateral obstructive hydronephrosis, and prior to irreversible renal damage. This alternative, however, must be balanced against the fact that "diagnostic errors of *in utero* ultrasonography can be significant" (Kramer, 1983, p. 375)—hence repeated studies, especially by real-time ultrasonography, are required to confirm findings.

In the present case, it is uncertain why the fetus's anomalies were undetected by the first ultrasound exam performed by the family obstetrician in his office at about 26 weeks gestation. Perhaps it was beyond his skill: for, while "more than 30% of obstetricians have ultrasound equipment in their own offices" and about 34% of all pregnant women in the United States who use an office-based obstetrician have at least one ultrasound exam (Perone et al., 1984, p. 801), minimum standards for such examinations have not yet been finally established. The recommended level of competency, however, will include recognition of "large pelvic masses," "amount of amniotic fluid," and other characteristics (p. 802). Additionally, it can be asked why the physician waited until the 26th week before performing the first ultrasound, since for those who use the procedure it is common to do so between weeks 7 and 13 (to check cardiac activity) and around 15 to 18 weeks (to check gestational age and fetal lie). In any case, performing ultrasound at 26 weeks effectively precluded the options of therapeutic abortion and of fetal surgery.

In a second issue, other studies strongly suggest that the prognosis of oligohydramnios with bilateral hydronephrosis for subsequent neonatal life is quite poor. For instance, Hobbins et al. (1984) reported in a study conducted between January 1, 1978, and April 1, 1983, that of the 25 fetuses with antenatal diagnosis of obstructive uropathy, 17 had bilateral obstruction. Of these 17 fetuses, 10 died of pulmonary hypoplasia, 3 women elected abortion "in the midtrimester," and 4 survived (all of which had serious problems). Furthermore, of the 17 fetuses, severe oligohydramnios was present, and this is one of the findings that best correlated with ultimately poor prognisis, even if the oligohydramnios developed later in gestation (pp. 870, 872). Finally, the incidence of other major anomalies in association with obstructive uropathy—reported at as high as 50% (Potter & Craig, 1976)—severely compromises intact survival and even survival itself.

In the Hobbins et al. (1984) study, it should be noted that the three abortions all fell within the Supreme Court's 1973 ruling on fetal viability: two at 22 weeks, and one at 24 weeks gestation. Of the 10 that died after delivery, all were between 31 and 38 weeks gestation (4 with normal vaginal delivery, 6 by cesarean section), but no data were supplied on length of survival. It is also interesting to note that of the 13 fetuses that did not survive (abortion or after delivery), *none* of the latter were diagnosed early enough to meet the accepted criterion for permissible abortion, as their first ultrasonographic diagnosis came *after* the 24-week limit (one at 25.2 weeks, one at 26, one at 29, and seven between 30 and 35.5). It seems clear, then, that in our case, the young woman's fetus would in all likelihood not survive, or at most that neonatal life would be quite brief (a matter of hours or days at most).

Clearly, the concept of *viability* as defined by the Supreme Court in *Roe v. Wade* (1973) has been the central factor in such cases, and probably in those in which ultrasonographic or other antenatal diagnostic technologies pick up other fetal anomalies (Clewell et al., 1982; Depp, Sabbagha, Brown, Tamura, & Reedy, 1983; Michejda et al., 1984; Sun, 1983). But here again, emphasis falls on *early* diagnosis if *in utero* surgery or therapeutic abortion are to be real options, as opposed to the otherwise distressing alternative of forcing a woman to continue her pregnancy in the full knowledge that her fetus is afflicted with seriously compromising and possibly lethal anomalies.

The issue that these cases make prominent is this: Is it at all medically coherent and morally fitting to require that these cases be judged in terms of the concept of "fetal viability" as currently defined? In different terms, it has been judged legally correct to hold that parents and children have the right to recover damages from wrongful birth—*Gleitman v. Cosgrove* (1967) and *Stewart v. Long Island College Hospital* (1968). The same has been held in torts for wrongful life, when infants are born with multiple congenital or genetic anomalies that severely compromise their lives, if not also causing their early deaths—as in *Curlender v. Bio-Science Laboratories* (1980), in which damages both to parents and child were awarded, and in *Turpin v. Sortini* (1982), which awarded damages to the parents only. In these latter cases especially, as Englehardt (1985) has suggested, "the general principle that one may be liable to both parents and their children for not having given adequate information that would have influenced reasonable individuals in their choices regarding contraception and abortion remains in place" (p. 314).

Given these decisions, might it not also be morally (and even legally) correct to hold that these same parents should have been allowed to abort regardless of the 20–24 week gestation ruling on viability? In a sense, the *Curlender* court seemed to intimate that conclusion: Faced with the issue of incorrect transmission of information with regard to whether a couple carried Tay-Sachs disease, and an affected child was born, the court not only awarded damages to both parents and child but also raised the possibility that parents could be held liable for damages for continuing a pregnancy that they knew would likely result in a multiply damaged infant. Furthermore, the Washington State case of *Harbeson v. Parke-Davis, Inc.* (1983) found that parents had the right to prevent the birth of a defective child. Neither case, however, mentions the standard of viability, so presumably such parents could prevent birth *only* prior to the 24th week gestation (absent a threat to the life or health of the mother). Thus, in the cases that concern me here, not even these court decisions prove very helpful, as they have all involved post–24-week fetuses. (That parents whose afflicted fetuses were first diagnosed earlier could, of course, elect to continue then later change their minds is true, but not at issue here.)

Regarding a third issue, Fost, Chudwin, and Wikler (1980) have written that every definition of viability is either too limited or fails to recognize that viability is an essentially relative notion expressive of a developmental process. There simply is no "single event in a fetus's development" at which viability occurs. Instead, viability "can refer to a variety of points . . . depending on such variables as the environment into which the fetus would hypothetically be born and the imagined duration of survival" it might have (p. 12), where "environment" must include both "natural" supports (food, warmth, etc.) for some infants, and "artificial" supports (ventilator, shunts, etc.) for others.

After analyzing various proposed definitions of viability, including the Supreme Court's—the point at which the fetus is "potentially able to live outside the mother's womb, albeit with artificial aid"—Fost et al. (1980), noting that this includes neither a specified length of time of survival nor a mention of the *kinds* of "artificial aid" necessary, concluded that *any* definition of viability includes "value judgments." The latter specifically relate to the environment (intrauterine or extrauterine) and the amount of neonatal survival time believed to be appropriate. When one uses "viability," that is, one must include some idea of both of these, as well as what kinds of "artificial aids" are acceptable. The authors concluded, however, that, as "value judgments," these variables are essentially "arbitrary." Which sort of environment, what types of "aids," and how long the survival must be to give specific content to the concept, all of these are "a matter of individual preferences" or "conventions." For that reason, even though "viability" does have a useful role in clinical decisions, it has only "limited moral significance" in moral theory and legal or social policies (pp. 11, 12).

But that conclusion, in addition to being very dubious on other grounds, is too strong for the arguments given. For the central problem with the viability criterion is *not* that it involves personal preferences or conventions, but rather that it has been tied to a *specific gestational age*. It is not "viability" that is arbitrary; it is its limitation to 20–24 weeks gestation. The reason for this is made decisively, if also tragically, clear by cases like those considered here: the post–24-week fetuses in question hardly seem "viable." In different terms, if the prognosis for such a fetus is likely death soon after delivery, then it seems legally, and certainly morally, incoherent to regard the fetus as "viable" while still a fetus simply because it is 25, 29, or 38 weeks gestational age. To be fair, the Supreme Court's ruling can be interpreted as merely *suggesting,* based on then-current medical evidence, that "viability" occurs at about 20–24 weeks.

One of the main issues concerning viability that has been focused on in the abortion dispute is the likelihood that newer and newer technologies will eventually make it possible for younger and younger fetuses to be supported outside the mother's womb, and thus be "viable." Now, while this must surely be a legitimate concern, it does not change in the least the serious dilemmas that are presented by the fetuses considered here. Indeed, few if any researchers or scholars touch on this issue: For *whether or not* even younger fetuses could become viable, we *still* face the awesome and tragic issue of whether diagnostically determined anomalies such as those discussed here do not seriously compromise the limiting of viability to merely one gestational age (or, for that matter, to a certain birth weight, or any other single event or stage in fetal life). Such cases can, moreover, be expected to increase as antenatal diagnostic capabilities become more accurate.

In different terms, if there are sound reasons (medical as well as moral) for "withholding" treatments from multiply afflicted infants (those whose lives or "viability" is seriously in doubt, that is, who are "terminal" and for whom "treatment" is "futile" or "virtually futile"), it does not seem unreasonable to suggest that the same reasons would be appropriate for post–24-week fetuses diagnosed as having the kinds of impairments already discussed. Continuing with "pregnancies" seems as "inhumane" in the one case as continuing "treatments" is said to be in the other.

Proposed Research Agendas

Several profoundly necessary areas for research stand out.

1. First, if it is true, as Fost et al. (1980) allege, that clinical decisions include "value judgments"—about desirable or preferable environments, survival-times, and technologies—just how true is it that these reflect merely "personal preferences" or "conventions"? What are these "preferences" or "conventions"? For instance, hospital policies, NICU protocols, legal or statutory regulations, as well as moral commitments of individual physicians and parents, could all be classed in one or

the other category—but it is unclear just which way to classify them, without first of all finding out what they are, why they are held, and what their status is believed to be by those who hold them.

2. To what extent, if any, do physicians or parents include in their respective "preferences" something like quality of life considerations? (Fost et al. in fact include it in their list of relevant factors for clinical decisions, without, however, specifying it in any way.) In different terms, if it is true, as these authors allege, that "a judgment of viability, though partly moral in nature, does not in and of itself necessarily demand a course of action" (p. 12), then what else is or is thought to be necessary for a course of action by physicians, by parents, by policy makers, or by judges?

3. If "viability" is retained as a criterion, but is no longer tied to any one event or stage of fetal development, what content can be given to it? Or, just how is this notion used by practicing physicians, when it is not tied to a single event or stage? If, as Fost et al., and others, suggest, viability *cannot* be tied to one event or stage of fetal development, then how precisely can viability be judged?

4. Finally, what do prospective parents themselves believe when they face such a difficult pregnancy? What exactly are they told, how is this information actually related, and how well do they understand what they have been told? When they are informed that their child-to-be is multiply damaged, are they nevertheless capable of making decisions? If they are told *after* the current 24-week limit, what do they feel and believe about no longer being able to have an abortion performed? What factors go into making such a parent a capable decision maker?

The Clewell et al. (1982) study had included a "theologian and a neonatologist" to "serve as advocates for fetuses who are candidates for intrauterine therapy" (p. 1325). In response to this, Benfield (1982) raised a number of penetrating questions about such "advocates," about their actual authority and role, and repeated the results of his study of parental decision making concerning their own afflicted infants. He and his colleagues (Benfield, Leib, & Vollman, 1978; see also Duff, 1981; Elliot & Heim, 1978; Fost, 1981; Rowe et al., 1978; Watchko, 1983) found that parents (without advocates) can indeed be effective, caring decision makers as partners with physicians, and Benfield (1982) adds in his response to Clewell et al. (1982) that the same conclusion seems reasonable for prospective parents with difficult pregnancies. He wonders, indeed, whether "physicians may be too stressed or too biased to offer the information and support that parents need to act responsibly" (p. 1212).

So far as I can tell, however, few if any studies have been done regarding parental ability to make crucial decisions about their damaged fetuses, much less studies of what "good decision making" consists. Hence, Benfield's surmise must surely be tested by research, not only regarding parents but equally about the possible bias and stress on the part of physicians.

CONCLUSION

One issue seems clear-cut and overriding in importance regarding both difficult pregnancies and imperiled infants. It may well be that it is simply impossible fully to reject so-called quality of life considerations from intervention or nonintervention decisions regarding currently defined viable fetuses or imperiled infants. One thing that seems consistently included in such considerations is the future mental status, specifically the extent or degree of mental retardation, which can be reasonably expected (a matter that, neurologists and psychologists inform us, is exceedingly difficult if not impossible in many cases to predict). The question that must be posed here concerns this connection: Does being mentally retarded or compromised diminish the quality of life of the person with retardation and, if so, precisely how? In an age deeply set within "quantitative" modes of thinking, so much so that proposals to "quantify" the quality of life are taken more seriously than proposals to examine it "qualitatively," and where the "quantity" of life is often given as much if not more weight than its "quality," one has to wonder whether the phrase *can*, without radically new approaches, be given any concrete sense at all.

There is, however, another side to the problem that I ought at least to address here. Many parental and physician decisions to discontinue pregnancies, or supports and treatments for "viable" fetuses or imperiled infants, appeal to the needless "pain and suffering" they will undergo, or to the fact that prolonging the life of either is both pointless and "inhumane." Such decisions are most often said to be in the fetus's "best interests." Sometimes, of course, the quality of life of the fetus or infant is given as a reason for discontinuation.

On the one hand, however, it is difficult if not impossible to differentiate "pain and suffering" from "quality of life," for surely the latter, whatever else it may mean, includes references to the former. Pain and suffering diminishes the quality of the person's life. Not even the DHHS interpretation of "congressional intent" can so easily restrict the sense of "inhumane" to merely the "pain and suffering" of the "treatment itself" for a dying infant, for if the fetus's life continues at all, even if only for a few hours, its quality of life has to be a factor. The pain and suffering from the treatment can be said to "outweigh" the slight potential benefit only if the *quality* of the fetus's remaining life is the factor that *defines* the difference between the two.

On the other hand, the strict requirement to comfort such an infant by continuing to provide appropriate medication, nutrition, and hydration cannot itself be seriously distinguished from considerations relating to the "quality" of its remaining life either. Thus, the point made by Fost et al. (1980) about "viability"—that the factor virtually undiscussed in the abortion literature, namely the *duration* of survival, turns out to be a critical variable for *any* definition of "viability"—has a correlate here. Even if it be for only a few hours or days, the life of a dying infant, or that of a grievously afflicted post–24-week fetus, must be taken into consideration and decisions made at least partly on that basis. My suggestion is merely that such considerations—as, for instance, that continued treatment is "inhumane," or that there is a reasonable requirement for continued medication, nutrition, and hydration—are inseparably part of the quality of the life in question. What is accordingly seriously needed here, I think, is not only sound empirical research but also hard conceptual work to grapple with the nature of *quality* and of *life*, and of their relationships.

Infant and fetal pathologies present numerous issues needing careful moral, psychological, sociological, and other forms of research. I have tried to keep to that agenda here, and to concern myself strictly with certain of those issues. My conviction is that moral and ethical analysis within medicine must become deeply informed of the different factual data obtainable only through empirical research focused on the moral dimensions of medical practices, fetal and neonatal life, and that of the families concerned. This conviction—only slowly arrived at, and with considerable resistance from myself as well as from others—stems from another conviction, also arrived at only gradually and with much initial perplexity: Moral issues are presented solely within the contexts of their actual occurrence, and within the lives of those to whom the problems relate. To be responsive to clinical medicine, or to empirical concerns focused on persons with severe retardation, or to the concerns of policy makers, those of us in ethics must not only learn to benefit from the research of others but must also learn ourselves to conduct research into the actual moral lives of the people who are responsible for making intervention decisions. Only time and alert, careful criticism will determine what will eventually come from these "ethics research" efforts, or from a clinically oriented ethics discipline. From the way things now appear, however, such a discipline—clinical and research ethics—not only has much to learn but also seems to have a remarkably fruitful potential.

REFERENCES

Beal v. Doe, 432 U.S. 438 (1977).
Benfield, D.G. (1982). To the editor. *New England Journal of Medicine, 307*(19), 1212.
Benfield, D.G., Leib, S.A., & Vollman, J.H. (1978). Grief response of parents to neonatal death and parent participation in deciding care. *Pediatrics, 62,* 171–177.

Blane, C.E., Doff, S.A., Bowerman, R.A., & Barr, M. (1983). Nonobstructive fetal surgery for hydrocephalus: Sonographic recognition and therapeutic implications. *Radiology, 147*(1), 95–99.

Cadkin, A.W., Ginsberg, N.A., Pergament, E., & Verlinski, Y. (1984). Chorionic villi sampling: A new technique for detection of genetic abnormalities in the first trimester. *Radiology, 151*(1), 159–162.

Clewell, W.H., Johnson, M.L., Meier, P.R., Newkirk, J.B., Zide, S.I., Hendee, R.W., Bowes, W.A., Hecht, F., O'Keefe, D., Henry, G.P., & Shikes, R.H. (1982). A surgical approach to the treatment of fetal hydrocephalus. *New England Journal of Medicine, 306*(22), 1320–1325.

Curlender v. Bio-Science Laboratories, 165 C 477 (Cal. App., 1980).

Depp, R., Sabbagha, R.E., Brown, J.T., Tamura, R.K., & Reedy, N.J. (1983). Fetal surgery for hydrocephalus: Successful in utero ventriculoamniotic shunt for Dandy-Walker syndrome. *American Journal of Obstetrics and Gynecology, 61*(6), 710–714.

Doe v. Bolton, 410 U.S. 197 (1973).

Duff, R.S. (1981). Counseling families and deciding care of severely defective children: A way of coping with "Medical Vietnam." *Pediatrics, 62*(1), 315–320.

Elliot, B.A., & Heim, H.A. (1978). Neonatal death: Reflections for physicians. *Pediatrics, 62*(1), 96–100.

Englehardt, H.T., Jr. (1985). Current controversies in obstetrics: Wrongful life and forced fetal surgical procedures. *American Journal of Obstetrics and Gynecology, 151* (3) 313–318.

Federal Register. (1983, July 5). Washington, DC: U.S. Government Printing Office.

Federal Register. (1984a, January 12). Washington, DC: U.S. Government Printing Office.

Federal Register. (1984b, December 10). Washington, DC: U.S. Government Printing Office.

Federal Register. (1985, April 15). Washington, DC: U.S. Government Printing Office.

Fost, N. (1981, March). Counseling families who have a child with a severe anomoly. *Pediatrics, 67*(3), 321–324.

Fost, N., Chudwin, D., & Wikler, D. (1980, December). The limited moral significance of "fetal viability." *Hastings Center Report, 10*(6), 12.

Gleitman v. Cosgrove, 227 A2d 689 (NH 1967).

Harbeson v. Parke-Davis, Inc., 656 P2d 483 (1983).

Harris v. McRae, 48 LW 4941 (1980).

Hobbins, J.C., Romero, R., Grannum, P., Berkowitz, R.L., Cullen, M., & Mahoney, M. (1984). Antenatal diagnosis of renal anomalies with ultrasound. *American Journal of Obstetrics and Gynecology, 148*(7), 868–877.

Kolata, G. B. (1980). Mass screening for neural tube defects. *Hastings Center Report, 10*(6), 8–10.

Kramer, S.A. (1983). Current status of fetal intervention for congenital hydronephrosis. *Journal of Urology, 130*(4), 641–646.

Maher v. Roe, 432 U.S. 464 (1977).

Michejda, M., Patronas, N., Di Chiro, G., & Hodgen, G.D. (1984). Fetal hydrocephalus: Amelioration of fetal porencephaly by in utero therapy in nonhuman primates. *Journal of the American Medical Association, 251*(19), 2548–2552.

Perone, N., Carpenter, R.J., & Robertson, J.A. (1984). Legal liability in the use of ultrasound by office-based obstetricians. *American Journal of Obstetrics and Gynecology, 150*(7), 801–804.

Poelker v. Doe, 432 U.S. 519 (1977).

Potter, E.L., & Craig, J.M. (1976). *Pathology of the fetus and infant.* Chicago: Year Book Medical Publishers, Inc.

Rodeck, C.H., & Morsman, J.M. (1984). First trimester chorion biopsy. *British Medical Bulletin, 39*(4), 338–342.

Roe v. Wade, 410 U.S. 113 (1973).

Rowe, J., Clyman, R., Green, C., Mikkelsen, C., Haight, J., & Ataide, L. (1978). Follow-up of families who experience a perinatal death. *Pediatrics 62*(2), 166–170.

Smith, M.F. (1982, July 28). Handicapped newborns: Current issues and legislation [Report]. *Congressional Research Service,* p. 6.

Stewart v. Long Island College Hospital, 296 NYS2d 41 (1968).

Strong, C. (1983). The tiniest newborns. *Hastings Center Report, 12*(1), 14–19.

Sun, M. (1983, July). FDA draws criticism on prenatal test. *Science, 221,* 440–441.

Turpin v. Sortini, 643 P2d 954 (Cal 1982).

Watchko, J.F. (1983). Decision making on critically ill infants by parents. *American Journal of Diseases of Children, 137*(8), 795–798.

Weir, R.F. (1983). The government and selective nontreatment of handicapped infants. *New England Journal of Medicine, 309*(11), 662.

Wright, E.E., & Shaw, M.W. (1981). Legal liability in genetic screening, genetic counseling, and prenatal diagnosis. *Clinical Obstetrics and Gynecology, 24*(4), 1133–1149.

Response

BIOLOGICAL BEING
AND QUALITY OF LIFE

John Lachs

THERE ARE TWO REASONS why I find it difficult to disagree with much in Richard Zaner's rich, sensitive, and thoughtful chapter. The first is that he shows himself impressively judicious in his opinions. The second has to do with the nature and conception of his presentation. His aim is to identify research areas of relevance to the ethics of dealing with imperiled infants, and at this he is signally successful. This plan, however, does not lend itself to argumentation, and, accordingly, he makes no controversial substantive claims.

I tend to be less circumspect than my esteemed friend and colleague, and will accordingly spell out several theses to which his discussion points. I do not attribute these views to Zaner; they are merely thoughts one might naturally come to entertain upon reflecting on his comments. These judgments, moreover, are highly controversial and easily misinterpreted. There is little to recommend them from the standpoint of our emotions, and the only reason I chance voicing them is that I think they are clearly true.

The 1984 amendment to the Child Abuse Prevention and Treatment Act and the related regulations of the U.S. Department of Health and Human Services amply demonstrate that those who seek ethical subtlety and moral wisdom had better look elsewhere. The amendment deals with intensely emotional issues: the political pressure exerted by fervid interest groups made it impossible to crystallize their legitimate concerns in a thoughtful and balanced piece of legislation.

The law, the presumed congressional intent, and the effectuating regulations are all flawed in exactly the way Zaner indicates: in the hurry to protect biological life, no attention is paid to the values that render such life worthwhile. The idea of the unconditional value of physical existence comes closer to being a sacrilege than an adequate expression of the Judeo-Christian ethic. The religious issue after all, is the health of one's soul; to hold on to life as if it were something of supreme relevance is quietly to deny our spiritual nature and supernatural destiny. All sound human traditions leave room for circumstances when life is no longer worth having to the person who lives it. But whether our life is good or a burden best laid down, its value is a function of what it contains. Biological being is the neutral substratum of the good and evil that can come our way; it is itself, intrinsically, neither good nor bad. Quality of life considerations can, therefore, never be absent when we choose for ourselves or decide on how to treat others.

ARE LAWS ALWAYS USEFUL?

Poor laws aside, there is the question of whether, concerning some matters, we should have any laws at all. We have acquired a lamentable tendency to resolve social problems by regulation. Those who write the laws earnestly seek a narrow, definable good. But they are incapable of deeper ethical analysis, cannot predict long-range consequences, overlook the systemic effects of the law they want, and rarely ask its cost in money, welfare, and human liberty.

The uniformity that law assures is itself not always a good; shall we opt for McDonald's over the local French cuisine? A democratic society must trust its citizens, yet the premise of the sort of regulation we face is that only judges, lawyers, and a tough district attorney can be relied on to do what is right. Is it unreasonable to suppose that even without the aid of politicians, nurses and physicians can intelligently further the interests of their patients? Is it not scurrilous to imply that parents are incapable or disinclined to choose what will benefit their child? To be sure, there are bad eggs among physicians and parents (as there are among lawyers and judges), but that justifies little more than helpful guidelines and education instead of the criminal sanctions of the law.

Laws in our area of concern cease to be merely inappropriate and become a positive mischief when they impose rigid substantive duties instead of providing procedural safeguards. In medicine, the development of technology tends to render substantive and specific legal edicts irrelevant or outmoded. And the complexity of individual situations makes the application of such rules sometimes clearly harmful, even tragic. The situational judgments of which much of clinical medicine consists are not well served by extensive and precise regulations, even when these regulations leave some room for clinical judgment. All the circumstances relevant to difficult cases (such as Professor Zaner discusses, for instance) cannot be written into law; it is futile if not absurd, therefore, to try to gain more control over complex practices than is required in terms of fair procedures for the protection of basic rights.

A SEA OF IGNORANCE

Vital decisions affecting the life and well-being of imperiled infants and those with retardation are now made in a sea of ignorance. Some of the ignorance, such as the inability to predict the outcome of complex conditions and novel treatments, is unavoidable. But considerable nescience is due to historical, institutional, and personal causes; such ignorance is avoidable, and we ought to work hard to eradicate it.

Too often, parents are poorly informed about the medical condition of their child, and guilt, worry, or lack of education makes it difficult for them to assimilate what they are told. Physicians are not great communicators, and are themselves largely unaware of the psychological and systematic moral dimensions of the problems with which they deal. Ethicists and patient advocates, on the other hand, are hampered by inadequate understanding of the medical facts. We could eliminate individual ignorance and make truly informed communal judgments in a series of extensive conferences between parents and the members of the treatment team. But the quickness with which decisions have to be made and pressures on everyone's time render such discussions impractical. The solution is broad and multifaceted education prior to the crisis point. The world is a perilous place; since we or our loved ones may at any time become patients of high technology medicine, we simply cannot afford to remain ignorant of our bodies and of the stages and conditions of normal development.

QUALITY OF LIFE

There is one area in which we are ready to claim ignorance, yet know significantly more than we suppose. Perhaps we cannot articulate a defensible concept of the quality of life, but we make complex quality of life decisions every day and do so with considerable skill. The worth of a life, from the standpoint of the one who lives it, should not be measured by the rare peaks of achievement or delight, but by the tone and temper of its everyday. All the choices that affect our daily existence are, in this way, quality of life decisions in the miniature. Consciousness of what we are doing, research into how we do it, and suitable generalization of the principles of our choice will go a long way toward articulating a shared standard of the quality of life.

Even without this detailed research, however, some ideas appear both clear and true. Since there are ineradicably subjective elements in how we value things, people should be allowed to make their own decisions about the quality of their existence. Although this may seem innocuous, in fact it has profound implications for the right to suicide, the social acceptability of euthanasia, and the liberty to refuse unwanted treatment. If an individual (an infant, for example) cannot make such decisions, we may have to step in to make them for him or her. We should do this only reluctantly, ever mindful not only of what is good for the individual but also of what, to the best of our ability to determine it, he or she would choose. The key fallacy to avoid here is generalizing from our own experience and supposing that if another cannot lead the sort of life we choose for ourselves, his or her existence is without redeeming grace. The most pernicious form of such egocentrism is the intellectualist fallacy that maintains that whoever is unable to attain a certain level of cognitive achievement or a measure of intelligent long-term control over his or her life cannot enjoy an existence that is worth preserving. Yet many Down syndrome children, for example, lead lives more tender and emotionally more rewarding than do most chief executives. The fact that others differ from us in values or behavior is not a reason for supposing that their condition is lamentable.

In spite of the variety of values that give meaning to our lives, it is clear that there are cases in which there simply is no meaning. One's quality of life can reach a level so low that existence becomes a burden and the efforts of those who would sustain us immoral violence. Infants with severe defects, born to a short life of mindless misery, have no achievement to anticipate and no conscious delight to redeem their suffering. To continue to feed and medicate such hopeless, tragic wrecks in the full knowledge that each new day brings but renewed misery is an immoral act. To require us to do it, as the 1984 amendment does, is a moral outrage whose wickedness is not abated by the fact that it is the work of well-meaning individuals.

It is not that I cast my lot with those who favor the traditional course of passive euthanasia, allowing the hopelessly defective to expire without food and drink. To starve an infant to death is an abject and cowardly deed. The only humane course is to ease such individuals out of their sad and afflicted existence in a way that is both painless and lovingly swift.

Chapter 6

EARLY INTERVENTION FOR CHILDREN AT EDUCATIONAL RISK
SOME SIDELIGHTS FOR LEARNERS WITH SEVERE MENTAL RETARDATION

Susan W. Gray

IN THIS BOOK on ethical aspects of intervention decisions for persons with severe retardation, I am in one sense an interloper. My own research has been primarily with children and families from low-income homes. Such children are frequently considered at risk for sociocultural retardation. The incidence of severe retardation, however, among low-income families is not great, and I have had little experience even with this small number. Yet we are all human together, and parents of children at risk and with retardation have many needs in common. Perhaps, then, my experiences may shed some sidelights on some of the ethical issues that arise in intervention research with children with severe retardation and their families.

The issues I have chosen are ones that have concerned my colleagues and me when we have planned and conducted intervention research with young children at risk and with their families. For purposes of this chapter, the term *intervention research* is used in the limited sense of meaning behavioral research that involves a treatment lasting months or years, is relatively broad in its approach, and is expected to have, if successful, a substantial and enduring effect upon the participants.

GOALS

For all of us who conduct intervention research, our primary questions must be ones of goals. What anticipated outcomes, and the means by which we reach them, will be truly ethical?

Our answer depends to a considerable degree upon our values. Such values are not always explicit; often we are not clearly aware of their origins or of their influence on our thinking. My own experiences and research efforts have led me, by a path not always easy, to be especially sensitive to problems that arise when working with people from other socioeconomic backgrounds and ethnic groups. There is no need to rehearse the tired but still valid observation that most of us who write in books such as this and those who conduct research are white and middle-class. Inevitably, our views of the good life are seen through the lenses of our own middle-class experiences and opportunities. There is also what the French call "déformation profession-nelle," the particular distortion, or refractive error, contributed by our professional outlook. An easy pitfall for most of us is to select characteristics of an idealized mainstream culture as our goal. Or as academes, even more rarified in our contacts, we look at people like ourselves and our families, and consider what we see as good. We smile ruefully at Michael Harrington's (1984) tale of the woman who, when asked to which social class she and her husband belonged, said, "Oh, we're middle class. We go out every week for beer and pizzas; that makes us middle class." Or, alternatively, we may cringe a little at the glowingly portrayed life-style of the Young Urban Professional. But how shall we select values, if we are justified in selecting any at all? How can we overcome our class, ethnic, and professional biases in viewing the world, or at least render those biases less powerful?

The answer, I think, may lie in how we view and respond to the constraints and such freedoms as exist for those families with whom we work. Low-income persons have few choices. A lack of resources of every kind means that they are constantly stalked by necessity. The paycheck has many claimants well before it is earned, and one is lucky to have any kind of job, let alone a good one. Imagine for a moment a woman who, after a hard day of work for minimum wage or less, comes home to a cramped, disordered house with three fretful children clamoring for attention and their supper. Small wonder she does nothing but try to cope with the immediate situation as best she can—the so-called reactive life-style. Or imagine the man whose only way to earn money today is to stand at some hiring point in the line of those looking for a day's work, hoping for someone to hire him for a long day of hard labor and small pay. If you live in Nashville you may have seen these men early in the morning, lunch in hand, down by the river waiting for someone to come by and offer them a day's work, if they are fortunate.

Granted these two examples may come from a small segment of the population, yet there are many in this relatively small percentage of our nation. All one needs to do is to read census reports or commentaries thereon to be aware that the proportion of low-income people in America has increased in the last several years; this is especially true among children (see for example, Jencks, 1985). These children and their parents have many constraints, and restricted freedom of choice.

Parents of children with severe retardation, even when affluent, as well as the children themselves, have limited options. Robert Moroney, for example, in Chapter 10 in this book presents some telling data on the impact of such reduced options on the families of persons with severe retardation. The remainder of this paper draws some parallels between low-income families and other families whose reduced options originate in attempting to meet the needs of a child with severe retardation.

THE DOUBLY VULNERABLE

Any caring parent is vulnerable where his or her children are concerned. When caring parents have few resources or have many demands upon them, their vulnerability is great enough that exploiting their needs, or doing harm, is easy.

Children by their very status are vulnerable, less able to defend or protect themselves. They are accustomed to obeying adults, to looking upon them as authorities. The less competent the child, the more vulnerable is that child to possible hurt, or simply unpleasantness, which a more capable child could avoid. Thus, intervention with parents and children with retardation becomes an undertaking fraught with possible dangers.

Most of us have good intentions. We as practitioners hope we are doing good when we develop and put in place intervention programs designed to enhance the competence of the individuals with whom we intervene. But good intentions, unaccompanied by wisdom and sensitivity, do not suffice. Not only may our interventions be unhelpful, but upon occasion the evidence suggests that they can be harmful. Many of us could contribute a horror story to illustrate the perils. One that haunts me is the Cambridge-Somerville study (McCord, 1978). As you may recall, some 500 young adolescents at risk for juvenile delinquency were randomly assigned either to a group that received counseling or to a nontreatment group. A follow-up of the sample 30 years later indicated only seven significant differences on 57 indices of social competence. These seven favored the control group. In this particular case, one can perhaps assign such undesirable consequences as existed to the singling out of one group as potentially delinquent. Or the counseling may have been inadequate. Often the problem stems from the fact that long-term interventions take place in a matrix of other events and relationships, and extend over time. In a word, intervention always occurs within a system. The possibility is ever there that one may disrupt a functioning system. Aversive side effects can and sometimes do occur.

My own longitudinal study, begun in 1962, involved in the early years an extended treatment for children of preschool age and their caregivers (usually mothers) from low-income families. We became concerned with the consequences of the intervention upon the other children in the family. Our first examination, I am happy to say, actually revealed what appeared to be a benign effect. The home visitors believed the younger siblings were benefiting from the program. We decided to put it to the empirical test. On the Stanford-Binet Intelligence Test, the younger siblings of experimental children showed IQs 14 points higher than those of younger siblings of the control children. We labeled this effect vertical diffusion. In a later study, we attempted to determine whether the effect came through the mother or the older sibling, since both possible agents were confounded in the earlier research. You will not be surprised to learn that in the second study only the children whose mothers were involved in the intervention showed such a positive effect.

With the older siblings we did not expect to find a positive change. Instead, we were concerned lest the attention focused on the target child might have negative effects, in the form of jealousy or lower self-esteem, for example, upon the older child. Since the intervention improved the school competence of the target children (Klaus & Gray, 1968), parents and also teachers might make invidious comparisons. When the target children were in the first grade, we examined the school achievement, ratings by teachers of classroom behavior, and school competence of the older siblings. We also administered the Family Relations Test by Anthony and Bene in order to examine the older child's perception of his or her place in the family. Our findings for the most part were the weak ones of not being able to reject the null hypothesis. In this case, of course, we were relieved that no significant differences, and thus no clearly aversive effects, were shown. In retrospect, I am pleased and almost surprised that we had the wit to make these inquiries two decades ago. From an ethical standpoint, we were at least reassured. Our efforts suggest that one does well to look to the side as well as straight ahead when assessing the effects of an intervention.

Yet, at the same time, there is such a thing as being entirely too cautious. One thinks of the parable of the talents. Doing nothing is a form of doing something. Indecision can mean some other intervention by default. The risk-benefit analysis that each researcher must make involves a delicate balance. The decision needs sensitivity and a careful look at accumulated wisdom and experience. Good intentions should be buttressed by good thinking.

THE ARROWSMITH DILEMMA

As students, we all had dinned into us that the research plan of choice in the behavioral sciences is the so-called true experimental design, which involves assigning one's participants to two or more treatment groups by random selection, and then testing for a difference in effects of the treatment by setting up the null hypothesis. We set up the null hypothesis in order to reject it. In strict terms, even if in the real world there is no difference in our two populations, and no matter how carefully controlled is our procedure, our test does not allow us to accept the null hypothesis. As we learned, all we can do is fail to reject it. From a statistical standpoint, there are clear advantages for such comparisons of having one treatment group as a control, or "no treatment" group, especially when the groups have been constituted by random assignment. Some methodologists (Meehl, 1967; Serlin & Lapsley, 1985) consider that in the behavioral sciences, where multiple causation is almost always the rule, the particular experimental design behavioral scientists have adopted has had unfortunate consequences, since by its use equality cannot be demonstrated. There is always the "other things being equal" qualifier, and human organisms are never exactly equal. Even though such criticisms of the typical research design as those of Meehl and of Serlin and Lapsley appear to be well founded, behavioral researchers continue to favor the traditional null-hypothesis comparison. And they must live with its limitations.

The ethical issue that follows from this experimental design of choice is not far to seek: How can one deny a potentially valuable treatment to some of one's participants? I have called this the Arrowsmith dilemma. Some of you of my generation may have been impressed as I was in my young days with Sinclair Lewis's novel of the young medical researcher who discovered a promising substance that appeared to destroy bacteria. The novel was written in the early 1920s, well before the advent of even the sulfonamides. Lewis's young researcher was faced with the dilemma of whether to test this promising substance with a control group when the need for a destroyer of bacteria was urgent. How could he deny his magical treatment to anyone who needed it? His professor and mentor attempted to make clear to him where his ultimate responsibility lay.

Fortunately for most of us who engage in intervention research of the kind I am discussing, our decisions are usually less urgent, the experiment less perilous. And there are also the constraints of institutional review boards. What we may require is a large measure of ingenuity—and funds—in order to reconcile the need to make adequate tests of our hypotheses with our ethical responsibility to those whom we assign to our control groups. Today we think in terms of providing certain desired services for our control or comparison groups. This is now usual, and some clever solutions have been worked out by researchers. There are a number of relatively complex problems, and some pitfalls, in setting up such comparison groups, but one can find guidance, as well as good illustrations, in the literature on design in nonlaboratory settings, such as the book by Cook and Campbell (1978).

Faced by the need for control groups formed by random assignment, the researcher is likely to invoke the principle of scarce resources, or even the "tragedy of the commons," the original cautionary tale by Hardin (1968). In

Hardin's fable, if everyone grazed his or her sheep on the village common, share and share alike, the pasturage would of course be destroyed, and no one would benefit. His point was that where resources are limited, equal distribution may mean that no one is helped. Scarcity of resources may be a valid point, but it is not a sufficient excuse for failing to use as much wit and foresight as possible in order to avoid having to tell those of your shepherds randomly assigned to the control group, "Sorry, there's not enough pasturage for all the sheep, so you are out of luck."

One solution sometimes proposed for this dilemma is to tell the shepherds ahead of time that you are going to have to draw lots, that if they are willing to participate in the lottery they have a good chance of obtaining pasturage. The analogy could be pursued, but suffice it to say that such a solution sometimes has a serious drawback; it may exploit those participants who are most desperate.

I expect the reason I have gone into the Arrowsmith dilemma at such length is because of my own feelings of discomfort over the years with the control groups of the Early Training Project. When we planned the study back in 1960, a century ago it now seems, we were hardly the only ones with no more than moderate qualms about establishing a no-treatment group. At that time we were far from confident that our treatment would prove successful; certainly our resources were not abundant. As the treatment began to show positive results, however, qualms appeared in earnest. The qualms did not take away our belief that our control groups were essential, but they did arouse feelings of being unkind. We had paid a very modest amount to the parents of the children in the distal control group, in another town, each time their children were tested. We had not done this for the local control group, since we were advised not to do so by the school officers of the town. We did, however, try to do a number of little things for the control group, such as occasional play periods and small gifts.

Yet of all the things we did for the control groups, the one that seemed to have the most impact was simply expressing our gratitude on many occasions to the parents and the participants in the two control groups. These individuals gave much but had little to gain. Over the years we have tried to build a modest esprit de corps among the young people and their parents, with emphasis on the importance of the contribution they have made to a research enterprise that has already had some influence on enhancing educational opportunities for children from families like theirs. Yet that is small return for what they have given us.

A favorite question asked of longitudinal researchers is, What would you do differently, if you had it to do over again? Aside from the obvious response, run in the opposite direction as fast as possible, I think first of trying our hardest to set up a study so that the knowledge of 1985 might provide a better solution to our Arrowsmith dilemma of over two decades ago.

PROTECTING THE DIGNITY OF ONE'S PARTICIPANTS

Respect for one's research participants, or clientele, as an ethical principle, probably needs little explication. There are, however, one or two facets of this principle that may be worth mentioning, ones that concern participants and families who live in poverty.

First, it is easy to forget that the proportion of the American population living in poverty today is about as great as it was in the early years of the War on Poverty. The status of elderly poor has improved; the status of children has worsened. Danziger, Haveman, and Plotnick (1985) in their analysis of Census Bureau publications show that poverty among the elderly, when adjusted for in-kind transfer such as Medicare, declined almost 90% from 1964 to 1983. The official figure for those 65 years of age or older was 28.5% in 1966, the first year such figures were published; the figure for 1983 was 14.1%. For children under 18, figures for the same two years, respectively, are 20.7% and 22.2%. Thus, at least one in five children today lives in a family below the poverty line. As all of us are at least tangentially aware, the gap between the poor and the nonpoor has widened, or perhaps deepened, in the last two decades. National figures suggest that the American people as a whole are more affluent than ever before. But the affluence of the majority has been purchased at the price of increased poverty for a sizable minority. As Michael Harrington elucidates in his recent book, *The New American Poverty* (1984), today's poverty is structural, built into the current worldwide economic system; it will not go away with a few quick fixes to the U.S. economy.

As the gap widens, the lack of empathy with the least fortunate grows; those who have never been poor have little concept of what it means in day-to-day living. Over two decades ago, Michael Harrington (1963) made the point that for most Americans the poor were invisible. And even earlier in the century, Bertolt Brecht expressed this invisibility in the last lines of the final chorus of *The Three Penny Opera.*

Denn die einen sind im Dunkeln
Und die andern sind im Licht
Und man siehet die im Lichte
Denn im Dunkeln sieht man nicht.

(For some are in the darkness
and others in the light.
One sees those in the light,
but in the dark one does not see.)

Most people of my generation have known what it is to be poor, for we lived through the Great Depression. I sometimes wonder how those born since the mid-thirties can ever have any grasp of what grinding poverty really means. But even those of us who were the children of the Depression had the solace that everyone else we knew was in the same boat. Poverty today is unlike that of half a century ago: today's poor are continually bombarbed by television and other media with visions of the affluent, even opulent, life—a life they see spread before them in a superficial way, but which they cannot enter. I like the phrase "the glass curtain"—bountiful and glamorous goods of every conceivable type are displayed, ones that can be viewed at the turn of a dial, but not touched, let alone possessed. An empathic awareness of what life is like for those who watch from the other side of the glass curtain may be difficult to come by, but it is not impossible. And it is probably the first step in developing appropriate regard for the dignity of those who live in poverty and who must struggle each day for mere subsistence.

Honoring the dignity of one's participants imposes additional demands when one is concerned with children and those persons, children or adults, who have severe retardation. It is not always easy to show genuine regard for the dignity of the very immature. Adults are too used to thinking they know best. In some ways, respect for the child has improved over the years. This change is in part attributable to increasing evidence that children are active shapers of their environment and of the people in it, anything but passive lumps of clay (e.g., see Bell & Harper, 1977). A qualifier is necessary, in some ways, because this change in perception of the child's capacities and autonomy has not been accompanied by increases in support for programs designed to benefit children. Every time a state legislature or the U.S. Congress attacks the problem of the budget we see evidence of where the money fails to go. Children do not vote.

Another aspect of regard for the dignity of the child participant stems from the fact that what is good for a child, as perceived by the child's parents in all sincerity, is not necessarily what is good for the child from the researcher's standpoint, or what the child might ultimately desire. Thus the conflicting loyalties that workers with children and families sometimes experience. In the late 19th century and the early part of the 20th, this conflict was seen dramatically in disparities between values held by immigrants and their American offspring. It is still seen occasionally in media accounts of the ever-fascinating but often little understood Anabaptist sects, the Mennonites, the Old Order Amish, and the Hutterites. One can honor and respect the convictions and desires of these groups to rear their children according to their religious convictions and a life-style centuries old. But one can also understand why some of the children are drawn to "go into the world."

Embedded in the general principle of respect for the dignity of one's research participants are at least three other ethical principles generally considered in codes of ethics and by institutional review boards, ones with particular regard for the individual's rights and autonomy. These are: the protection of confidentiality, avoidance of the invasion of privacy, and informed consent. Each of these is discussed on the succeeding pages as it applies to intervention research with families at risk.

Protection of Confidentiality

The usual cautions and caveats apply on the confidentiality of information gathered in an intervention program. Such programs tend to be relatively public; they take place in schools, day-care centers, and university classrooms and laboratories, where many people come. Those of you who work with children with severe retardation are at least as familiar as I am with matters of confidentiality in such intervention settings, and the problems therein. When a study becomes a longitudinal one, and extends over years, additional issues come into play.

Records on participants in a long-term study accumulate at a fearful pace as the years go by. Standards of what is ethical, and even legal, in conducting research change somewhat as accumulated wisdom, public attitudes, and communication technology change. In the research in which my colleagues and I have been involved for some 20 years, we did not originally plan the Early Training Project to extend beyond 4 years of study. Partly for this reason, and probably because we lacked sufficient foresight, it is only recently that we have faced up to the desirability of placing our records in proper form for a research archive. In attempting to carry out this wish we have encountered some problems with ethical overtones.

When we began, ethical codes for psychology were in their infancy. We were fortunate in having as colleagues some psychologists who were involved in the development of the early codes. As I look back, we were sensitive in general to most of the ethical principles that concern the profession today. Over the years, however, new problems have arisen.

Our study might be characterized as one featuring a lot about a little, in comparison with the panel studies of sociologists that number their participants in the thousands. We, on the other hand, have less than 100 individuals, although we have a great deal of information about each of them. There are available certain statistical techniques that can make identification of individual participants virtually impossible (e.g., see Boruch & Cecil, 1979). These techniques involve the loss of a few degrees of freedom, immaterial if one has 20,000 respondents, but a serious matter for the 70 to 85 persons on whom we do our analyses. A little triangulation on demographic data could identify individuals, if someone wished to do so. The probability of this happening is low, but it is not zero. When a study is well known in professional circles and also in the institutions of higher learning in the communities involved, such a recognition of one's fellow participants is not impossible, unless we are extremely careful. We might contrast our study with the Terman Study of Children of High Ability (Terman, Sears, Cronbach, & Sears, 1983). The Terman participants, generally speaking, appear pleased to be identified as some of "Terman's geniuses." Most psychologists know someone who was in the original study and is proud of it. It is unlikely that our young people are proud of their selection for the research, although we have tried to foster a sense of pride in their participation in a study that has shown some lasting effects and has had some impact on public policies toward children. We are inclined to think that some sort of gatekeeping may be needed for the archive, if we are to honor our promises of confidentiality to our participants. In other words, some of our data may not be suitable for sharing for every academic use, such as classroom demonstrations. And yet the whole purpose of a research archive is to share one's data. We must perform a neat balancing act.

Invasion of Privacy

Guarding against the invasion of privacy is always an important aspect of ethical research with human beings. Research with vulnerable participants not only makes the principle salient, but it imposes special problems. Much of the intervention research in which I have been involved has been carried out in the home. All the tact and sensitivity the home visitor can muster is needed to work in the home of a highly vulnerable parent, one who perceives your presence as indicating that she, or rarely he, has been evaluated negatively by someone and judged to need help. In a general way, the inference is of course correct. I have often discussed this issue with our home visitors. An especially perceptive and skilled individual among them has said to me that she has learned to be selectively blind and deaf when she goes into a home, oblivious to dirt and disorder, with never an eyebrow raised at what she may see or hear. She tries never to forget she is a guest in the home and the parent she is visiting is the host or hostess. She tries to present her role and that of the parent as a partnership formed in the interest of the child. In discussing how to establish a sense of trust with the parent-host/hostess she says, "You must learn just where the line is drawn between being nosy and having a friendly interest in the other person. What makes this so hard is that the line is different in every home." In one home a failure to inquire into the concerns of the family is taken as a lack of interest; in another, such questions are seen as unwarranted inquisitiveness. One can learn fairly easily not to pry; locating the thin line between appropriate concern and intrusiveness is far more difficult.

A problem we have encountered occasionally as we have tried to protect the privacy of our families stems from the fact that work with poor young children makes good copy in the public media, especially around holiday time. We have faced a difficult dilemma. Our long-term aim has been to contribute to efforts to improve the lot of low-income families. More public attention focused on the problems of families living in poverty may have some positive influence on changing public opinion. It is difficult to provide recognition, however, without some invasion of privacy, particularly if one is dealing with local media in communities where people are likely to be known. A partial solution for us has been to avoid all possible publicity until a study, or a major phase of it, has been completed. At that point, we believe we have an obligation to communicate findings of substance. But one cannot always avoid premature publicity, and many of the group today could contribute sad examples of this point. We have tried to work with reporters of local newspapers and television stations to explain why we believe it important to withhold publicity at a given time. Anticipation of problems must be one's guide.

Informed Consent and Implied Contracts

By definition, research is designed to find the answer to a question for which one has at best only a provisional answer. Informed consent thus becomes a cardinal principle in ethical research. Participants need to know what they are getting into. I assume that for the purposes of this volume we are less concerned with matters of deception than with issues of how we obtain, or fail to obtain, consent that is adequately informed. Especially relevant are the inferences participants draw from our words and behavior about the nature of the research and its possible outcomes.

Most of the families with whom we have worked for extended periods of time have been low-income, often for generations. Their educational level has usually been less than high school completion. As a whole they have not been comfortable dealing with abstractions or with time frames extending into the distant future. If you are wondering where next month's rent, or even the next meal, is coming from, your outlook tends to be immediate and concrete. The goals of intervention research are usually long-term and often, for most of us, relatively abstract. There is nothing wrong with being either concrete or abstract, except that between the two approaches there may exist a broad gap, one the researcher must make efforts to bridge, and to do so in a manner neither condescending nor distorting.

The approach to this general problem that we have found most helpful is to discuss the various issues involved with persons familiar with the population with whom we hope to work. The home visitor just quoted would be an example of the kind of person who could provide help for researchers who lack experience in wording information in simple concrete terms, enabling them to explain intermediate goals more effectively, and to describe the actual participation expected of the individual. The rift, or sometimes chasm, in understanding is reminiscent of George Bernard Shaw's quip that America and England are two nations separated by a common language. Middle-class investigators may find that some familiar words have different meanings to low-income people or to members of other ethnic groups. I remember perusing the transcript of an interview with one of our young women who gave birth to a child out of wedlock. When asked about the father's attitude toward the infant she responded that he said it could not be his child, because the baby was too bright. I thought he was referring to the child's intelligence, which seemed a trifle strange, until someone enlightened me; the young man was referring to the child's skin color.

Long-term intervention programs are frequently molded by what has come to be called formative evaluation—the evaluation that helps the program developer reshape the program in accordance with the results so far obtained. Practically, the use of such continuing evaluation means that the researcher cannot inform to the fullest extent those people being asked to serve as participants, for the program itself is being shaped as time goes on. This course of events usually should pose no great problem, but at least it needs recognizing by intervention researchers and their institutional review boards. It also means that the researcher may find it desirable to check periodically on the adequacy of the information participants actually have about the nature of the on-going research.

Individuals agree to participate in research not only because of what is said but also because of their perceptions, accurate or sometimes distorted, of the purposes and possible outcomes of the research, the activities in which they expect to be involved, and their judgment of the person who asks them to participate. An empathic and sensitive interviewer creates the impression that the participant will find empathy and sensitivity in the people who will conduct the research. So far, so good; but what if the participants, because their need is great, expect or at least hope for more than is being promised? I should think this clutching at a hope, and reading more into an offer than is there, would be particularly likely to occur with the parents of children with severe retardation. Extreme caution is needed.

A problem we encountered in the Early Training Project surfaced during our follow-up data collection when we asked the parents to evaluate the project. In answer to what they saw as the purpose of the early intervention program, a typical reply was that the program was intended to get their children ready for school. In a general way, the parents were right; our goal had been to offset the progressive retardation in schooling often observed in children from low-income homes. But if the parents expected that the program was designed to give the children a specific foretaste of what first grade would be like, or that it would involve such primary grade activities as reading, writing, and arithmetic, they must have been disappointed. We deliberately made no attempts, except purely incidental ones, to teach the children to read or to write, or much in the way of learning numbers. If an experimental child did poorly, did the parent blame it on us? If a control child did poorly, was that also our fault for denying treatment to the child?

A related facet of the consent issue is compliance or acquiescence set. Our families were not only low income; they were also black. In the early 1960s in the South, most black people were likely to be compliant, at least on the surface, with middle-class whites, saying what they thought the white person wanted to hear. Our interviewers were all black, but the school officials and most of the researchers were white. Our parents may have found it hard to say no, particularly since the school officials were enthusiastic about the project and told the parents it would be a good thing to have their children take part. In general, however, our impression was not one of superficial compliance. As a whole, the intervention program was an attractive one for them. It meant that a school bus came by, with a driver familiar to them, and took the children to school. There the children were fed a substantial lunch and were returned home with specimens of their artwork, songs to sing, or picture books to show their parents. Still, compliance set may have helped our recruitment.

An enlightening contrast appeared in evaluations of the intervention program, when we compared the responses given by parents in the local and distal control groups to the question of whether they thought the program had been a good thing for their children. The local control group, who were randomly assigned from the same pool from which the experimental children came, tended to be either neutral or slightly negative as to the effect upon their children. They of course had a basis for comparison. No one likes for his or her child to fail to receive what is seen as a benefit. Yet these control parents, with two possible exceptions, were cooperative. Interestingly enough, of all the young people whom we have been able to contact so far, and that is nearly all, only two have refused to allow their records to be placed in the research archive, and these were from the two families just mentioned. Refusal was of course their right, and all we have said is, sorry, but thanks for your contribution up to now.

On the other hand, the majority of the distal control group parents, who had not had contact with the experimental groups, and who were paid a modest amount for their children's participation, replied that they thought the program had been a good thing for their children, a response that makes us feel rather ashamed. The only positive thing for them in taking part, besides the $5 per time, was a little attention for their children at the periodic testing times. We assume that the response indicated acquiescence set, but it is worth noting that acquiescence set appeared less powerful when there was a basis for comparison, when the parent had an opportunity to observe what was going

on with others of the neighborhood children in the experimental group. Informed consent, then, is not easy; neither can it be taken care of once and for
all at the outset of a study.

CONCLUSION

Now, to endeavor to tie a knot in the string of ethical issues and principles I
have discussed and to relate these to the concerns of those whose research
involves persons with severe retardation and their parents or guardians.

As in other research with human participants, the overarching ethical
principle seems to be that of truly honoring and respecting the dignity of each
individual involved in one's research. Empathy and sensitivity are the key
words. But empathy and sensitivity do not occur in a vacuum, or simply by
deciding that as of tomorrow one intends to respect the dignity of one's
research participants. Furthermore, such resolutions may not touch those
staff members who actually deliver the intervention treatment. Willing is not
enough, and wishing will not make it so. But there are some obvious approaches that may help. To me, where staff are concerned, the key is selection. One selects staff who have had extended experience in working with
parents and children similar to those who are to be involved in the research.
They should have demonstrated already that they can be accepting and non-
judgmental of others, and have an in-depth awareness of the day-by-day
demands these participants have upon them. It is not impossible to teach some
of these perspectives to staff members, but attitudes change slowly, at best.
There is much that can be learned, however, from persons with experience in
working with a wide spectrum of families and from those wise in examining
the ethical issues that must be faced in research with vulnerable human
beings. All of us are vulnerable to some extent. But when demands upon
individuals are great and resources few, researchers must tread delicately on
an eggshell-strewn pathway.

At the start of this chapter the question of superordinate goals was raised.
What goals are genuinely ethical in intervention research with human beings
with retardation, whether their retardation is mild or severe? Unless one
rejects all relativism in the sphere of morals and ethics, one faces the serious
question of whether the light that is within you may not be darkness instead
for the ones with whom you are working. How sure are you that you are on
the right track? A strong dose of humility is probably good for most of us. In
my own thinking I often come back to the words of Oliver Cromwell in his
letter to the General Assembly of the Church of Scotland: ''I beseech you, in
the bowels of Christ, think it possible that you can be mistaken'' (Cromwell,
1650; cited in Bartlett, 1980, p. 272). Our belief, sincere as it is, as to what is
best for another may not be the other's view nor the view of those who are

wiser than we. Or it may not be what the future will bring. We must think it possible that we can be mistaken.

Yet there is a way out of our dilemma, not perfect, but workable, and ethical as many would see it. This way out is based on a point already made, that the families of children with sociocultural retardation and with severe retardation, regardless of social status, have sharply limited options, few alternatives, as they attempt to cope daily with the demands that comprise so large a part of their lives. Worthy goals for would-be interventionists can be those of trying to increase options or alternatives for their participants, and of enabling these participants to take advantage of the options already existing or of new ones they create for themselves.

A story that has gladdened my heart comes from one of our home visitors. A mother in one of our intervention programs had decided she would like to enroll her younger child in a Head Start program at a nearby public school. She took the child to the school but was turned away because, according to the director, the child was too immature. The mother went back home, gathered up the proof of her son's readiness and competencies, took him back to the school, proved her point, and enrolled him in Head Start. The home visitor asked her, "What would you have done, if it hadn't been for your experiences in the program?" The mother replied, "I would have gone back down the hill to my house and stayed there."

Our goals must often be modest; we cannot open up the whole world to our participants. But even a little more in the way of skills, in knowledge of the outside world and how it operates, and in the growth of feelings of competence may set in motion processes that can help those in our programs and others like them come a little nearer to realizing the goals they have set for themselves. I could wish for no more ethical way to approach the setting of goals for all the participants who contribute so greatly to the research in which we are engaged.

REFERENCES

Bell, R.Q., & Harper, L.V. (1977). *Child effects on adults.* Hillsdale, NJ: Lawrence Erlbaum Associates.

Berrueta-Clement, J.R., Schweinhart, L.J., Barnett, W.S., Epstein, A.S., & Weikart, D.P. (1984). Changed Lives: The effects of the Perry Preschool Program on youths through age 19. *Monographs of the High/Scope Educational Research Foundation* (No. 8). Ypsilanti, MI: High/Scope.

Boruch, R.F., & Cecil, J.S. (1979). *Assuring the confidentiality of social research data.* Philadelphia: University of Pennsylvania Press.

Cook, T.D., & Campbell, D.T. (1978). *Quasi-experimentation: Design and analysis issues for field settings.* Boston: Houghton Mifflin Co.

Cromwell, O. (1650, August 3). [Letter to the General Assembly of the Church of Scotland]. In J. Bartlett (Ed.), (1980), *Familiar quotations* (15th ed., p. 272). Boston: Little, Brown.

Danziger, S., Haveman, R., & Plotnick, R. (1984). Antipoverty policy: Effects on the poor and the nonpoor. Paper prepared for conference on "Poverty and Policy: Retrospect and Prospects," Williamsburg, VA, December 6–8 (Revised, March 1985). Ann Arbor: Institute for Research on Poverty, University of Michigan.

Gray, S.W., & Wandersman, L.P. (1980). The methodology of home-based intervention studies: Problems and promising strategies. *Child Development, 51,* 993–1009.

Hardin, G.J. (1968). The tragedy of the commons. *Science, 162,* 1243–1248.

Harrington, M. (1963). *The other America.* New York: Macmillan Publishing Co.

Harrington, M. (1984). *The new American poverty.* New York: Holt, Rinehart & Winston.

Jencks, C. (1985, May 9). Review of *Losing ground: American social policy, 1950–1980,* by Charles Murray. *New York Review of Books, 32*(8), 41–49.

Karnes, M.B., Schwedel, A.M., & Williams, M.B. (1983). A comparison of five approaches for educating young children from low-income homes. In *As the twig is bent: Lasting effects of preschool programs* (pp. 133–170). Consortium for Longitudinal Studies. Hillsdale, NJ: Lawrence Erlbaum Associates.

Klaus, R.A., & Gray, S.W. (1968). The Early Training Project for disadvantaged children: A report after five years. *Monographs of the Society for Research in Child Development, 33*(4, Serial No. 120).

McCord, J.A. (1978). Thirty year follow-up of treatment effects. *American Psychologist, 33,* 284–289.

Meehl, P. (1967). Theoretical risks and tabular asterisks: Sir Karl, Sir Ronald, and the slow progress of soft psychology. *Journal of Consulting and Clinical Psychology, 46,* 806–834.

Miller, L.B., & Bizzell, R.P. (1984). Long-term effects of four preschool programs: Ninth and tenth grade results. *Child Development, 55,* 1570–1587.

Serlin, R.C., & Lapsley, D.K. (1985). Rationality in psychological research: The good-enough principle. *American Psychologist, 40*(1), 73–83.

Terman, I.M., Sears, R.R., Cronbach, L.J., & Sears, P.S. (1983). *Terman Life Cycle Study of Children of High Ability, 1922–1982.* Ann Arbor, MI: Inter-University Consortium for Political and Social Research.

Response

ISSUES OF CONTENT AND CONTEXT REGARDING EDUCATIONAL DECISION MAKING FOR YOUNG CHILDREN WITH SEVERE RETARDATION

Susan C. Hupp

I ADMIRE SUSAN GRAY'S work focused on ethical considerations for intervention with young children with severe retardation, and view this opportunity to discuss and react to the ideas of someone with as rich a background as hers as exciting.

Gray's discussion of ethical issues relevant to early intervention was extensive. Rather than highlight all aspects of her paper that merit further thought, I have chosen to discuss two specific ideas that she presented: the first relating to looking at intervention as a system and the second relating to the provision of greater options for children with handicaps and their families.

INTERVENTION AS A SYSTEM

Based on the work of researchers interested in families, Ann P. Turnbull notable among them, the field has oriented itself of late toward systems analysis. As Gray aptly pointed out, "Intervention always occurs within a system. The possibility is ever there that one may disrupt a functioning system. Aversive side effects can and sometimes do occur." Although family systems have received increasing attention, I would like to examine more closely the notion of child-centered systems, particularly the system we refer to as child development.

Intervention with children with severe retardation has focused primarily on the acquisition of discrete skills. Historically, this focus was justified on the basis that persons with severe retardation were considered uneducable, perhaps even untrainable. We now have demonstrated with reasonable assurance that persons with severe retardation can learn. Less attention has been paid to the long-term effects of the teaching strategies that we have chosen to facilitate skill acquisition. Symptoms of problems have begun to present themselves. Children are not maintaining acquired skills, they are not generalizing them appropriately, and the skills they have acquired often are not functional for performing activities that occur in the children's everyday environments.

The field has responded enthusiastically to correcting these problems. We now advocate analyzing the environment to determine those skills that occur in daily activities, we teach clusters of skills that tend to occur simultaneously, we present multiple examples during training to increase the probability of generalization, and we use naturally occurring contingencies to ensure maintenance of acquired skills. These approaches to research have been admirable, but they represent only one avenue of exploration.

We need to consider new perspectives. While we may be able to remediate some learning problems through more sophisticated behavioral programming, we need to examine the *source* of learning problems more extensively. Perhaps, inadvertently, we directly caused some of these learning problems through application of the very technology that we used successfully to demonstrate that these children could profit from instruction. For example, when we teach a child to respond to an event in the environment with a specific response or a limited set of responses, and consequate the child systematically with reinforcement or error correction, we may be undermining a basic process of hypothesis testing that some say underlies development. The child may now look to others to direct learning, rather than relying on his or her own trial and error or postulating cause and effect to exert control over the environment.

To cite another example, and an issue pertaining to my own research, we need to examine our current approaches for exploring strategies to enhance generalization. To assess a child's ability to generalize learning, we tend to look for the occurrence of a previously trained response in novel, yet similar, situations. Is that consistent with the notion of development, however? To some, development implies not only accommodation but also adaptation. When we succeed in facilitating generalization as defined by most current dependent measures, will we actually have blocked the process of development rather than enhanced it?

There are no quick fixes for these new problems. These problems are not caused by ill-intentioned researchers and practitioners, but are inherent in our intervention and research agendas. On the other hand, no matter how strong our defense of the state of the art, we must challenge ourselves to set aside time to go back to the drawing board to develop new blueprints for the future. Dr. Gray justified this type of challenge by remarking that ''good intentions, unaccompanied by wisdom and sensitivity, do not suffice.''

How might we operationalize the challenge? I would propose three strategies. First, we understand precious little about the process of child development. We understand something about the way in which we can directly change behavior. We understand something about sequences of behavior change that occur with most nonhandicapped children. However, we know very little about the reasons for these developmental sequences, and even less about the courses of development of children with various handicapping conditions. This suggests that we need to study child development in greater depth, both in nonhandicapped populations and in populations with handicaps. As a corollary, it may be helpful for us to focus on the development of assessment tools that can describe the level of, and perhaps more importantly the nature of, development that a child has attained. Finally, it may be profitable for us to look at the effects of intervention programmatically. A point that has been raised time and again in recent years is that learning is a multivariate process. Dependent measures do not occur in isolation. Neither do independent measures. Variables interact over time, and these interactions need to be studied.

PROVIDING OPTIONS

A second issue concerning ethical considerations that was elaborated by Gray relates to increasing options of young children and their families. As Gray mentioned, persons with limited income have few options. Parents of children with severe retardation may also have limited options. How can we best help these families increase their options? Moreover, what options are we willing to assist families to pursue? Interventionists and researchers have an incredible impact on children and families. By and large, they are considered experts in child development and intervention planning. As is the responsibility of all in positions of authority and power, continued scrutiny of one's impact is essential.

I am convinced that most researchers and practitioners believe that they have fairly liberal views regarding the value of different life-styles. Literature on intervention has discussed extensively the nature of middle-class values. We as practitioners have to some degree tried to understand the functional nature of our actions within our environment and the potential reasons for actions that may be exhibited by persons of different income groups and cultural backgrounds.

Yet, even given this degree of inquiry, I have been puzzled by interactions of mine and others that suggest a strong, perhaps unnegotiable, bias regarding how children should be incorporated within families. In the course of reading Gray's paper, the source of some of my biases became clearer. While I recognize myself as a person with a "middle-class" background, I tend not to think about another source of my values, that of academia. Likewise, most researchers are academicians and most practitioners have extensive academic histories.

What are some of the values held by academicians who are interested in mental retardation? I think, first, that we tend to value education in its own right and that, in fact, we value overachievement. We value systematicity and validation. We value civil rights in general, although we may disagree about what they are and how to achieve them, and we value advocacy. Finally, we value investing in the future. For the most part, these values complement our life-style.

With these values in mind, what options are we willing to provide young children with handicaps and their families, who may have different life-styles than our own? What is our probable reaction when a family tells us verbally or through their actions that they do not value education? Are we likely to try earnestly to increase their options to engage in activities that may not only be noneducational but that may also in our best judgment interfere with development? And what is our reaction likely to be when a family tells us that they do not value validation? Although the suggestions that we have to offer a family may be logically constructed and systematically verified, it may well be the case that a family elects an alternative course of action.

Daily, practitioners are suggesting intervention goals and procedures that relate to, and perhaps embody, their own values. Decisions regarding such programming concerns as alternative language systems, systems of mobility, and the selection of social skills all potentially reflect our values. Those of us who have been in this position believe in our hearts that our suggestions will truly benefit the child. How do we then react when a parent does not support a suggestion we have made? Are we likely to agree that an alternative course of action would be of equal or greater benefit than that which we proposed? Are we likely to admit that we may not have considered some variables essential to the decision? There is a growing body of literature describing problems experienced by educational planning teams in trying to develop coordinated instructional programs based on joint decision making, indicating that we have great difficulty letting go of our well-reasoned opinions.

I am not certain that we as academicians have adequately explored our values concerning education and the process of systematic inquiry in order to truly respect alternative values that families of children with handicaps may have. Moreover, I am concerned about the tactics that we have at our disposal to impose our values on others. Various ones of us are well-versed in educational, psychological, and legal jargon. We have practiced the style of debate. And we are considered by many as experts. Have we developed with equal expertise strategies for values clarification that could enable us to be fair in our interactions with families of children with handicaps? Perhaps we have some learning to do.

I admire Gray because she saw difficult challenges and had the bravery to pursue them. One might say that she took "the path of most resistance," and as such has made significant contributions to the field. Her own words serve to underscore the courage and insight that interventionists must exhibit: "In retrospect, I am pleased and almost surprised that we had the wit to make these inquiries. . . . From an ethical standpoint, we were at least reassured. Our efforts suggest that one does well to look to the side as well as straight ahead when assessing the effects of an intervention."

Chapter 7

FAMILY RESEARCH AND INTERVENTION

A VALUE AND ETHICAL EXAMINATION

Ann P. Turnbull, Martha Blue-Banning,
Shirley Behr, and Georgia Kerns

THE GOAL OF THIS chapter is to analyze the values inherent in family research and intervention as a means for examining the ethical dimensions of professional practice. Rather than relying strictly on the professional literature, we use divergent sources of information—perspectives of parents and persons with disabilities, and even marketing literature of a professional organization. Our purpose is to create a clash in perspectives to accomplish what we hope is a fresh look at some age-old issues. We have heeded Baumeister's (1981) statement: "Truth is ultimately a moral test, the outcome of the confrontation of values; truth does not depend on scientific methods" (p. 451). With this admonition, we invite you to confront your own values and those represented in theory and practice related to family research and intervention.

PROFESSIONAL AND FAMILY
ANALYSIS OF RESEARCH AND INTERVENTION

A historical analysis of family research reveals discrete rather than continuous research emphases over the last 40 years. Research conducted from the 1940s through the early 1960s primarily investigated the impact of children with disabilities on their families in areas such as marital and sibling relationships (Farber, 1960; Farber & Jenne, 1963; Farber & Ryckman, 1965). The effects of institutionalization and counseling as interventions received primary emphasis. Case studies on stages of adjustment is a predominant theme in the literature of this period (Wolfensberger, 1970).

In the late 1960s and early 1970s a major research shift occurred, largely influenced by the success of behavioral interventions in clinical and educational settings. In contrast to the previous emphasis on the child's impact on the family, this period is characterized by studies of the mother's impact on the child's self-help, social, and cognitive development. The zeitgeist of the times was to "train" mothers in behavioral principles and techniques, with the expectation that mothers would then more positively influence their child's development. The fundamental value system of this work is summarized by Johnson and Katz (1973): "The advantage of parents as change agents is that they constitute a cheap, continuous treatment resource which is able to augment existing therapeutic manpower capabilities and work conveniently within the home" (p. 181).

An analysis of this quote suggests many value statements that are operating: children need to change rather than to grow and develop; parent time is cheap; parents can work continuously with their child and thus do not have competing responsibilities; it is in children's best interest to have continuous treatment; the appropriate role for parents is to augment what therapists do; home is a convenient place for therapy; and the values of therapists are an appropriate basis for determining what parents should do.

In light of these values it is not surprising that the result of many parent training interventions has been frustration on the part of professionals when parents did not live up to expectations (Baker, 1983). In one demonstration project, the parent trainers anticipated serving 130 families (Rosenberg, Reppucci, & Linney, 1983). By the end of the demonstration year, 48 parents had been referred and 25 had attended at least one group meeting.

Bernal (1984) described barriers to effective parent training as follows:

> There are some personal and demographic characteristics of parents that have the potential for reducing the effectiveness of parent training, even if the parent does not drop out before the end of treatment. Among these characteristics are marital problems (Cole & Morrow, 1976; Johnson & Lobitz, 1974; Margolin & Christensen, 1981; Oltmanns, Broderick, & O'Leary, 1977; Wahler, 1980); depression (McMahon, Forehand, Griest, Wells, 1981); social isolation (Wahler, 1980); low socioeconomic status (Blechman, Budd, Christophersen, Szykula, Wahler, & Embry, 1981); child-rearing philosophies that conflict with parent training philosophy (Bernal & Klinnert, 1981; Sloop, 1974); a severely negative, critical view of the child (Bernal & Klinnert, 1981; Cole & Morrow, 1976); and inability or unwillingness to devote sufficient time to carrying out parent training programs (Bernal & Klinnert, 1981). . . .
>
> My personal view of behavioral parent training is that it is best suited for white middle- and upper-class families, since it was developed primarily for service to these families. Issues arise relevant to the match or mismatch between parent training (as well as parent trainers) and diverse populations, such as low-income and culturally or ethnically different families. The parent trainer who

attempts to work with low-income families soon learns that the required appointments, homework, and monitoring of parent and child behavior are not family priorities when economic pressures and uncertainties disrupt schedules, plans, and availability of resources on a daily basis. These families may have needs for which a parent training approach may be inappropriate. (pp. 488–489)

Current research appears to be a synthesis of the two former periods. The bidirectionality of impact of the family member with a disability on other family members is increasingly being recognized. In fact, the family is being viewed as an ecological system with formal and informal networks operating both within and beyond the family (Bristol & Gallagher, in press).

Several reviews of different facets of family research have been published recently (Blacher, 1984; Crnic, Friedrich, & Greenberg, 1983; Dangel & Polster, 1984; Snell & Beckman-Brindley, 1984; Turnbull, Summers, & Brotherson, 1984). An analysis of this literature suggests the following themes:

1. Most research fails to address theory related to successful family functioning. The result is that research frequently becomes an end in itself, since the meaning of the relationships between variables was never conceptualized. The question is rarely asked: What are the implications of this research for family life?

2. Family adjustment and acceptance are frequently identified as the outcome measures, but have not been conceptually and operationally defined. What is a positive adjustment to a child with a disability? What is acceptance? A father illustrated the double-bind of acceptance as follows:

   I believe that parents should love their handicapped children as they are and work with everything they've got to help them reach their highest potential. But there is a fine line involved in doing this, almost a paradox. To love them as they are might tempt parents to not encourage them to achieve their highest potential, but rather to be content. On the other hand, emphasizing reaching their highest potential could lead parents to dwell on what they can't do. The result could be that it is harder to love them as they are. (Winton, Turnbull, & Blacher, 1984, p. 55)

   Does acceptance mean loving the child as he or she is? Or encouraging the child to reach his or her highest potential? Or both? Or neither? Family research lacks specificity on these issues.

3. Research methodologies and instruments have often failed to address issues of ecological validity (Brooks & Baumeister, 1983). The relevance of this point was underscored by a parent who made the following comment after participating in a research study that used an open-ended interview to gather data:

   I'm so glad someone's talking to me instead of giving me forms to fill out and questionnaires. Last time I said, "There are no answers to any of these questions." They really should do some checking before they ask some of these questions because some of these parents don't even know what you're talking about because of the language [used]. I've got a handicapped youngster . . . talk to me on my level. (Winton et al., 1984, p. viii)

4. Research subjects have primarily been nonemployed, married mothers with a middle-class or upper-middle-class background, and then generalizations have been made to "all families."

5. Much of the research is based on a limited view of persons with disabilities and their families, one that unduly emphasizes the "pathology" view of family stresses and burdens of care.

This last point came to the attention of some families in Lawrence, Kansas, when they were preparing funding requests for a program (Families Together, 1985) that provides weekend workshops and recreation for families with children having disabilities. The material that caused them concern reads as follows:

> The impetus for forming Families Together was the recognition that families with a disabled child encounter many challenges that may result in stress and, subsequently, a distabilization [sic] of the family. These effects on families with a disabled child are well documented (cf. Farger, 1975; Fotheringham, Shelton, and Hodelinotl, 1972; Friedrich & Friedrich, 1981). Gath (1977), for example, in a comparative study, found "severe marital disharmony" in approximately one-third of the families with a disabled child. This is not an unlikely consequence in light of the evidence that families with a disabled child are more likely to face additional financial costs, social isolation, limitations in recreational activities, stigma, additional time spent in personal care of the child, difficulty in handling problem behaviors, and hold pessimistic views of the future (Moroney, 1981). In addition, these families frequently encounter difficulty in taking vacations, participating in community activities, locating sitters (Farber and Ryckman, 1965); providing complicated diets or treatments, extra housework (Travis, 1976); and maladjustment in siblings (Gath, 1973).[1]

The families became insulted that their public image was so negatively construed. They did not recognize themselves in the pathological description, and began to fear that the professionals working with them might hold these negative stereotypes about them. They organized a discussion group at the next Families Together weekend, entitled *Who Are These Researchers and Why Are They Saying These Things about Us?* (1985). We had the privilege of sitting in on these discussion groups and learning about parental views on research—an opportunity too rarely afforded in academic circles. Following are the many questions parents raised for discussion:

> When you read the cover sheet [the material just presented] how did it make you feel?
> Who is doing research on families with handicapped children?

---

[1]Bibliographic data in this quotation were not provided in the original Families Together material.

Why would anyone want to do research on our families?

Who is paying for this research?

Who is benefiting from this research?

Where do they get the families that they do research on?

Do all professionals read this research before they start to work with our children? Does this research make them think that families with handicapped children are all troubled?

Are there a lot of books for professionals to read that are about families with handicapped children?

How do researchers decide what kind of research to do?

Why hasn't anyone asked the parents what kind of research would help them?

Does it help young professionals do a better job if they have read a lot of studies on families, or does it just create problems for them by giving them a picture that may not be a true picture?

Do you find it frightening to think that someone is doing research on families like ours? What would happen if the results of the research studies were very very wrong?

What kind of research would help you as a parent? What kind of research could hurt your family?

How much research is being done now on families with handicapped children?

Is the research being done now very different from the research that was done 10 years ago? If someone doesn't read all the latest research could they believe things about our families that have been proven wrong by newer studies?

Is this research good or bad for our families?

In response to these questions, staff members of Families Together asked the families, first, if they recognized themselves in the cover-sheet description. Some of the families commented that they had experienced severe stress similar to the description, others described the effect their child had on the family as neutral, and still others described the joy and satisfaction they derived from their child. A general consensus was expressed by a parent who said that researchers tend to "lump all families together and to assume that if you have a handicapped child it means you have a problem. Professionals ignore the positive aspects in families, because they don't believe it and they don't want to hear about it. They only want to hear negative reports." There was discussion about the premise that research "should be done with an open mind." There was strong agreement on the point that "researchers are part of the rest of the world in which a disability is viewed as a terrible thing. Their focus, like everyone else's, is to find out what's wrong."

Second, much discussion focused on the manner in which physicians initially told these families about the presence of a disability. This communication was characterized as being "unduly pessimistic." One father commented that "when normal children are born, the doctors do not recount for parents all of the problems that could happen to their child like drug involvement, flunking out of college, sexual promiscuity, or teenage suicide; however, when a child with Down syndrome is born, the doctors only point out the negative." Another parent said that "when you go into something expecting it to be bad, it naturally is going to influence your adjustment." They commented that "if physicians read this research, no wonder they can only see problems." The families identified the following chain reaction: Society influences researchers to interpret disability with a negative bias, researchers influence physicians to think that family dysfunction prevails, physicians influence families to expect their child to be wholly burdensome, families made decisions to provide or withhold treatment based on a burdensome view of their child, and families begin their relationship with their child from a negatively biased perspective.

One grandfather suggested the idea of having a public relations expert review some of the research on families and come to a discussion group (such as the one the families were having) to gain information on the nature of the negative bias that is being projected. Then the public relations expert could suggest strategies whereby families could most effectively address this problem through the major media. He said that "families need more specific expertise on changing societal attitudes which would result in a ripple effect on researcher, physician, and family attitudes." Isn't it paradoxical that researchers often inquire into the attitudes of families toward their children; and now families are not only inquiring, but devising strategies to change, researcher's attitudes toward these same children? We were struck, in addition, by the irony of these parents wanting to hire persons with expertise in marketing and advertising to counteract the bias that they believe researchers hold. From their perspective, could it be that some researchers might be contributing to the creation of problems rather than solutions?

Third, most families expressed surprise over the research described in the program announcement, because they commented that they had never read *any* research findings. One mother (the wife of a pediatrician) stated that her major source of research information was telethons, and a few other parents mentioned an occasional magazine article. A lively discussion focused on whether the purpose of research was "to help professionals advance themselves or help parents get along in their situations." The consensus was that "the purpose must be for professional gain, since research is not made available to families and the kind of research in the handout is not very helpful anyway."

Finally, the parents questioned why so much money, time, and effort is spent on studying all the ways children with disabilities can be problems. They affirmed that the role of research was "to solve problems, not merely highlight them." They specified some questions that they would like to see researched (Families Together, 1985):

> How can persons with disabilities develop relationships with persons of the opposite sex?
> How can the first encounter between parents and professionals be improved?

How can one get employment without losing government benefits?
What is the economic impact of disability on the family and how can money be spent proportionally?
What are potential successes we can have with our children?
How have other families coped well?
What makes the difference between successful and unsuccessful families?

As university researchers, we naturally found ourselves in an uncomfortable position in this discussion group, because we recognized elements of truth in many of the statements. The following week we read in a University of Kansas publication:

> University: The word is compelling, daunting, magical, even a bit arrogant. In using it, we boast of having fashioned a world in miniature, an environment sufficient unto itself. The creating and maintenance of a university is an idealistic act performed by people who aspire to gather and nurture the best that is known and thought. But, though we often speak of a university as a thing apart, an ivory tower, the ideal world of our creation cannot forswear the laws of the Newtonian universe: If unaffected by its surroundings, it remains inert; if prodded, it reacts with equal vigor. (Marsh, 1985, p. 1)

We offer here two recommendations. First, that university researchers conducting family research form partnerships with families and organizations representing their interests (e.g., Association for Retarded Citizens/United States). An appropriate starting point could be the two sets of questions just posed. By mutual prodding of each other's thinking, academicians and parents can enable research to have its best chance to fulfill the promise. Second, that the emphasis in graduate education programs on the philosophy of science is increased. Focusing on *how* to do research is necessary but not sufficient. It is equally important to know *why* to do research, to know *what* questions are important to ask, and *what* to do with the results of research.

TOWARD A FAMILY-PROFESSIONAL PARTNERSHIP

We have just suggested that a partnership be formed with families. We recognize the ease of merely suggesting; it appears almost trite because of the overuse of the concept of family-professional partnership in policy and interventions. Yet one encounters formidable barriers in attempting to establish a successful partnership. Following is an examination of the influences that shape our notions about such a partnership.

Law and policy have been a major impetus to establishing a family-professional partnership in the service delivery system. A fundamental theme permeating the myriad PL 94-142 requirements is the legal empowerment of parents to be educational decision makers. Indeed, an analysis of the *Congressional Record* during the PL 94-142 debates reveals the assumption on the part of the U.S. Congress that schools needed a monitor to ensure that they would follow through on their responsibility to provide a free, appropriate public education; therefore, parents needed to be empowered to be the monitor and to hold the school accountable (Turnbull, Turnbull, & Wheat, 1982). This parental empowerment is in the form of notification, consent, involvement in program planning, and access to records. The primary forum for educational decision making is the individualized education program (IEP) conference. Policy clarifications, prepared by the Office of Special Education in the U.S. Department of Education, stated the intended nature of the family-professional partnership:

> The parents of a handicapped child are expected to be equal participants, along with school personnel, in developing, reviewing, and revising the child's IEP. This is an active role in which the parents (1) participate in the discussion about the child's needs for special education and related services, and (2) join with the other participants in deciding what services the agency will provide to the child. (*Federal Register*, January 19, 1981, p. 5468)

The value of equality is clearly embedded in this policy interpretation.

Does policy change educational practice? One of the roles of research is to provide factual information to answer that question. Given the substantial time and effort that schools have invested in the IEP process (Price & Goodman, 1980; Safer, Morrissey, Kaufman, & Lewis, 1978), it is disconcerting that such a limited amount of research has been directed at models for enhancing a family-professional partnership. The research that has been conducted indicates a consistent trend of passive parental participation in the IEP conferences (Gilliam & Coleman, 1981; Goldstein, Strickland, Turnbull, & Curry, 1980; Lynch & Stein, 1982; Yoshida, Fenton, Kaufman, & Maxwell, 1978). Many barriers to a meaningful partnership have been cited in the literature, including logistical (Price & Goodman, 1980; Safer et al., 1978; Witt, Miller, McIntyre, & Smith, 1984), educational (Malmberg, 1984; Thompson, 1982), and psychological (Ferguson, 1984; Gilliam & Coleman, 1981; Pistono, 1977). One barrier that has not been squarely addressed is the gap, indeed the chasm, between the policy expectation for equal participation in decision making and the reluctance of professionals to form a partnership characterized by equality and dignity.

This chasm was vividly crystallized for us recently when we saw an advertisement in the fall 1984 issue of the *Kappan*. It is noteworthy that the *Kappan* is the journal of the professional education organization Phi Delta Kappa, which states its purpose as follows:

> an international professional fraternity for men and women in education. The membership is composed of recognized leaders in the profession and graduate students in education whose leadership potential has been identified. . . . The purpose of Phi Delta Kappa as stated in the fraternity's constitution is as follows: "The purpose of Phi Delta Kappa shall be to promote quality education, with particular emphasis on publicly supported education, as essential to the development and maintenance of a democratic way of life. This purpose shall be accomplished through the genuine acceptance, continuing interpretation, and appropri-

ate implementation of the ideal of high quality leadership through research, teaching, and other professional services concerned with and directed to the improvement of education, especially of publicly supported and universally available education. (Phi Delta Kappa, 1985)

The advertisement in question was for the purpose of selling mugs, each mug carrying an intended humorous cartoon. One cartoon is related to family-professional communication: A teacher, depicted to be gregarious and assertive in his body language, is saying to a mother, cast into a timid and reticent character, "Well, you see, Mrs. Smith, the reason your son is doing poorly in school is that he's dumb." The advertisement itself says:

DRINK AND BE MERRY!
Liven up your coffee break with a Kappan Cartoon Mug. . . . Order your favorite for yourself or a friend who needs a lift. Better yet, order all four and quadruple the fun. These mugs will also make unusual Christmas gifts for your PDK friends.

It appears that the message in this cartoon and advertisement is that the spirits of teachers can be lifted by putting down a child and parent. What does this say about values? What are the implications of a professional organization giving this message? What is the likely impact of a student with disabilities seeing this mug on the teacher's desk, or that of a student without disabilities seeing it, or family members of either group of students? Would Phi Delta Kappa have allowed a cartoon with an ethnic slur? If not, why are disability slurs considered acceptable?

The executive director of Phi Delta Kappa responded to letters of concern about the cartoon as follows:

I appreciate your taking time to write relative to the cartoon mug. Yours is one of a half dozen letters we have received regarding the particular cartoon. It is of course, one that appeared in an issue of the KAPPAN. We received no objection to it at that time. When the cartoons were selected for the mugs, we circulated over 150 cartoons to a large number of PDK members. The cartoon in question was picked by far the largest number. More significantly, no one objected to the cartoon.

The first objection came after the mugs had been produced and distributed. The mug in question was, by far, the best seller. I have, however, found in talking with others, that parents do not generally regard it as humorous. Had we realized that in advance, we would not have included it in the series. (L. C. Rose, personal communication, 1985)

Here we receive more disturbing information: The overwhelming endorsement of the cartoon by professional educators suggests that the morality of being sensitive to those included in the "universally applicable education" that Phi Delta Kappa seeks, and of doing no harm to those who are vulnerable, was not a decision-making criterion. There is also the claim that the mug would not have been included had the administrative staff or Phi Delta Kappa members realized it was demeaning. We truly believe that that is so; however, if we follow the ethical reciprocity doctrine of putting ourselves in the place of the mother or her son in the cartoon, can we come to any conclusion other than that the cartoon is demeaning? What is the distinction between humor and human degradation from the mother's perspective? From a student's perspective?

Now let us put ourselves in the role of professionals who find the cartoon humorous. The very fact that this cartoon sold more than any other is notable. Does it indicate a high frustration level on the part of professionals in communicating with parents? Or working with certain types of children? Or even having to relate to *those* parents and *those* children? Is it a warning that professionals need alternatives other than humor to defuse their frustration? Would professionals find it equally funny if a reverse cartoon had been printed in which parents degraded their competency? It may be that calling the child "dumb" is falling into the trap of "blaming the victim."

This seemingly innocuous advertisement suggests that as a profession we need to start asking many questions, including: What is the role of research in formulating strategies to enhance family-professional partnerships? How is preparation for such a partnership being addressed in preservice and inservice training programs for teachers, psychologists, administrators, and related service providers? How can time be reasonably allocated to parent conferences within the busy daily schedules of professionals and parents? What is the role of values in forging a family-professional partnership?

As a profession, how can we best ensure the promotion of ethical practice? Until we are willing to engage in ethical analyses of our own behavior, simply calling for a family-professional partnership can be likened to rearranging the chairs on the deck of the Titanic.

AN ALTERNATIVE TO A NEGATIVE BIAS TOWARD FAMILIES

Twenty-five years ago, an article in the *American Journal of Mental Deficiency* outlined the needs of parents as well as the positive contributions that may be derived from family experiences with a child having a disability. The author, also the mother of a child with mental retardation, shared this perspective on positive contributions:

> Even though we as parents of retarded children are faced with a multitude of problems, many unanswerable questions and a great deal of grief, yet we *do* have our compensations. . . . It has been my privilege to have talked with hundreds of parents of retarded children. One of the favorite themes . . . is how much our children have meant to us. This thought runs like a bright golden thread through the dark tapestry of our sorrow. We learn so much from our children, retarded children are wonderful teachers if we are not too proud to learn from them and the grief of parents leaves little room for pride. We learn so much in patience, in humility, in gratitude . . . ; so much in tolerance; so much in faith . . . ; so much in compassion for our fellowman; and yes, even so much in wisdom about

the eternal values of life because deep agony of spirit is the one thing which can turn us from the superficialities of life to those things that really matter. We also gain much in developing a strange kind of courage which enables us to face life without cringing because in one sense we have borne the ultimate that life has to offer in sorrow and pain.

Where, in all of this wide, wide world could we go to learn such lessons as these—lessons dealing with the real meaning of life?

Where else could we ever learn so much from those who know so little? (Murray, 1959, pp. 1087–1088)

Where is the research on positive contributions? Only a minute amount has been done. Where are the instruments designed to identify the nature and degree of positive contributions? They have not been developed. Why do the vast majority of instruments in the family area assess problems, stress, and burden of care? If actions are the by-products of values, what does a negative focus infer about the values of researchers toward the meaning of disability?

Although minimal references to positive contributions have appeared in the professional literature, the popular literature has tended to emphasize the positive aspects of disability much more frequently. Many books written by parents tend to point out both the benefits and drawbacks of raising their children (Featherstone, 1980; H. R. Turnbull & Turnbull, 1985). We wonder how many family researchers read parent-written accounts as a source of insight into the formulation of relevant research questions.

There is minimal indication in the professional literature that researchers recognize the existence of positive contributions. On the contrary, a negative bias frequently exists. We have identified two types of biasing statements. The first is a pervasive negative generalization. An example of such a generalization from a professional journal is: "In most families in which there is a defective member, pervasive guilt permeates the family and is expressed in its characteristic style. The birth of a retarded child, his presence in the home, and even the knowledge that such a child once lived at home, greatly exacerbates this existential guilt" (Martino & Newman, 1974, p. 168). A second type of bias occurs when researchers explain unexpected positive findings through a negative interpretation. An example of this is:

> Jacobs (1969) . . . found that most of the normal brothers and sisters of a group of retarded children were sympathetic, helpful, and understanding and did not seem to have been adversely affected by their mentally retarded siblings. It is quite possible, however, that these siblings were outwardly helpful and cooperative while manifesting adjustment problems in other ways. (Wasserman, 1983, p. 622)

Wikler, Wasow, and Hatfield (1983) commented candidly on an earlier study of theirs (1981) that had focused on an examination of chronic sorrow. In the 1981 study, parents were asked whether raising a child with developmental disabilities had made them stronger or weaker. Of the 27 respondents, 75% reported that their parental experiences had made them stronger. In

1981, the authors discounted these responses, attributing a positive finding to methodological problems; however, data on stress from the same questionnaire were not discounted. In 1983, they noted the initial dismissal of positive findings "to be another example of a pervasive stance adopted among professionals, in which problems instead of strength and instances of coping are concentrated on in dealing with families of developmentally disabled children" (p. 313).

A PROGRAM TO STUDY POSITIVE CONTRIBUTIONS

As a team of investigators, we are in the initial stages of developing a research program to investigate the nature of positive contributions. Our work to date has been in several phases. The first phase involved a collaborative project with H.R. Turnbull and P.D. Guess. We obtained copies of letters sent by parents or relatives and individuals who themselves have disabilities to the U.S. Department of Health and Human Services to comment on the 1983 proposed regulations concerning the medical treatment of newborns with disabilities. We were interested in knowing whether persons in these three groups supported the regulations and their reasons for or against. Like the department itself, we found that these respondents unanimously supported the regulations. The qualitative analysis of 174 letters resulted in the identification of eight categories of reasons for support, along with the number and percentage of responses for each type of respondent and for the total respondents (see Table 1). (Letters frequently included more than one reason for supporting the regulations; thus, each reason cited was coded.)

Of particular interest to our discussion are the two categories of positive attributes and positive contributions. Differences among the respondents were most apparent in these two categories. Persons with disabilities (64%) listed their own positive attributes as a common reason for supporting the regulations, whereas parents (39%) and relatives (48%) noted the positive contributions that their family member with a disability has made to them.

The specific positive attributes that were the most frequently cited included the subcategories of experiencing love, developmental/academic achievement, being happy, and positive physical (e.g., beautiful) and personality (e.g., caring and personable) characteristics. The positive attribute most frequently mentioned was experiencing love. Here is an example of a comment:

> My only daughter is profoundly retarded. She's loved and in return she's lovely. She's not able to walk or talk, but she can smile and laugh. She is loved.

The four major subcategories related to positive contributions to others included experiencing love, source of joy, a blessing to others, and a source of learning life's lessons. An example of each is as follows:

Table 1. Categories, frequency, and percentage of respondents' reasons for supporting treatment regulations

Categories of reasons for supporting regulations	Persons with disability		Parent of person with disability		Relative of person with disability		Total	
	N	%	N	%	N	%	N	%
Sanctity of life	5	15	18	18	12	29	35	20
Positive attributes of person	21	64	36	36	16	38	73	42
Positive contributions to others	2	6	39	39	20	48	61	35
Equal treatment	27	82	63	64	31	74	121	70
Repeating historical abuses	1	3	2	2	0	0	3	2
The line-drawing problem	2	6	4	4	2	4	8	5
Loss of confidence	9	27	30	30	14	33	53	30
Inaccurate medical predictions	5	15	8	8	3	7	16	9

Experiencing love:

Anyone who feels that someone else is a burden has not learned to love. Love feels someone else's needs above their own. My son, Matthew, was not useless. . . . If he served no other purpose than to give me love, then he served that one and if he served no other purpose than to teach me love, he served that one.

Source of joy:

I am a thirty-five year old parent of a sixteen month old child diagnosed as having Down's syndrome and a severe congenital heart defect. And yet, as imperfect as he may appear to many "professionals" and "intellectuals" of our day, I wouldn't trade him for any other child in this world. I cannot begin to sufficiently articulate the profound joy this child has brought into our lives. He has added a dimension of completeness and fulfillment that I have never experienced previously. He may never grow up to be president of anything, but that surely doesn't mean that he does not contribute in a positive way. His life is so very precious to us.

Blessing to others:

We are the parents of a brain-damaged son. Todd is now 20 years old and although we encountered some very stressful times during his early years, we believe very definitely that God allowed him to be born in our family. Although he is somewhat handicapped mentally he is . . . a blessing and encouragement to many (including us). I shudder to think that someone might have decided that he had no right to live.

Source of learning life's lessons:

My life and the lives of my family were changed forever on January 18, 1980. At about 6:00 p.m. our daughter Sarah was born. She weighed three pounds. Her diagnosis from the doctors was hopeless, 24 hours to live, deaf, blind, severely retarded.

As I looked at her, fighting to live, held her in the palm of my hands, amazed that this little one was my daughter, hope became eternal for me.

For the next 26 months she taught us more about love, courage, faith and life than most of us could teach or learn in 100 years.

Our other work at the University of Kansas on this topic involves the development of an instrument to assess positive contributions. We are just completing a qualitative study with 20 families. The data are being categorized to develop an item pool for the construction of a questionnaire. The qualitative data will enable us to generate items from the perspectives of parents and to state them in the language patterns that parents use to describe their experiences. We eagerly anticipate using the questionnaire to assess the relationship between positive contributions and demographic characteristics, ideological style, life-cycle stage, family subsystems, and disability descriptors. We believe this research is important for several reasons: 1) it has the potential of ensuring equal treatment for persons with disabilities, since it will fairly delineate the benefits they contribute to their families as well as the drawbacks that have already been documented; 2) it has the potential of decreasing stigma that accrues when persons are viewed as wholly negative; and 3) it has the potential for providing intervention strategies aimed at supporting families in accentuating the positive aspects of their circumstance.

We are enthusiastic about the potential of intervention capitalizing on the positive aspects of disability. We were struck by the comment of an individual with a disability in his letter on the treatment regulations: "It [the disability] is the greatest thing that has happened to me. For without these limitations, I would not have been able to acquire some of the important character qualities of life." There is a theme here consistent with the insights of persons who have encountered other types of limitations and won. We remember President John F. Kennedy's reply to the question, "How did you become a war hero?" He said: "It was involuntary. They sank my ship." We can also turn to Victor Frankl's (1963) theory of logotherapy and existential analysis:

We who lived in concentration camps can remember the men who walked through the huts comforting others, giving away their last piece of bread. They may have been few in number, but they offer sufficient proof that everything can be taken from a man but one thing: the last of the human freedoms—to choose one's attitude in any given set of circumstances, to choose one's own way.

And there were always choices to make. Every day, every hour, offered the opportunity to make a decision, a decision which determined whether you would or would not submit to those powers which threatened to rob you of your very self, your inner freedom; which determined whether or not you would become the plaything of circumstance, renouncing freedom and dignity to become molded into the form of the typical inmate. . . . It becomes clear that the sort of person the prisoner became was the result of an inner decision, and not the result of camp influences alone. Fundamentally, therefore, any man can, even under such circumstances, decide what shall become of him—mentally and spiritually. (pp. 104–105)

We believe that research can be a means to the end of supporting families and individuals with disabilities to use their limitations as a catalyst for positive outcomes.

GROWING UP WITH DISABILITIES WITHIN THE FAMILY

In this section, we ask you to take the "shoes test" (Boggs, 1985) by asking yourself: What would a person with mental retardation do, standing in his own shoes, if he could fully grasp the consequences of actions and decision making for himself in light of his own values and preferences? Engaging in this kind of perspective-taking will help us gain insight into how to respond to the questions: When are intervention decisions ethical? What is an ethically relevant research agenda?

First, stand in the shoes of Kristin. You are 7 years old, cheerful, rambunctious. You have Down syndrome. When you were born no one expressed joy; neither the doctor, nor your friends, nor your neighbors said you were a "beautiful baby." Rather, people either said "too bad" or they didn't know what to say, so they ignored your birth. You have become a pro at going to school, if length of time is a criterion, for you have been enrolled in a formal program since you were 2 months old. Infancy, a time when children typically form primary attachments to their parents and develop a sense of trust, was also your time for therapy, stimulation, and intervention. You were loved, cuddled, and nurtured, but sadly, your Mom wasn't able to be nurtured in return because she, for so long, looked at you as someone who needed to be changed. She was determined to teach you to stack blocks and to be a normal person. You just wished that she could see that you really were a beautiful little piece of humanity rather than an imperfect object that needed to be repaired.

Your parents especially were at a loss as to how to deal with their own pain and the hostility toward disabilities that they perceived in the rest of the world. Your Mom went to the early intervention program as an open, empty cup. She hoped they would fill her cup. And the program did fill both her cup and her days with activities. The program was a haven of security when her emotions were in turmoil. They helped her begin the process of seeing you as a beautiful, worthwhile individual. There were teachers to help her help you, other parents who understood and cared, and new playmates for you. The program was very helpful to your whole family.

But there were some parts that bothered you. There sometimes appeared to be subtle competition among the moms in the program. It seemed to you that it was good to be the child to make the most progress. One of your classmates in particular was the pride and joy of the program. His mother worked with him a lot, and he really was a marvel. You sometimes felt that he was the "star." The staff would single him out when visitors came, to demonstrate what early intervention can accomplish. There was a great deal of pride in those kids who made the most progress in meeting what were called developmental milestones. You felt the undercurrent that being the Einstein of the retarded bunch made the professionals and parents very happy.

Sometimes your Mom felt guilty because she didn't "work" with you often at home. She desperately wanted you to be normal, and felt as though she were shirking her responsibility if you didn't do well enough. You hurt so much for her and just wished that she could see that it was okay for you and her to do fun things at home like tickling or reading, or snuggling . . . You also tried to convince her that throwing blocks was as much fun as stacking them, but she just couldn't see it. It made you feel crummy to disappoint her. But you worked hard, made a lot of progress, and were glad you could learn to do things.

Those years are now over and you are in the elementary special education class. Your mother's efforts to "fix" you have greatly subsided. She also seems to be smiling a whole lot more now. She helps you grow and learn about the world. You really get the idea that she is beginning to love you for who you are, rather than who you might become some day. It makes you feel swell to please your Mom, and it's also nice just to be a regular member of the family. If it hadn't been for early intervention, you wouldn't know nearly as much now. You are proud of what you know, and it helps you be successful in school. You just wish your Mom could have accepted you when you were a baby as she accepts you now. She no longer treats you as an object with broken pieces where she has to be glue. You are a whole person in your Mom's eyes and that makes all the difference.

The "shoes test" for practitioners reads: As Kristin, how could your parents help to fulfill your needs? What would constitute quality of life for you? What would you want researchers to study? What would you want family intervention programs to do?

We believe that, as a field, we need to pay more attention to the unintended consequences of the assumption in intervention that children with disabilities need to be "fixed" so they can become more "normal." Rousso (1984), a social worker who herself has a physical disability, shares insight into the implications of the "fix-it" philosophy for the parent-child relationship and the child's self-esteem:

> Disabled children need to have their bodies, disability and all, accepted, appreciated and loved, especially by significant parenting figures. This will solidify the sense of intactness.
>
> For all children, disabled or not, the "gleam in the mother's eye" in response to all aspects of the child's body and self is essential for the development of healthy self-esteem. This includes the parent's ability to show pride and pleasure in the disabled part of the body, as one valid aspect of the child, and to communicate appreciation and respect for the child's unique, often different-looking ways of doing things. The result can be an environment which allows children to develop their potential and develop positive body and self-feelings. It makes children think: "Mother thinks I am great, so I must be."
>
> Parents of congenitally disabled children may have difficulty loving the disabled parts of their child, often for many reasons. . . .
>
> As was the case with my mother, it may be difficult for them to understand that a disabled body could be experienced by a child as intact when they have learned to view disability as a defect and a deviance. As a result of these various reasons, parents too often communicate to their child, directly and indirectly, that the disability should be hidden or altered, if not purged—the child should strive toward appearing as "normal" and nondisabled as possible. This attitude can put the child into an identity crisis, causing him or her to push that feeling of intactness way underground. (1984, pp. 12–13)

Rousso helps us understand the discrepancy between Kristin's view of intactness and her mother's view:

> Being disabled and being intact at the same time is an extremely difficult notion for non-disabled people to make sense of. I keep thinking of my mother's words: "Why wouldn't you want to walk straight?" Even now, it is hard to explain that I may have wanted to walk straight, but I did not want to lose my sense of myself in the process. Perhaps the best I can say is that my perspective on disability, from the inside out, is different from my mother's, from the outside looking in. In our work with congenitally disabled clients, we must always be receptive and respectful of that difference. (1985, p. 12)

Now, let's experience disability from the perspective of an adolescent. You are Jay, 18 years old, enrolled in a special education program at the local high school, receiving vocational training for the first time, and trying to bring the raging hormones of adolescence under control. School has never been a particularly rewarding experience to you. You wonder why in the world you have to stay until you are 21 when other kids get to graduate at 18. Maybe that's what it means to have a disability—you are a perpetual student. It seems that the fun parts of the high school are things other people assume you are not interested in doing—joining clubs, singing in the chorus, going to the junior-senior prom, and getting a senior ring. While the other students are doing these things, you are expected to approach with gusto one more recreational outing to one more bowling alley. Enough is enough.

The big question with you, your parents, your grandparents, your teacher, and your friends is what happens to you when you leave high school. The words, "leave high school," are exactly what you mean, because you know that students without disabilities graduate, but ones with disabilities fade away. You truly believe that your parents have *finally* given you your life. You thought for years it would never happen, and it wasn't easy for them to give up the idea of molding you in their image. They are successful, achievement-oriented, love to learn, almost always rush, and so much wanted you to adopt their life-style. But their values are not for you. You believe a walk around the block is to smell the flowers rather than to reach your peak heart rate. They value activity; you value passivity. They value spontaneity; you value routine. They value achievement; you value contentment. You believe in "traveling light" through life rather than living on the fast-track. Your needs are relatively simple—loving relationships, good laughs, predictability in schedules, watching "Hee Haw" on Saturday night and on the VCR throughout the week, opportunities to be productive in the workplace and at home, a chance to worship, and the right to march to the beat of your own drummer.

Now that you have finally convinced your parents that you are entitled to be yourself, you sometimes believe that you will have to take on the human services profession next. It is amazing to you that people who have never even met you are so confident about what is in your best interest. Some say *you, all* classmates like you, and even *every* person with moderate and severe retardation in the United States should live in a group home; others say no one should live in a group home; and others say the ultimate accomplishment is to live alone in an apartment and prove you are independent, like doing your own laundry. You can't help but think that living alone in an apartment sounds awfully lonely; and your clear goal is to have enough money to pay someone to do your laundry. You've always questioned the teachers and psychologists who think doing laundry is so glorious. They probably don't even do their own.

And then there's all the debate about employment—sheltered workshops are fine, sheltered workshops are terrible; supportive employment is for everyone, supportive employment is not normalizing; competitive employment is the only way, competitive employment is unrealistic. The thing that really gets you is that none of the proponents have acknowledged your right to decide for yourself where you work.

Several other things puzzle you, too. It seems that people get all excited when you spend time with people who aren't disabled. It's as if they are more desirable friends and are higher up in the pecking order of acceptability. You may be retarded, but you still catch on to the message that you and your buddies with disabilities are viewed by many people as "second-class friends." This really gets under your skin, because you have a strong sense that when people are with you they are in good company. Also, you value friendships that are equal, people who choose to be with you because they truly enjoy you. Peer tutoring and citizen advocacy are fine, but they are a far cry from having a date tell you that you're handsome. Other people may think being with your girlfriend who is retarded is stigmatizing, but you think she's terrific. You know better than to use the presence or absence of a disability as a criterion for friendship. Why can't professionals know this?

You believe that people should live and let live. You don't restrict the choices of others; why do they restrict yours? You know that the professionals who are working to create opportunities for you are doing it because they really want you to have a good life. It's such a relief from the ones who thought you couldn't work at all. Part of your fear, however, is that if you choose to not take advantage of their opportunities, they will consider you a failure. It boils down to the fact that part of a good life is making your own decisions. You are forever reminded of your double disability. Mental retardation is not the toughest part; it's having your personhood denied that's really demeaning. All you ask is to own your life. Yes, you need assistance and advice but, ultimately, you are content to be who you are.

For too long independence has been simplistically defined as the process of completing tasks unassisted. On the contrary, we believe that independence means "choosing how to live one's own life within one's inherent capacities and other means and consistent with personal values and preferences" (A. P. Turnbull & Turnbull, 1985). Thus, this definition of independence allows the option of choosing to do tasks with assistance and choosing on whom one will depend (Scott, 1984).

An important research direction is to assist individuals with disabilities and their families in passing the torch of autonomy, to the extent possible, from one generation to another. This direction is consistent with the values of consent, choice, and self-direction.

The "shoes test" for practitioners reads: As Jay, what intervention would be ethical? What values would undergird an ethically relevant research agenda?

CONCLUSION

The confrontation of values has no simple formula for next steps. It is a complex process that must be addressed first by individuals prior to considering systemic changes for an ethically relevant research and intervention agenda. As Burton Blatt (1975) so rightly advised:

> And I, too, own a part of my family, a part of the University, a part of society, a part of the total "action." I, too, must think and do, not only for others, but for myself. But what I must do most urgently is change. For the world to change, I must change. If I blame an evil world, a stupid system, ineffective leaders, or man's obvious imperfections, I may be right. But if it means that I do not have to change, I contribute to the evil. Before we can change humanity, we must change ourselves. (p. 419)

REFERENCES

Baker, B.L. (1983). Parents as teachers: Issues in training. In J.A. Mulick & S.M. Pueschel (Eds.), *Parent professional partnerships in developmental disability services*. Cambridge, MA: Ware Press.

Baumeister, A.A. (1981). Mental retardation policy and research: The unfulfilled promise. *American Journal of Mental Deficiency, 85*(5), 449–456.

Bernal, M.E. (1984). Consumer issues in parent training. In R.F. Dangel & R.A. Polster (Eds.), *Parent Training* (pp. 477–503). New York: Guilford Press.

Bernal, M.E., & Klinnert, M.D. (1981). *Further insights on the results of a parent training outcome study*. Paper presented at the XIII Banff International Conference on Behavioral Sciences, Banff, Canada.

Blacher, J. (Ed.). (1984). *Severely handicapped young children and their families: Research in review*. New York: Academic Press.

Blatt, B. (1975). Toward an understanding of people with special needs. In J.M. Kauffman & J.S. Payne (Eds.), *Mental retardation: Introduction and personal perspectives*. Columbus, OH: Charles E. Merrill Publishing Co.

Blechman, E.A., Budd, K.S., Christophersen, E.R., Szykula, S., Wahler, R., & Embry, L.H. (1981). Engagement in behavioral family therapy: A multi-site investigation. *Behavior Therapy, 12,* 461–472.

Boggs, E.M. (1985). Who is putting whose head in the sand? (or in the clouds as the case may be). In H.R. Turnbull & A.P. Turnbull (Eds.), *Parents speak out: Then and now*. Columbus, OH: Charles E. Merrill Publishing Co.

Bristol, M.M. & Gallagher, J.J. (in press). Psychological research on fathers of young handicapped children: Evolution review, and some future directions. In J.J. Gallagher & P. Vietze (Eds.), *Families of handicapped persons: Current research, treatment, and policy issues*. Baltimore: Paul H. Brookes Publishing Co.

Brooks, P.H., & Baumeister, A.A. (1983). A plea for consideration of ecological validity in the experimental psychology of mental retardation. *Peabody Journal of Education, 60*(3), 45–59.

Cole, C., & Morrow, W.R. (1976). Refractory parent behaviors in behavior modification training groups. *Psychotherapy: Theory, Research and Practice, 13,* 162–169.

Crnic, K.A., Friedrich, W.N., & Greenberg, M.T. (1983). Adaptation of families with mentally retarded children: A model of stress, coping, and family ecology. *American Journal of Mental Deficiency, 88*(2), 125–138.

Dangel, R.F., & Polster, R.A. (Eds.). (1984). *Parent Training*. New York: Guilford Press.

Families Together. (1985, February). *Who are these researchers and why are they saying these things about us?* Discussion conducted at the meeting of Families Together, Inc., Lawrence, KS.

Farber, B. (1960). Family organization and crisis: Maintenance of integration in families with a severely retarded child. *Monographs of the Society for Research in Child Development, 25*(1, Serial No. 75).

Farber, B., & Jenne, W.C. (1963). Family organizations and parent-child communication: Parents and siblings of a retarded child. *Monographs of the Society for Research in Child Development, 28* (7, Serial No. 91).

Farber, B., & Ryckman, D.B. (1965). Effects of severely mentally retarded children on family relationships. *Mental Retardation Abstracts, 2,* 1–17.

Featherstone, H. (1980). *A difference in the family*. New York: Basic Books.

Federal Register. (1981, January 19). Washington, DC: U.S. Government Printing Office.

Ferguson, D.L. (1984). Parent advocacy network. *Exceptional Parent, 14,* 41–45.

Frankl, V.E. (1963). *Man's search for meaning.* Boston: Beacon Press.

Gilliam, J.E., & Coleman, M.C. (1981). Who influences IEP committee decisions? *Exceptional Children, 47*(8), 642–644.

Goldstein, S., Strickland, B., Turnbull, A.P., & Curry, L. (1980). An observational analysis of the IEP conference. *Exceptional Children, 46,* 278–286.

Jacobs, J. (1969). *The search for help.* New York: Brunner/Mazel.

Johnson, C.A., & Katz, G.K. (1973). Using parents as change agents for their children: A review. *Journal of Clinical Psychology and Psychiatry, 4,* 181–200.

Johnson, S.M., & Lobitz, G.K. (1974). The personal and marital adjustment of parents as related to observed child deviance and parenting behaviors. *Journal of Abnormal Child Psychology, 2,* 192–207.

Lynch, E.W., & Stein, R. (1982). Perspectives on parent participation in special education. *Exceptional Education Quarterly, 3*(2), 56–63.

Malmberg, P.A. (1984). *Development of field tested special education placement committee parent education materials.* Unpublished doctoral dissertation, Virginia Polytechnic Institute at State University, Blacksburg.

Margolin, G., & Christensen, A. (1981). *Treatment of multiproblem families: Specific and general effects of marital and family therapy.* Paper presented at the XIII Banff International Conference on Behavioral Sciences, Banff, Canada.

Marsh, C. (1985). To the core. *Kansas Alumni Magazine.* Lawrence, KS: Alumni Association of the University of Kansas.

Martino, M.S., & Newman, M.B. (1974). Siblings of retarded children: A population at risk. *Child Psychiatry and Human Development, 4*(3), 168–177.

McMahon, R.J., Forehand, R., Griest, D.L., & Wells, K.C. (1981). Who drops out of treatment during behavioral training? *Behavioral Counseling Quarterly, 1,* 79–85.

Murray, M.A. (1959). Needs of parents of mentally retarded children. *American Journal of Mental Deficiency, 63,* 1078–1088.

Oltmanns, T.F., Broderick, J.E., & O'Leary, K.D. (1977). Marital adjustment and the efficacy of behavior therapy with children. *Journal of Consulting and Clinical Psychology, 45,* 724–729.

Phi Delta Kappa. (1985). *An introduction to Phi Delta Kappa.* Bloomington, IN: Author.

Pistono, W.J. (1977). The relationships between certain identified variables and parental participation during the educational planning and placement committee meeting for handicapped students in Michigan. *Dissertation Abstracts International, 38*(5).

Price, M., & Goodman, L. (1980). Individualized education programs: A cost study. *Exceptional Children, 46*(6), 446–458.

Rosenberg, M.S., Reppucci, N.D., & Linney, J.A. (1983). Issues in the implementation of human service programs: Examples from a parent training project for high-risk families. *Analysis and Intervention in Developmental Disabilities, 3,* 215–225.

Rousso, H. (1984). Fostering healthy self esteem, Part One. *Exceptional Parent, 14*(1), 9–14.

Rousso, H. (1985). Fostering self esteem, Part Two. *Exceptional Parent, 15*(1), 9–12.

Safer, N.D., Morrissey, P.A., Kaufmann, M.J., & Lewis, L. (1978). Implementation of IEPs: New teacher roles and requisite support systems. *Focus on Exceptional Children, 10*(1), 1–20.

Scott, S. (1984). *Family systems.* Unpublished manuscript, University of Kansas, Research and Training Center on Independent Living, Lawrence.

Sloop, E.W. (1974). *Problems with parents as behavior modifiers: How to fail and how to succeed.* Paper presented at the meeting of the Southeastern Psychological Association, Hollywood Beach, FL.

Snell, M.E., & Beckman-Brindley, S. (1984). Family involvement in intervention with children having severe handicaps. *Journal of Speech and Hearing, 3,* 213–230.

Thompson, T.M. (1982). An investigation and comparison of public school personnel's perception and interpretation of P.L. 94-142. *Dissertation Abstracts International, 43,* 2840A.

Turnbull, A.P., Summers, J.A., & Brotherson, M.J. (1984). *Working with families with disabled members: A family systems perspective.* Lawrence: University of Kansas, Research and Training Center on Independent Living.

Turnbull, A.P., & Turnbull, H.R. (1985). Developing independence. *Journal of Adolescent Health Care, 6*(2), 108–119.

Turnbull, H.R., & Turnbull, A.P. (1985). *Parents speak out: Then and now.* Columbus, OH: Charles E. Merrill Publishing Co.

Turnbull, H.R., Turnbull, A.P., & Wheat, M. (1982). Assumptions about parental participation: A legislative history. *Exceptional Education Quarterly, 3*(2), 1–8.

Wahler, R.G. (1980). The multiply entrapped parent: Obstacles to change in parent-child problems. In J.P. Vincent (Ed.), *Advances in family intervention, assessment, and theory* (Vol. 1). Greenwich, CT: JAI Press.

Wasserman, R. (1983). Identifying the counseling needs of the siblings of mentally retarded children. *Personnel and Guidance Journal, 61*(10), 622–627.

Wikler, L., Wasow, M., & Hatfield, E. (1981). Chronic sorrow revisited: Parent vs. professional depiction of the adjustment of parents of mentally retarded children. *American Journal of Orthopsychiatry, 51*(1), 63–70.

Wikler, L., Wasow, M., & Hatfield, E. (1983). Seeking strengths in families of developmentally disabled children. *Social Work,* 313–315.

Winton, P.J., Turnbull, A.P., & Blacher, J. (1984). *Selecting a preschool: A guide for parents of handicapped children.* Austin, TX: Pro-Ed.

Witt, J.C., Miller, C.D., McIntyre, R.M., & Smith, D. (1984). Effects of variables on parental perceptions of staffings. *Exceptional Children, 51*(1), 27–32.

Wolfensberger, W. (1970). Counseling the parents of the retarded. In A.A. Baumeister (Ed.), *Mental retardation: Appraisal, education, and rehabilitation* (pp. 329–400). Chicago: Aldine Publishing Co.

Yoshida, R.K., Fenton, K.S., Kaufman, M.J., & Maxwell, J.P. (1978). Parental involvement in the special education pupil planning process: The school's perspective. *Exceptional Children,* 531–534.

Response

ILLNESS AND THE CHILD
PATHOLOGY AND DEVELOPMENT

James M. Perrin

ANN P. TURNBULL AND her colleagues have done important things to help us all, and her paper provides a helpful framework from which to view research and clinical interactions with children and families. Despite my background as a pediatrician, my response ventures into ethics in choosing five issues from Turnbull et al.'s chapter. Many of the issues raised there apply equally to children with long-term health conditions and their families, an area we have focused on recently in research at Vanderbilt University (Hobbs, Perrin, & Ireys, 1985).

ABNORMAL OR ALTERNATIVE

First, what is pathological and what is normal? Turnbull argues that there is a bright side to disability. There is an important distinction among disease, disability, and handicap (Court, 1976). Disease reflects the physiological process. A child's disease may be arthritis. His or her disability may be a knee that functions poorly. Handicap reflects the way that the dysfunctional knee interferes with the child's ability to carry out his or her daily activities: walking up steps, going to school, participating in the band, whatever else. Conceptually, professionals have tended to define "normal" pathways of development, or "normal" pathways of action. Variations from those pathways are typically considered deviant or pathological. Often these different pathways are socially determined, as with different methods of toilet training or sleeping arrangements for children. Are these different pathways pathologic or deviant, or are they alternate pathways? Much can be learned from considering different pathways not as abnormal but as alternative, not as pathological but as potentially enriching the breadth and variety of normal pathways available to human development (Gliedman & Roth, 1980).

The idea that variations from usual behavior are alternative rather than deviant can be applied with equal force to sociology, to social development, or to how groups interact. And certainly one can apply it to medicine, as will be demonstrated here.

THE DISEASE OR THE CHILD

Second, many professionals overgeneralize from the illness or the condition to the child. The medical literature discusses the leukemic, the asthmatic, the arthritic, or the cystic rather than the child. This problem faces not only professionals but many others interacting with people with illness. Parents are greatly relieved when emphasis is placed on the child. He or she then becomes primarily a child who happens to have asthma; the child is not replaced by an asthmatic. In our own clinical care, we avoid terms such as leukemic or asthmatic for that reason.

This is more than a semantic issue, because that overgeneralization, as Turnbull et al. eloquently demonstrate, drives services. Treatment becomes limited to the leukemia, often neglecting the developmental, educational, or emotional needs of the child. Overgeneralization also creates certain expectations. For example, leukemia is a commonly fatal disease, and the specter of fatality may diminish expectations for the child. As many children with arthritis are crippled and unable to get around, one may mistakenly assume that this is true for all children with arthritis. This conceptualization encourages services narrowly conceived and limits our expectations of what children can do. One saving grace of children is that they often have different expectations from those of professionals. Frequently, children can break through the boundaries of professional or parental expectations (Gliedman & Roth, 1980). But there is a tendency to assume their capacity is limited.

OUTCOME AND ITS MEASUREMENT

The third topic to be touched upon here from Turnbull et al.'s work is the issue of defining appropriate outcomes. The authors discuss family outcomes. How are these measured? A preliminary question is, "How are appropriate child treatment outcomes measured in medical realms?" In medicine, the focus is mainly on physiologic outcomes. Quality of life is often defined as quality of physiology. If the system works right and the hypertension is controlled, then the person is doing fine. Diet, however, may interfere with that person's family life, or medications to control hypertension may render the male impotent. Broad family and social issues are important.

In the last few years, it has become clear that outcome, even individual outcome, is a complex concept. It includes the presence or absence of disease. But it also includes pain or discomfort, and estimates of personal achievement, resilience, coping—all measures of an individual's capacity (Starfield, 1974). Physiologic parameters are easier to measure than are many of these other elements of outcome. It is crucial that we develop adequate and broad-based measures of outcome. As Turnbull et al. note, the measures must extend beyond the child to the family.

A number of researchers are looking carefully at the development of measures of family adjustment, which are crucial to the area of childhood chronic illness (Pless & Satterwhite, 1973; Stein & Jessop, 1984). One of the conceptual advances that pediatricians have recently come to recognize is that there is much commonality across diseases (Stein & Jessop, 1982a, 1982b). Until recently, most clinicians assumed that each disease had its own characteristics. There was no similarity between a child or a family with arthritis and a child or family with leukemia. We now acknowledge that chronicity itself has special meaning for children and families, and this recognition has fostered the development of cross-disease measurements of child functioning and of family functioning (Stein & Jessop, 1984).

IMPACT OF ILLNESS

Fourth, what is known about the impact of illness on family stability and functioning? Turnbull et al.'s chapter addresses the question of the impact of disability on family functioning. The chronic illness literature is afflicted with conceptualizations similar to those of the disability literature. Older theories assumed, for example, that there is an arthritic personality, and earlier psychiatric work suggested that people get disease partly because their personality makes them susceptible. More recent evidence suggests the absence of a specific arthritic personality or of personality types characteristic of other specific diseases. From the work of Stein and Jessop (1982a, 1984) and others, it is clear there is much more variation *within* disease than *between* disease with respect to essentially all family, personality, or child psychological measures available.

In a related fashion, until recently it had been assumed that all families whose children had chronic illness were highly burdened and faced tremendous psychological risks, and that this stress led to divorce and family disability (Pless & Pinkerton, 1975). The most recent evidence is that childhood chronic illness does not seem to influence divorce rates (Sabbeth & Leventhal, 1984). This finding may mainly reflect the high background static rate of divorce. The more important data to share are that the numerous studies that have examined psychological impacts on the child (not the family, because much less work has been done there) of having a chronic physical disorder do indicate an increased risk of psychological adjustment problems among children with chronic illnesses. That risk, however, seems to be much less than previously assumed (Drotar & Bush, 1985).

Furthermore, the average child copes well. The mode is for children who have long-term illnesses to be splendid people, to grow up, to participate well, to become cheerleaders, and so forth. These coping processes are not well understood. Turnbull et al. suggest that we need better theoretical bases on which to do research. For children, there is a need for research on theories of vulnerability or, more important, on theories of invulnerability (Starfield, 1985). How do people cope with various stressors, including the stress of long-term illness? Children with arthritis, for example, have tremendous variations in the degree of disability of their joints. Yet many children who have severe disabling arthritis—such as horrible knees—head the school drama club, are cheerleaders, or are active in debate. Other children with minimal disease, those in whom clinicians demonstrate little arthritis, may miss three days of school a week. Greater understanding of these interactions and of how most children cope is needed.

ETHICS OF DECISIONS

The fifth issue concerns decision making. What are professional judgments, and what are family judgments? Where do they interact? Are any fully professional? What about uncertainty? One of the hardest things to teach medical students is that there are rarely clear-cut answers to anything in medicine (Fox, 1979). There is so much biologic variability among people that one cannot predict accurately whether an antihypertensive drug will work for an individual. Uncertainty is tremendously difficult. It is hard for clinicians to accept; they prefer to believe that they hold the answers. And most families demand clear answers as well. Yet, much of what is known about long-term chronic illness is that it is fraught with unknowns. Fifteen years ago, for instance, it was generally certain that a child with acute lymphocytic leukemia would die. Now that child has a good risk of surviving, although it is less clear for how long, or whether the child will be fully cured, or whether he or she will develop a second malignancy years later.

When do the issues of public versus private resources play a role in decision making? We have followed a 15-year-old retarded young woman with a very rare disease: agammaglobulinemia. She lacks some of the normal ways to fight infections and thus is subject to frequent severe illnesses. About 3 or 4 years ago, she had frequent bouts of arthritis, sometimes a consequence of this particular disease. It was unclear whether this was an infectious arthritis or an immune arthritis, or something else. We treated her occasionally with antibiotics, although we were unsure of their benefit to her. When treated with antibiotics, she was in the hospital for several weeks each time. She lives 2 hours from Nashville and her mother usually stayed with her, leaving three other children at home (Perrin, 1985).

Who should make what decisions in this situation? This 15-year-old girl currently has the intellectual capacity of a 7-year-old. Should she participate in decisions regarding hospitalization or the use of antibiotics, not knowing their efficacy (when the clinicians also do not know if antibiotics will help)? Should the mother participate? Should this be a decision for the physicians, with advice from infectious disease specialists?

Moreover, some of the services for this child are covered by the Crippled Children's Service Program, a program poorly funded in most of the southern states including Tennessee. She is a very expensive patient. As a medical consultant to the Crippled Children's Service Program, I help staff make policy decisions about the allocation of resources. If this child is hospitalized, there will be other children who cannot be hospitalized because the program will run out of money. How should that information enter into clinical decision making? Should this problem of resources be shared with the family in their decision making?

The problem of obtaining adequate resources for children with high-cost service needs is complex, and the solutions are not easy. But a measure of a society's compassion and quality is its ability to provide services needed to strengthen the capacity of children with long-term health needs and their families.

REFERENCES

Court, S.D.M. (1976, December). *Fit for the future, the report of the Committee on Child Health Services*. London: Her Majesty's Stationery Office.

Drotar, D., & Bush, M. (1985). The mental health of chronically ill children and their families. In N. Hobbs and J. Perrin (Eds.), *Issues in the care of children with chronic illness* (pp. 514–550). San Francisco: Jossey-Bass.

Fox, R.C. (1979). Training for uncertainty. In R.C. Fox, *Essays in medical sociology*. New York: John Wiley & Sons.

Gliedman, J., & Roth, W. (1980). *The unexpected minority*. New York: Harcourt Brace Jovanovich.

Hobbs, N., Perrin, J.M., & Ireys, H.T. (1985). *Chronically ill children and their families*. San Francisco: Jossey-Bass.

Perrin, J.M. (1985). Clinical ethics and resource allocation: The problem of chronic illness in childhood. In J.C. Moskop and L. Kopelman (Eds.), *Ethics and critical care medicine (pp. 105–116)*. Amsterdam: D. Riedel Publishing Co.

Pless, I.B., & Pinkerton, P. (1975). *Chronic childhood disorder: Promoting patterns of adjustment*. Chicago: Year Book Medical Publishers.

Pless, I.B., & Satterwhite, B.B. (1973). A measure of family functioning and its application. *Social Science and Medicine, 7*, 613–621.

Sabbeth, B., & Leventhal, J. (1984). Marital adjustment to chronic childhood illness. *Pediatrics, 73*, 763–768.

Starfield, B. (1974). Measurement of outcome: A proposed scheme. *Milbank Memorial Fund Quarterly, 52,* 39–50.

Starfield, B. (1985). The state of research on chronic illness in childhood. In N. Hobbs and J. Perrin (Eds.), *Issues in the care of children with chronic illness* (pp. 109–132). San Francisco: Jossey-Bass.

Stein, R.E.K., & Jessop, D.J. (1982a). A noncategorical approach to chronic illness. *Public Health Reports, 97,* 354–362.

Stein, R.E.K., & Jessop, D.J. (1982b). *What diagnosis does not tell.* Paper presented at annual meeting of the Society for Pediatric Research, Washington, DC.

Stein, R.E.K., & Jessop, D.J. (1984). Relationship between health status and psychological adjustment among children with chronic conditions. *Pediatrics, 73,* 169–174.

Chapter 8

THE ISSUE OF EDUCABILITY

Donald M. Baer

DEVELOPMENTAL DEFICIENCY needs study. It is one of the most fundamental of human problems; it is basic to understanding who we are and how we work. I think that we shall not understand the fullness of development until we understand all its possible forms, especially its deviations, and most especially those that we have chosen to call its deficiencies. Furthermore, our society tries to deal constructively with developmental deficiency as a social problem. I think that we shall not truly understand our society until we understand how and why it deals with this problem, and how it can be brought to deal with it better, or at least differently. This is truly a case of applied science, and we may well learn something about how to use our science, if we can comprehend this problem.

Furthermore, I think that this is not a casual moment in the history of our knowledge of and approach to developmental deficiency. Some important, desirable, and illuminating trends are emerging worldwide in its study; at the same time, some quite undesirable trends are developing in our society's perception of developmental deficiency. In this chapter I want to celebrate the sudden illumination of developmental deficiency, while warning of any social perceptions that ignore that sudden illumination; and I want to do both with a strong sense of urgency.

Portions of this chapter are reprinted with minor modifications, with permission, from Baer, D.M. (1981). A hung jury and a Scottish verdict: "Not proven." *Analysis and Intervention in Developmental Disabilities, 1,* 91–97, © 1981 by Pergamon Press; and Baer, D.M. (1984). We already have multiple jeopardy; why try for unending jeopardy? In W.L. Heward, T.E. Heron, D.S. Hill, & J. Trap-Porter (Eds.), *Focus on behavior analysis in education* (pp. 296–299). Columbus, OH: Charles E. Merrill Publishing Co. Copyright © 1984 by Charles E. Merrill Publishing Company.

This chapter is lovingly dedicated to my adored wife, Jacqui Baer, whose extraordinary sense of science is matched by her sense of ethics, not only for science and its applications but for our life.

ADVANCES IN STUDYING DEVELOPMENTAL DEFICIENCY

First, the celebration. For a long time, developmental deficiency was studied descriptively, and, in my opinion, exploitatively. People with retardation and other handicaps were studied to see the essence of their retardation, their difference from the normal. The problem was to explain why these persons had retardation, in terms of then-current ideas in educational, psychological, and physiological theory. That study too often was meant to show only the goodness of those ideas, by showing that they could analyze developmental deficiency as well as the more usual cases to which they were applied, and from which they had been derived. As a result, this kind of study of persons with developmental deficiency enriched only the study, not the persons being studied. Indeed, persons with deficiencies sometimes emerged more deficient, in that some of those theories concluded that their deficiency was inevitable and irremediable, and so *assigned* helplessness to them.

The cause for celebration is that the last two decades have reversed that trend in at least two major approaches to the study of persons with developmental deficiencies—the cognitive and the behavioral. The cognitive analysis of behavior, and of deficiencies in behavior, once was inferential and mainly tautological. When it examined the differences between normal persons and those with deficiencies, it imagined what profound mental processes present in the normal must be either absent or deformed in those with deficiencies, such that those differences would result. Too often, the resulting inferences were of mental processes too abstract, too vague, or too fundamental to be either observable or teachable; the inferences only explained—and condemned.

Currently, the cognitive analysis of behavior allows for a great deal more positive action on behalf of the individual. It still looks at the differences in behavior between normal persons and those with deficiencies, as a means of inferring what varying mental processes could be operating. But now, its imaginings more often emerge as testable hypotheses rather than inaccessible presumptions. More important, its imaginings tend to be practical, and specific to much smaller domains of mental functioning. The antecedents of *these* mental processes might well be observed, and better yet, might well be taught experimentally. Most important of all, modern cognitive analysis sometimes agrees that the experimental teaching of these imagined mental skills is the best possible test of these skills. If these skills are taught, say the analysts, what will the observable results be in the future functioning of the student, whether normal or deficient?

To answer this question requires a very good science of teaching technique—of behavior change—to show us how to teach those hypothetical skills. Interestingly, applied behavior analysis, in these same two decades, has been busy building just that technology. It has found that a systematic understanding of reinforcement and stimulus control automatically brings with it a powerful and systematic set of teaching procedures. Those procedures sometimes prove so effective that applied behavior analysts have begun to wonder if a thorough technology of teaching will in itself prove to be a good enough analysis of developmental deficiency: Are persons with developmental deficiencies simply those who require the best and most perfectly task-analyzed teaching, and have not yet received it for as thorough a curriculum as they need? In this disarmingly simple query, the behavior analysts sometimes have denied that a cognitive analysis would prove necessary, mainly because they doubted that an analysis based on unobservable processes could ever be confirmed or made practical.

And indeed, when cognitive analysis imagined overly vague and abstract processes as being at issue, the applied behavior analysts probably were correct: those ideas were neither verifiable nor actionable. But the new cognitive analysis is doing much better than that; it is proposing teachable skills as the training ground for the mental processes that it now thinks are at issue. While those mental processes may be unobservable, teaching them is not—it may well be a thoroughly real and practical goal, just the kind of goal that the applied behavior analysts like to learn how to teach. After all, they already know a good deal about how to teach a variety of lessons with power and generality.

Obviously, on both theoretical and pragmatic grounds, a worthwhile alliance is possible. I believe that that alliance is now forming, despite the arrogance of some cognitive analysts in proclaiming that a noncognitive behavioral analysis cannot possibly be complete and thus useful, and despite the arrogance of some behavior analysts in damning any proposal with even one unobservable component as unnecessarily frivolous and ultimately unscientific. Fortunately, we can allow both sides a bit of rhetoric now and then without declaring war.

This alliance is not just a theoretical encounter. In recent years, both sides have shown considerable practical power. The subjects with retardation who have been the focus of their studies have not only benefited the sciences those studies represent, but have sometimes emerged from the studies with less retardation than when they entered. That is entirely reasonable: the technological power of applied behavior analysis, especially if allied to the conceptual breadth of targets characteristic of cognitive analysis, should begin to improve the crucial capabilities even of individuals with the most profound deficiencies. What a marvelous moment in our field. Surely its excellence will be second only to the realization of its potential that can be seen for the next moment, perhaps a few decades hence.

REVIVED SOCIETAL PESSIMISM

If I am not too euphoric, then this is the moment for general optimism about the future of individuals with developmental deficiencies. But, paradoxically, it is a moment of revived pessimism on this subject instead. Instead of satisfying my former urge to celebrate, then, I can only view this pessimism with alarm, argue against it, and hope that it is but temporary. I offer here an example of an argument against that pessimistic stance, as a kind of preventive public-health measure.

The context for this pessimism and my argument in opposition to it came to a focus in 1972, when a suit (*Wyatt v. Stickney*) brought in a federal district court in Alabama charged that the conditions of the institutions maintained by the state of Alabama for a child institutionalized with retardation, named Ricky Wyatt, and other such children, were so poor that habilitation of this boy and his peers was impossible. It was further argued that the U.S. Constitution could be interpreted to establish a right of all children to an education, which Wyatt and his peers were not receiving, and indeed were systematically excluded from by the conditions of Alabama's institutions.

Federal Judge Frank M. Johnson did not affirm that constitutional right; instead, he ruled that citizens of the United States could not be confined to institutions in deprivation of their liberty, except by due process of the courts, which was rarely the case for persons with retardation or mental illness who were confined to the institutions. The only justification permitted for confining such persons, Judge Johnson argued, was for the betterment of a condition that constituted a danger to themselves or others. If the institutions of Alabama were not accomplishing that betterment, at least slowly, then those persons were unconstitutionally confined to those institutions. Judge Johnson's examination of the facts of institutionalization in Alabama led him to conclude that *no* betterment was taking place, and therefore that the confinement was unlawful.

Consequently, Judge Johnson ordered Alabama to improve its conditions of institutionalization, and specified in more than 50 particular ways how this was to be done. Some of those ways simply established humane conditions of life; others, significantly, established conditions that were to begin in order to habilitate and educate each resident. For example, the judge ordered some form of educational or habilitative programming for each resident for at least 6 hours each weekday. Interestingly, he did not require that this programming succeed; he only required that it take the form of the most enlightened habilitative or educational programming available at the time.

The state of Alabama both resisted Judge Johnson's order and began to comply with it. Over the next several years, repeated cases were brought before his court in the name of Ricky Wyatt, mainly charging that the state still was not complying with the important components of the 1972 order. In general, those charges were found to be true, and the 1972 order was reaffirmed. In an episode that occurred in the *Wyatt v. Hardin* case in 1975, an expert witness doubted the potential of persons with retardation for development—for education and habilitation. That expert testimony was given in support of a petition that Alabama be allowed to exclude some children from habilitative or educational programming on the grounds that these children were incapable of profiting from it, and that therefore the 1972 order's continuing imposition on them was a trial and a burden to them as well as to the state.

Nearly a dozen distinguished psychologists testified to the effect that indeed, some children with retardation were ineducable and incapable of benefiting from habilitative programming, and that Alabama ought to be excused from providing that programming in their cases. That such pessimism was present in the thinking and teaching of that many respected psychologists is cause for alarm. It is also a paradox, considering the exciting, powerful arena to which the sciences dealing directly with developmental deficiency are just entering.

I work in applied behavior analysis, and in my field, ignoring undesirable social behavior is one of the strongest tactics known for eliminating it. My sense of this case, however, is that the pessimism it reflects is too urgent to ignore. Apparently many other psychologists share my sense of urgency. Conferences geared exclusively to developmental deficiency, such as the Gatlinberg conference, have given much time to debating this issue. It is also a persistent topic in the professional literature. One of our newest journals, *Analysis and Intervention in Developmental Disabilities,* devoted its entire first issue to it. (In fact, much of the argument that follows is taken from my contribution to that issue of the journal.)

Arguing the educability or ineducability of any person with developmental deficiencies can lead to some profound propositions about the nature of human behavior. As the argument has developed so far, however, it has also produced a number of distracting elements. These are discussed next in order to clear the way for what I consider to be an ethical policy position.

DISTRACTING ELEMENTS

It is distracting, first, to argue that the *Wyatt* case and others have created a problem of teaching every person with retardation and other handicaps in our society to live, to be taught, and to work in the community rather than in an institution. The essence of these cases is that such persons cannot constitutionally be kept in institutions if those institutions are not offering them some form of habilitation. In my opinion, the court's definition of habilitation is essentially behavior change in the direction of those skills that together allow community living. "In the direction of" is not the same as "arrival" there, as best I understand Judge Johnson; it only means steady programming that could logically be expected to produce progress toward that goal. If the issue were whether or not it is possible now to move every institutionalized person into effective community placement, there would be no issue—that is not possible now. But the issue is "probably progressing in the direction of," not "arrival," and so, if institutions can program their efforts for residents "in the direction of" that goal, then the issue of actual community placement is distracting.

Second, it is distracting to argue that the persistent application of unsuccessful training programs to a person with retardation is demeaning and aversive to that person. The aversiveness of a teaching program for its student is independent of its success, in my experience. If a teaching program is well designed, it finds some response in the student to reinforce, and even if no progress is made from that level (from the teacher's point of view), the student nevertheless collects many reinforcers every session for the repetition of at least one response well within his or her capability. In my experience, residents who are not progressing in what was meant to be a teaching program still can come happily to and leave happily from their fruitless daily sessions. Such sessions are fruitless only for me (the program designer and analyst); they are full of reinforcers for the student. Projecting what to me is aversive about such sessions onto the student is distracting. (This is not to say that I cannot design a teaching program that will be both unsuccessful and aversive to the student. It is only to say that the pleasantness of a teaching program need not be related to its success.)

Third, it is distracting to show that a great deal of expert opinion doubts that all people can be taught effectively. The authorities who so testified in the latest round of *Wyatt* have devoted their research to analyzing how persons with retardation differ from normal persons. They believe that such research may finally give us some understanding of what retardation is, out of which may emerge better tactics for dealing with it. Much of their research is admirable, and I wish them the best of luck with that tactic, although I would never try it myself. What is distracting is that such retardation-analytic research usually concentrates on ways in which people with retardation *fail* to learn. In arguing the educability or ineducability of persons with retardation, would not a more objective view be gained by asking the opinion of those whose professional lives have been spent finding ways to make people with retardation *learn*—professionals not reinforced by the inference of yet another fundamental deficit "explaining" the person with retardation?

A fourth distracting element is to argue that the literature does not prove that all students can be taught effectively. The literature is not designed to do that. Even in its applied journals, it is open to innovation and resistant to the repetition of cases that it thinks it has already published. Studies proving that a certain technique, already shown effective for certain behaviors of some students in particular settings, also is effective for other behaviors, other students, and other settings, will meet a cool reception in the editorial-review process of most journals.

Finally, and more important than the latter point, it is distracting to argue that any literature of any journal *could* show that all people can be taught effectively. Neither the principle that all people can be taught effectively nor the principle that some people cannot be taught effectively has been proven, simply because neither of them *can* be proven.

AN ETHICAL POLICY POSITION

It seems appropriate to exemplify this argument from my own experience. I testified in the 1975 *Wyatt v. Hardin* case concerning a motion by the Alabama defendants to modify the original *Wyatt* order of 1972 (*Wyatt v. Stickney*). The defendants asked the court's agreement to define as unteachable certain residents of their state's institutions who had retardation, to recognize that continuing efforts to teach these residents were bad for them, and to allow alternative programs free of efforts to habilitate them. As already indicated, the court did not agree. My role was to testify that in my experience, I had often failed in my initial efforts to teach certain persons who had profound retardation; but that when I then tried different approaches (sometimes slight variations on the original approach, sometimes quite different tacks), I often found that eventually some such variation yielded at least the beginning of the desired behavior change. I said, in effect, that this had happened to me often enough to encourage an inductive leap: that if I could do it that often, perhaps it could always be done.

An Inductive Leap

No one asked me to state that I was making an inductive leap, although I had tried to make it clear that it was, and would have been happy to say so explicitly. No one asked me to agree that inductive leaps are not proofs, although I would have wholeheartedly agreed. No one asked me if, in the face of initial failure, I knew exactly how to go about trying the "slight variations" or "quite different tacks" that might eventually succeed, although I would have said immediately that often I did not know and frequently proceeded intuitively or even less systematically than that. No one asked me if there were other educators like me in sufficient numbers to go around, although I would have modestly doubted it. Most important, however, no one asked me if, considering the triviality of a mere inductive leap, there was a better course of action. I would have responded, fervently, that I could see no other *ethical* choice but to make the leap.

To reiterate:

I cannot prove that all people are capable of learning under instruction;
I cannot prove that some people are incapable of learning under instruction;

I have initially failed to teach some persons with profound retardation, yet in the face of those failures I have succeeded often enough in teaching them by trying something different, to allow me to affirm, not as a statement of fact but as one of ethical policy, that I *will* proceed as if all people are capable of learning under instruction, no matter how severe their retardation.

This is a very comfortable statement at the level of policy. If I proceed in this way, sometimes—perhaps often—I will be right, and that will be good for persons with retardation, good for our society, and good for behavioral science. To elaborate: What will be good is not that I will have been right (much as I enjoy that), but rather that some people whom we otherwise might have thought could not learn now will learn at least something useful to them, and that will be good for them. To the extent that such efforts make it clear that society means to do its best for even the least fortunate of its people, that is good for the society's ethics and therefore for all of its people, even if those least fortunate progress only one response toward better self-help in a year's programming. And to the extent that we sometimes finally succeed in teaching a person whom we have consistently failed to teach in many previous efforts, we may learn something about teaching technique and about the nature of behavioral prerequisites to behavior changes.

Arguments Against An Opposed Ethical Policy

By contrast, if we assume that some persons with profound retardation cannot be taught, then we forgo some of these outcomes. If we declare only a few people to be incapable of learning, then only a few will not learn, and society will look only a little less devoted to even the least of its people. (Never mind that one of the better known Jewish philosophers implied that how we treat the least of us is how we treat God—there is so little of that religion in practice today.) But we still will lose an exceptionally important part of the third benefit of always trying to teach everyone: we lose perhaps the best encounters we could have for learning about the nature of behavior and how it is really taught. Too often, in my opinion, we study the teaching of children who are not only capable of teaching themselves but eager to do so; in their wisdom, they cheat us of the opportunity to learn completely how the trick is done, because they do some of it for us, and they do it privately. It is when children cannot do much if any of it for us that *we* get to find out how to do all of it ourselves, as teachers. That opportunity is not merely a complicated *tour de force* or an irritatingly difficult chore; it is probably the most basic opportunity available to us for learning about the fundamentals of behavior change. Thus, declaring even a small number of people unteachable, if it stops us from trying to teach them, is destructive of better behavioral science, and that is intrinsically bad social policy.

Economics of the Ethical Policy

My statement of policy is also economically comfortable, at least for me. I am proceeding as if all people are capable of learning under instruction. I am already being paid by my society for proceeding in some direction relevant to human development; it will cost no more if I proceed in this direction than in its opposite, and in the long run it should cost less. I am, however, merely a researcher. Many argue that large-scale societal attempts to teach those whose retardation is most profound are expensive, and that society simply will not pay the costs much longer, especially if those attempts always fail. To this, there are at least four responses:

1. The legal response, which is that society does not get that choice unless it amends the Constitution or changes the judiciary;
2. The pragmatic response, which is that there is a large number of cheap ways to proceed with teaching that may work well but have rarely been tried;
3. My case, which, if applied to the many people involved in institutional care, suggests that those people already are being paid to proceed in some helpful direction, and may as well proceed in this one;
4. The cost-effectiveness argument, which I will symbolically attribute to the U.S. Office of Management and Budget. The amount that we spend on attempts to teach those with profound retardation can and always should be compared to the amount that we spend on liquor and tobacco, photographs of Saturn's rings, designer jeans, ballistic and antiballistic missiles of unknown necessity, nonfunctional tanks, skirts that are a different length yearly, lapels that are a different width yearly, nuclear alternatives to oil, the uncollectible loans that our banks make to desperate dictatorships, and the wars of our clients. The essence of these comparisons is not that we spend money foolishly, but that the amount we spend on anything is determined not by its necessity, its wisdom, its value, or even its cost, so much as by behavior modification, most often in the forms of style epidemics, advertising, and politics. Thus, spending is always open to remodification, usually called negotiation. If the parents and friends of our citizens with retardation think they can convince sufficient politicians to invest another millipercentage of the gross national product into teaching those with profound retardation, the point is either to help these parents and concerned friends, hinder them, or watch them, but hardly to suggest that they are flying in the face of natural law. Indeed, they are merely acting as if politicians are capable of learning under instruction; they are trying to develop the most effective techniques of that instruction. The argument against assuming that persons with profound retardation cannot learn is the same as that of assuming that the society cannot learn to continue investing in teaching them. Ultimately, it

is bad social policy to assume that either is impossible. Arguments that you personally do not wish to invest in teaching persons with profound retardation are of course intrinsically defensible in this society, as are arguments that you *do* wish to make just that investment. It is arguments that the society *will not* or *cannot* continue doing so that seem both indefensible and Machiavellian.

If my statement of policy is comfortable at the level of policy, it is, nevertheless, as I have stated, uncomfortable at the level of fact, since I have no way to prove that all people can be taught effectively. A universal proposition like that might be affirmed by induction, by succeeding in all our attempts to teach effectively every person ever presented for education. But any such induction is always susceptible to disproof by a single contrary case. I have a number of cases whom I have failed to teach so far, despite repeated efforts to do so. But I cannot affirm that any one of them is the "single contrary case," because many of my earlier initial failures, somewhere in the train of repeated or different teaching attempts that I could recall or invent, finally learned after all. So it is always possible that our so-far-unteachable cases will eventually turn out to be teachable. I cannot predict whom I can eventually succeed in teaching and whom I cannot; I can only testify that sometimes, despite repeated earlier failures to teach, I eventually succeed.

THE NATURE OF TEACHING

I cannot prove that some people *cannot* be taught effectively, either. On analysis, that turns out to be a universal proposition about teaching techniques. Teaching is a set of procedures. If it were a relatively small, thoroughly known set, it would be possible to exhaust the entire set in an attempt to teach a given student. Failing to teach effectively by any one or any combination of those procedures would let us affirm that this student was not teachable. But teaching, far from being a small set of thoroughly understood procedures, is a very large set of procedures, some of them well understood, some of them partly understood, and most of them still waiting to be developed. Their underlying *principles* may be few; those *principles* may even be thoroughly understood. But the translation of principle into procedure remains for the most part undone, yet ready to be done. Paradoxically, this truth may be more obvious to those narrow individuals who know mainly applied behavior analysis than to those broader-based individuals who know something about almost everything and consequently know only a little of applied behavior analysis. I submit that if you know a good deal about behavior analysis, then you are also likely to know that its translation into procedure is largely unexplored so far, and that however well explored it ever becomes, it will always be only a set of procedures to be applied to a sequence of behaviors indicated as a curriculum.

A curriculum is a list of behaviors to be taught. The production of a list of behaviors, which, if taught in an indicated order, will undoubtedly accomplish a meaningful educational outcome is what applied behavior analysis respectfully calls a "response analysis" of that outcome—respectfully, because it is the least researched aspect of all the sciences dealing with the analysis of behavior, and yet logically is the most fundamental. Failure to teach a behavior, in the discipline of behavior analysis, can of course mean faulty technique, but it can also mean a faulty response analysis. Specifically, it may mean that the behavior being taught unsuccessfully has essential prerequisites, and that until *these* are identified and taught, the teaching of their dependent behavior will remain unsuccessful. By way of a homely example, consider the prospects of teaching a child long division before addition, subtraction, multiplication, and short division are mastered.

All this implies that there is no way to be sure that a given behavior is unteachable to a given student. The set of procedures to be tried is too large and not yet totally invented; the set and sequence of possible, reasonable prerequisite skills that, if taught first, would then render easy the teaching of the original target, is too large. A student cannot be declared unteachable, in fact, until teaching has been tried and has failed in its entirety, and such an experiment is too large to have ever happened within the lifetimes of the student or the student's teachers. This point can also be stated in mundane terms: The cost of truthfully affirming someone to be unteachable is no different from the cost of continuing to try new ways of teaching them.

Recognition of this premise has led recently to a more subtle denial of the worth of trying to teach persons with profound retardation: that even if each one of them should eventually prove teachable, that teaching can never be "effective" teaching because these students will never learn anything "meaningful." This position tells us that only trivial, delimited motor responses will be learned, and that these could never alter the quality of such a person's life. In my opinion, the best answer to that is not some philosophical abstraction but instead a simple example provided by a colleague who has long lived with a daughter with profound retardation. One day he realized how meaningful it would be if he taught his daughter the simple motor skill of managing the latch on the door that would allow her access to their fenced yard. Before she learned that very simple hand response, she had to be let out and let back in many times a day, all year long. But once the latch was mastered, she stopped being the burden to her family that she obviously had been, and they stopped being the burden to her that they obviously had been. She and her family have found that slight motor skill one of her profoundly meaningful accomplishments.

This family need not prove that their daughter will always be meaningfully educable; they need only continue to try to teach her useful things. Sometimes they will succeed in useful ways, sometimes in spectacularly useful ways—the door latch—and sometimes they will fail. They need only to be always ready to try the next possibility, to see how meaningful it might prove to be, and thus they will never need to argue that all children can be educated effectively. Such an argument is an eternal exercise in futility. Failure to see that futility makes the argument into a sort of projective test. Finding ourselves short of a proof of the general proposition, we get to operate on grounds much weaker than proof—that is, we get to assert what we most want to assert, uncontrolled by the moderating influence of any facts.

SOCIETAL RESPONSE: US VERSUS THEM

I have never been fond of projective tests, and this one I find intensely ugly. I think that our societal response to *this* projective test too often is the replaying of one of our oldest and most self-destructive dramas: "Us versus Them," written in antiquity by Nicholas Beelzebub, its first production starring Abel and Cain. We have been playing and replaying this one throughout our history, often starring Rich and Poor, Black and White, Management and Labor, Parent and Child, or Man and Woman. Currently, in response to what is only a projective test, we are rerunning "Us versus Them" starring Normal and Retarded. I would rather produce Pogo, just to hear its one-line correction: "We have met the enemy and they is *us*." While I await that revival, I quote a colleague who remarked bitterly that "a dollar spent on them [the apparently ineducable persons with retardation] was a dollar not spent on us." He was not describing his own position, but society's position.

Let me place beside that assessment the response of Judge Frank M. Johnson, the repeated arbiter of the *Wyatt* case. Judge Johnson, hearing the plea that Alabama could not afford to educate both Them and Us, answered in effect that either there was enough money in Alabama to give every child in Alabama a proper education, or there was not. But if there was not, that could only mean that there would be enough money in Alabama to give every child there the same improper education. In his court, there was not an "Us" and a "Them," there was just all of us, and if all that we were going to spend on our education was $3.75, then we could each have an equal share of whatever it bought.

Interestingly, Alabama immediately found more money at that point than it had seemed to own just before. Sometimes, it is better not to predict what "our society" is going to do, and instead point out that we *are* our society, and that we have repeatedly committed ourselves to do good things to ourselves as equitably as possible. Indeed, we have legislated this commitment; and despite the fact that we have institutionalized persons with retardation, we have even more forcefully constitutionalized our equality of opportunity. Perhaps our behavioral science should try to develop a teaching curriculum for all of us that would generalize that commitment to every case it fits.

I see that I have drifted away from dispassionate argument. As someone trained in science, I am used to dispassionate analysis. Yet this issue invariably dissolves my dispassion. Perhaps it is because every time that we produce "Us versus Them" starring Normal and Retarded, we try persons with retardation once again, and demean ourselves in the process. They—and we—have had our trial in Judge Johnson's court; we were found not guilty of ineducability. We had to be found not guilty—ineducability cannot be proven beyond a reasonable doubt. Every repetition of that trial constitutes double jeopardy, and we are committed not to do that to ourselves. Perhaps the function of "Us versus Them" dramas is to keep us from seeing that it *is* ourselves to whom we are doing it. Small wonder that I keep verging into passion; I detest self-injurious behavior, not only as injustice but also in simple self-defense.

CONCLUSION

In conclusion, as I hope to have made clear, we cannot prove that all people can be taught effectively, and we cannot prove that some people cannot be taught effectively. All issues that hinge on either of these propositions are eternally fruitless, which makes them useful only as red herrings in engineering a political stalemate for anyone desirous of maintaining the status quo. Perhaps that is why so many people dedicated to the problem of developmental deficiency have, finally, ignored any principle of universal educability or intrinsic ineducability, and instead have tried to continue to realize a policy of achieving however much educability could be managed given current knowledge of educational strategies.

If our future research realizes the potential for continuing educability that I described at the outset of this argument, it would weaken ineducability as the red herring of the next social debate and the next reallotment of our taxes. That would free us to decide how much money we were going to spend on the habilitation of those of us who have retardation, and would enable us to do so in a context of how much we recognized the value of their habilitation, rather than in a context of whether it was possible. A context of impossibility—of ineducability or of only meaningless educability—makes the debate viciously simple, counterfactual, and counterethical.

But if our research did realize the potential for educability, we would merely *enable* a political process more appropriate than a context of impossibility allows. The research in itself will not determine the outcome of that political process. But since the political process is a behavioral process, it too can be studied. The educability of our society and its politicians is as much a research target as is the educability of those of us who have retardation. If we were to study such educability from the point of view of application, as something to be understood and managed rather than as something to be understood and bemoaned, we behavioral scientists would learn even more valuable lessons about behavior change. Perhaps those lessons would not prove as basic as those we learn when we discover how to teach a new skill to a person with severe or profound retardation, but they would be instructive nonetheless. They would undoubtedly affect our continuing pattern of decisions to intervene into the lives of persons with severe retardation. They would also say something about the ongoing pattern of decisions to fund our research and, perhaps, our existence as state-supported scientists.

True, that knowledge might not seem to establish the ethics of such decisions. But the essence of my argument so far is that an understood, codified, disseminatable ability to manage some particular behavior often alters the ethics of doing so, especially relative to those moments in our history when it seems only a logical possibility that we might someday manage that behavior. If we studied the process of managing our future political decisions about how much to invest in the educability of those of us who have retardation, and learned enough not only to see who is now managing those decisions for us, and how, but also how to manage the process ourselves, and thoroughly, would we in the next breath discover what our ethics about doing so really are? Or make them what they then would really be? It would be fascinating to find out.

In summary, extremely difficult-to-teach people constitute a political challenge to their society and to the behavioral science of their society—that part of its science that deals with the remarkably fundamental teaching relevant to those with severe and profound retardation, and that part of its science that deals with the remarkably technological problem of managing the behavior of voters and politicians. I submit that our society and its behavioral science will be enriched, not impoverished, when it is assumed that all of us, those with retardation and politicians alike, can be taught effectively, and therefore will be taught effectively as soon as the knowledge of how to do so is available in a widely useful form.

REFERENCES

Baer, D.M. (1981). A hung jury and a Scottish verdict: "Not proven." *Analysis and Intervention in Developmental Disabilities, 1,* 91–97.

Baer, D.M. (1984). We already have multiple jeopardy; why try for unending jeopardy? In W.L. Heward, T.E. Heron, D.S. Hill, & J. Trap-Porter (Eds.), *Focus on behavior analysis in education* (pp. 296–299). Columbus, OH: Charles E. Merrill Publishing Co.

Wyatt v. Hardin, No. 3195-N (M.D. Ala. Feb. 28, 1975, modified July 1, 1975).

Wyatt v. Stickney, 344 F. Supp. 387 (M.D. Ala. 1972).

Response

LET'S TRY
INDIVIDUAL DIFFERENCES

H. Carl Haywood

DON BAER'S CHAPTER is, as is usually the case with his work, a model of erudition, clarity of presentation, and precision of ideas. It would be difficult to imagine a more compelling presentation of the particular point of view espoused in that chapter. Still, it is the point of view itself that merits some further discussion. The major issues come down to four: 1) Baer has misinterpreted the position that he argues against, that is, the position of the "12 distinguished psychologists" in the celebrated Alabama (*Wyatt v. Hardin,* 1975) case; 2) the position that Baer has defended is essentially antiscientific; 3) the question of what constitutes education requires further discussion; and 4) the ultimate question in this case is "How much effort is enough?"

One could hardly argue against Baer's assertion that "developmental deficiency" needs further study. Indeed, our state of knowledge in that field is so sparse that we should be especially reluctant to place our professional bets on any particular strategy for pursuing the care, treatment, education, and habilitation of citizens with mental retardation. Hardly has the author set that admirable tone when he forthwith subverts the good scientific intent by suggesting that research that only advances knowledge, and does not in the short range actually help the participants in that research in observable ways, is somehow reprehensible. A similar position was taken several years ago by the Association for Retarded Citizens. A very large question then as now was: If we know in advance that our manipulations will help the participants, why do we need to do the research? Are we, then, to be confined, in our search for the additional knowledge that we need so sorely, to further exploration of well-known domains? I have to ask, "What is wrong with research that we know in advance is not going to help anybody in the short range, so long as it also hurts nobody?" After all, most of our contemporary fund of knowledge, on which we have partially based the remarkable advances of the last 25 years in services to citizens with mental retardation, was developed without regard to the issue of its immediate benefits to mankind. This argument for supporting only that research that will have short-range benefits to its participants is not only specious, it is dangerous for science, for mankind, and most especially for the very persons with mental retardation that it is intended to protect, since it will ultimately deny those persons the benefits of a broad range of new knowledge.

There is some attractiveness in Baer's proposed alliance between cognitive psychology (a conceptually oriented discipline given to explanation) and experimental analysis of behavior (a technology with determinedly few and simple assumptions about unobserved events and processes). Theory needs technology. Even good notions about organismic processes that intervene between antecedent and consequent conditions cannot be tested directly without manipulation and observation of their behavioral manifestations. A good example of this mutual dependence is the controversy that raged for several years in learning theory over the question of the necessity of reinforcement for learning to occur. It was clear fairly early in these discussions that learning could not be observed directly, but had to be inferred from changes in performance. It soon became equally clear that changes in performance were materially aided by contingent reinforcement, a fact that led some psychologists to declare that reinforcement had indeed been shown to be a necessary condition for learning. Behavioral technology in this instance helped to establish changes in behavioral manifestations of an unobservable variable, and provided us with an observable basis for inference. I have to add, however, that the issue was not settled, partly because the nature of reinforcement itself was called into question, and partly because the relationship between the manifest variable (performance) and the latent variable (learning) was never shown to be clear and reliable. A technology without theory can certainly lead to all kinds of grief. We have already seen some of the negative consequences of unsophisticated application of the technology of experimental analysis by persons far less competent in both technology and theory than we all know Baer to be. Technology without theory is applied blindly to a narrow range of situations that can be anticipated and taught. When novel situations are encountered and there is no accompanying theory, technicians either are at a loss for what to do or they behave in logically (and theoretically) inconsistent ways. So, by all means, let us have a productive alliance between cognitive psychology and experimental analysis, especially if in that alliance the conceptual base of cognitive psychology can be shared with experimental analysis adherents, and if the rich and productive technology of experimental analysis can enable cognitive psychologists to manipulate behavior in ways that will reveal the nature of the underlying psychological processes.

As a means of doing research, examining the nature of any event or phenomenon by changing it is a very efficient scientific strategy. In this sense, science and "good works" move in the same direction, but only to the extent that one can be certain of the beneficial, or at least benign, nature of the changes. Thus, one may certainly set out to do good by one's subjects, to enhance their behavioral effectiveness, while simultaneously gathering data that bear upon important conceptual structures. At the same time, one may combine a conceptually oriented discipline with an anticonceptual technology, and assure oneself that only good can come of such benevolent intent. But is it not possible that evil consequences can follow from benevolent intent? Indeed it is! In the simplest case, doing behavioral "programming" for 6 or more hours per day with profoundly handicapped persons, while not necessarily doing direct harm, can deprive those persons of the potential benefits, if any exist, of other activities in which they might be engaged. This is analogous to the case of patent medical treatments for serious illnesses, which might themselves do no harm but they might keep the patients away from potentially more beneficial modes of treatment. In the worst case, it is not at all impossible that such programming, repeated and sustained in spite of the total absence of response, could result in a conditioned resistance to behavior change that might be based upon future, more moderate and tolerable, efforts. Let us, then, not confuse good intent with good effect!

Baer has missed the essential point of the "12 distinguished psychologists." He resists their supposed argument that "some retarded children were ineducable and incapable of benefiting from habilitative programming." The point of the 12 was this: the more severely retarded a person is, the less "educable" by definition, the more investment will be required to produce each increment of positive behavioral change, and the lower the ultimate level of functioning one might expect as a result of that "programming." The group argued further that there is a definable point at which the required investment is so great, the increments so small, and the result so insignificant that a full 6 hours per day of "programming" turns from treatment into molestation. At some point it becomes the philosophy of the treaters, not the welfare of the individual clients, that is served. The group also argued strenuously from an individual-differences perspective that: (a) there is huge interindividual variability among persons with mental retardation; (b) determinations of how much and what kinds of "programming" should be required ought to be made according to the characteristics and manifest needs of individual persons with mental retardation and not according to group-applied formulae; and (c) professional staff members should have greater flexibility in determining how to meet the individual needs of persons who differ so greatly from each other. All of these arguments were based on great respect for individual differences rather than upon assumptions of homogeneity within classifications, as well as upon the assumption that our contemporary state of knowledge is insufficient to warrant a blanket prescription, even of a predetermined number of hours of fairly loosely defined "programming," for all persons whose characteristics might make them fit into a descriptive category. From these standpoints, the position of the infamous "Alabama Twelve" was more, not less, humane and ethical than was the opposing position, espoused and defended by Baer and others. The essential position was that only individual *clinical determination by qualified professional persons could yield the most valid approaches to treatment and the most effective treatment plans.*

It was the position of this group that many persons with mental retardation were being deprived of adequate treatment from which they could be expected to derive benefit because of the necessity to concentrate limited resources on a few residents in the vain hope that available technology would somehow produce tiny improvements in their behavioral repertoires. This is the "most effective allocation of limited resources" argument. To be sure, we should all be lobbying for increased resources, and we should state clearly the needs of our clients as we see them without regard to the availability of resources to meet those needs. Calling attention to needs is one thing, and devising plans to allocate and apply present resources is another. At an abstract level, both a person with profound handicaps who has shown no responsiveness to training efforts and a person with mild/moderate handicaps who is being prepared for community placement have equal right to treatment (not in the constitutional sense; that is beyond the scope of this discussion). On any given day, however, the usual situation is that resources dedicated to the one will constitute resources withheld from the other. The "Alabama Twelve" did not advocate throwing anybody out of the lifeboat. They did resist the vain allocation of vast training resources over long periods of time to residents who continued to show no significant response to training efforts, with the certain knowledge that such a practice meant withholding training resources from persons who showed encouraging response.

Among Baer's "distractors" we find the "experts" accused of doubting ". . . that all people can be taught effectively." This particular one of those "experts" has certainly not spent his research career showing that persons with mental retardation are "different from normal" persons, but instead has spent much of it demonstrating conditions under which the performance of persons with mental retardation can be greatly improved. The central issues on that point are: how much, with how much effort, under what conditions, and with what methods?

Another of Baer's "distractors" is the notion that the "literature does not prove that all students (sic) can be taught effectively." This argument would distract me as well, since it violates the logical principle that "absence of evidence is not evidence of absence!" The more essential argument is that the literature does demonstrate that enormous investment can bring little or no result in many cases and with particular methods.

Baer argues that we should resist both the notions that "all people can be taught effectively" and that "some people cannot be taught effectively." That would be admirable, since neither can be proved, but Baer's own arguments assume the former.

Baer argues that the "ABA" (applied behavior analysis) approach is in its infancy, that there is much yet to be learned about how to develop the technology for teaching, and how to translate it into curricula. I accept his (vastly!) superior expertise in that realm, and suggest that for that very reason we not embue this approach with the orthodoxy of case law or the trappings of social policy. We should: (a) support continued research of behavioral technology, and (b) not institutionalize ideas such as "behavioral programming" (especially for specified periods of time in each day). Behavioral programming refers at this time specifically to operant conditioning technology and its derivatives. Alternative treatments, including some periods of rest, might be better, and we must have the flexibility to find out.

Baer argues against a social policy that would reflect the assumption that some persons are essentially ineducable, on the ground that such a policy would stop behavioral research on learning and teaching. There are three problems with that. First, one does not have to assume that some persons are ineducable in order to resist a rigid prescription of 6 hours per day of "behavioral programming." Second, the whole field needs a clear definition of "education." According to any classical—and in my view, reasonable—definition, most of what one does to teach persons with severe and profound mental retardation the "skills of daily living" is not education. The distinction between education and training has become unfashionable, but it was serviceable in that it helped to focus teaching attempts in person-appropriate directions. At extreme levels, learning to read appears to me to represent education, while learning to turn one's head in response to a tone or learning to button one's clothing represent training. Both involve learning, and both may require teaching. Certified educators may not be required for either, but are less likely to be required for the latter group. Third, our history suggests that even a policy under which some persons are defined as ineducable would not stop behavioral research on learning and teaching. Indeed, it was under just such a set of policies that behavioral research in these areas has had its most successful period. The existence of categories such as "trainable" and "educable" implied that some persons were neither trainable nor educable, and these categories persisted into the 1970s, but it was in the 1960s and 1970s that behavioral research in mental retardation, especially on learning and teaching, enjoyed a boom! While I do not advocate such a policy, it does no good to raise illogical and unsupportable bugaboos.

In short, while I greatly admire the dedication and passion with which Baer approaches the social-ecological issues in mental retardation, I do argue that those virtues are no less present in those who hold a different view of how to go about producing better circumstances of life for persons with mental retardation. The giving or withholding of particular treatments in specific dosages can be seen as an ethical issue only to the extent that we are certain of the *exclusive validity* of those treatments. Verdict: not proved!

REFERENCES
Wyatt v. Hardin, No. 3195-N (M.D. Ala., 1975).

Chapter 9

A MODEL FOR ANALYZING THE MORAL ASPECTS OF SPECIAL EDUCATION AND BEHAVIORAL INTERVENTIONS

THE MORAL ASPECTS OF AVERSIVE PROCEDURES

H. Rutherford Turnbull,III, and Doug Guess,
with Linda H. Backus, Patricia A. Barber,
Craig R. Fiedler, Edwin Helmstetter, and Jean Ann Summers

THIS CHAPTER DEVELOPS an approach for analyzing the moral aspects of special education and behavioral interventions with children and adults who have mental retardation or other developmental disabilities. Our purpose is to highlight the moral dimensions of some interventions, point out the shortcomings of existing professional discussions on the subject, propose a model for analyzing the moral aspects of those interventions, and illustrate how the model works by applying it to aversive interventions for self-injurious behavior of those with mental retardation or other developmental disabilities. First we define the term *aversive,* give our reasons for undertaking to examine its moral dimensions, and describe briefly our approach.

DEFINITION OF AVERSIVE INTERVENTION

For the purposes of this discussion, the term *aversive procedures/intervention* is any intervention that is applied as a result of a person's behaving in certain disapproved ways, and that is intended to have or has the effect of producing physical or emotional pain or discomfort. To focus our presentation, we use a relatively arbitrary paradigm. It is that aversive intervention is applied to three distinct behaviors: nail biting, pica, and head banging. In each case, a separate aversive intervention procedure is applied: hand slapping for nail biting, administration of Tabasco sauce to the person's mouth for pica, and electric shock for head banging. The behaviors and the contemplated intervention procedures are perceived, respectively, as progressively mild, moderate, and severe, although many persons probably would disagree with these descriptors.

Some people might argue that our definition is too narrow, and that *aversive* covers not only these and other similar painful interventions but also any interventions that are not "positive." Under this broader definition, seclusion, timeout, physical restraint, or chemical restraint are also aversive. Indeed, any procedure objected to by the recipient of the procedure could be called aversive. There would be no end to this slippery slope until a recipient regards a procedure as unobjectionable. (Of course, painful procedures could be unobjectionable and therefore not aversive.)

The slippery-slope argument implies that our method and conclusions about aversive intervention (as we have defined it) necessarily apply to other types of interventions that some people would call aversive. Indeed, we hope that our *approach* to the morality of aversive intervention will generalize to other interventions. With respect to the conclusions reached, however, our intent and expectations are different. We do not intend to say here that all other aversive interventions are moral or immoral. In fact, we have tried not to reach, and do not reach on the basis of our discussion, any conclusion concerning the morality of those other interventions. Our conclusions relate solely to the interventions we describe and to other interventions indistinguishable from them.

INADEQUATE MORAL CONSIDERATIONS—
EXAMINATIONS FROM THE LITERATURE

Aversive intervention is but one of many techniques subsumed under the term *behavior modification*. It is, however, one of the more controversial interventions and has been a lightning rod of legal and other professional concern. It is somewhat surprising, therefore, that the moral dimensions of aversive intervention have been given such short shrift, particularly by those professions (psychology, education, and law) that are most directly involved in its use and regulation. Following is a brief report of examples from the education and psychology literature. The legal analysis is presented later in this chapter.

Lovaas

Lovaas (1982) hints at the moral dimensions of aversive therapy, but does not deal with them. That is not to say, however, that his comments are not helpful, because they are. He posits that the only "right" approach to self-injurious behavior (SIB) is the learning theory approach and that all behaviors (including self-injurious ones) are learned and therefore can be unlearned. Relying on data that support the learning theory, he gives the label of "benevolent enslavement" to the psychodynamic approach, which he says seems compatible with Judeo-Christian values of unconditionally accepting the child with SIB, making no demands on him or her, and comforting, reassuring, and showing love and concern for the child. He alleges that such an approach is "totally harmful" since it reinforces a person for SIB. He singles out overcorrection as a more humane procedure than physical aversives and as highly effective. He notes that timeout is counterproductive, as it "may *worsen* self-destructive behavior" (Lovaas, 1982, p. 119). He applauds the use of more positive interventions to reduce SIB, and he likewise praises work that shows the relative merits of social extinction, DRO (differential reinforcement of other behavior), and other procedures for reducing SIB without physical aversives.

In a sense, Lovaas seems to suggest that physical aversives are morally wrong when positive interventions can work as well. And when he inquires into the motives of therapists and their choice of aversives as being grounded on considerations other than "hard data"—he says behaviorists may select aversives because of their own "anxiety" and thereby become aggressive themselves—he supports our own hypothesis that aversive procedures could be morally wrong because, among other reasons, they might have adverse effects on therapists.

Wood and Braaten

Wood and Braaten (1983) also just approach the water's edge of the moral ocean, but they barely put a toe into it. Indeed, they are somewhat ambivalent about aversive procedures. For example, they condemn corporal punishment for school children because of the "lack of empirical basis for use in classrooms" (p. 70). Nonetheless, and "regardless of the questions about (the) efficacy or appropriateness" (p. 68) of other aversive procedures, they do not condemn each of those procedures (physical restraint, physically enforced overcorrection, timeout, and electric shock). In fact, they explicitly condone restraint and timeout by developing guidelines for their use in public schools.

It is a curious posture that allows the use of procedures whose therapeutic effects lack "strong evidence." The moral situation is twisted even more by Wood and Braaten's (1983) acknowledgment that there is a "danger that appropriate, limited punishment may escalate in intensity until it becomes abusive unless its users follow well conceived guidelines" (p. 69). In other words, it is permissible to use some punishment, its efficacy notwithstanding, despite the fact that "aversive procedures are generally assumed to be seductive for those who use them" (p. 69)—that is, "the rewards resulting from the use of aversive procedures go largely to the punisher" (p. 69). Their concern, however, is not with the effects of aversive therapy on the teacher, only on its effects for the student.

Yet Wood and Braaten (1983) have raised an important issue, one that we deal with explicitly: Is a procedure "right" if it has "bad" effects for the user (as well as for the person on whom it is being used)? Indeed, the only justification for aversive procedures, say Wood and Braaten, is "the need for strong control measures in schools serving students who are highly disruptive or aggressive" (p. 69). This rationale, however, is seemingly contradicted by the authors: "Until the therapeutic value of punishment procedure can be convincingly demonstrated in field settings, we believe its use can be justified only in combination with positive procedures that teach desirable behavior to replace the punished behavior" (p. 70). Again we ask: Why use an intervention that is not demonstrably effective for the person with disabilities, that seems to have adverse consequences for the user, and that can be replaced by "positive" measures? Their answer: for control purposes. Is that "right"—is it a defensible conclusion on "moral" grounds? Wood and Braaten do not say. We attempt in this chapter to give an answer.

Professional Associations

The blue-ribbon reports of the Association for the Advancement of Behavioral Therapy (1982) and the American Psychological Association Commission (1978) do not adequately address the morality of aversive intervention. In particular, the American Psychological Association Commission that reported on ethical issues in behavior modification identified some of the ethical issues but did not attempt to pass judgment on whether any of the methods of behavior modification are moral in the sense of being right. That is a major failing.

Yet the commission has been helpful in that it addressed the power relationship between the therapist and the recipient and the potential discrepancy in their values. It cited the possibility of the abuse of behavior modification, the difficulty of defining what is deviant behavior, and the fact that all psychological interventions raise the same moral problems of goals and techniques as does behavior modification. The commission did not take a purely "learning theory" approach but instead acknowledged the role of "consent" and "choice" for the therapist and recipient: They may choose whether to act or intervene in certain ways. Despite its admission that it is "virtually impossible" to write guidelines for behavior modification, the commission proceeded to write them, not in order to resolve the moral issues but to raise them. In performing this limited but important task, the commission dealt with vital issues of the role of consent, of values, of the doctrine of the least restrictive alternative, and of the generalizability of a behavioral intervention. It also seemed to suggest the very difficult problem of the moral person who engages in immoral practice. In this chapter, we do more than the commission. We try to answer some of the questions it raises, and we raise even others.

Council for Exceptional Children

The Council for Exceptional Children (1983) recently adopted a Code of Ethics and Related Standards for Professional Practice. The code commits special educators to develop the highest educational and quality of life potential of exceptional children, to engage in only those professional activities that benefit children, and not to participate in "unethical or illegal acts" (p. 206). The council's standards relating to behavior management call for special educators to apply only those disciplinary methods and behavioral procedures that "do not undermine the dignity of the individual or the basic human rights of exceptional persons (such as corporal punishment)" (p. 206), to conform to legal requirements relating to the "judicious application of disciplinary methods and behavioral procedures" (p. 206), and to "refrain from aversive techniques unless repeated trials of other methods have failed and then only after consultation with parents and appropriate agency officials" (p. 206).

Here again, there is explicit outlawing of corporal punishment and explicit approval of aversive procedures, including apparently those that are painful and punishing (as corporal punishment is). It is somewhat unclear what relationship exists between the prohibition of practices that undermine an individual's dignity and the approval of aversive procedures. If the procedures undermine dignity, are they prohibited as a matter of ethical practice? If not, and if they conform to legal requirements, they apparently are permissible as a matter of the morals of one of the nation's special education organizations. This result begs the question of whether aversive procedures are morally right.

Other Commentators

Goldiamond (1974) considers the ethical and constitutional issues of applied behavior analysis in an elaborate article that, at heart, argues for the construction of behaviors, not merely their elimination, by the techniques of applied behaviorism. His concerns in the area of ethics and law focus on the use of behavioral techniques on "captive" populations in "total" institutions; on the power of behavioral control procedures to "shape and control the direction of future assent, dissent and, indeed, choice itself" (p. 4); on the necessity of the constitution to establish safeguards for the use of behavioral procedures; and on the effects of behavioral procedures on the recipient, the institutions and their employees, and society as a whole (p. 4). Clearly his concerns are about the therapeutic goals that are advanced by the means of behavioral procedures (p. 7).

Like Goldiamond, London (1969) is concerned about the control that behaviorism makes possible, but he shares a similar concern about the use of drugs and genetic code-cracking. In addition, he worries about the "threat to moral tradition" (p. 193) that can be removed by technology, particularly with respect to the effect of technology on religion and the family. For him, the three moral issues, "writ large by the tremendous power which technology confers," are "always the only three such questions in any social system: Who shall be controlled? By whom? How?" (p. 193).

Matson and DiLorenzo (1984) also see the adequacy of treatment goals as an ethical issue, but they also regard other issues to be ethical in nature: the adequacy of the choice of treatment; the obtaining of informed consent from the recipient; the clear identification of whom the client truly is; the adequacy of measurements of the treatment; confidentiality; referral to other specialists; qualifications of the professional; deprivation of primary reinforcers (such as food and water); and the painful nature of the stimulus, which they regard as a necessary and acceptable fact in light of the possibility of long-term consequences that will benefit the client.

Unfortunately, none of these commentators deal with the issue that underlies their legitimate concerns, which we share. That issue is the topic of this chapter: How does one analyze the moral aspects of a professional intervention, and with what results in the case of aversive interventions?

AVERSIVE INTERVENTION AS A PARADIGM AND LIMITATIONS OF THE PARADIGM

Based on the failure of the literature to address adequately the morality of aversive intervention, it seemed to us, therefore, that aversive intervention might well be a useful focus for developing a model for evaluating the morality of professional interventions with persons who have mental retardation or developmental disabilities. There were several other reasons for selecting aversive intervention. One is that very few other interventions in the lives of persons with disabilities seem to provoke so many strong and diverse feelings from practitioners in law, psychology, and education. Yet, as stated, none has attempted to answer whether aversive intervention is "right" or "wrong" from any one or more moral perspectives. Another reason is that, as noted earlier and in greater detail in upcoming paragraphs, professional abilities to address the morality of professional activities seem particularly weak in that attempts to deal with the rightness or wrongness of aversive intervention are noticeably absent. Any systematic effort to develop and apply a model for addressing these dimensions thus seemed valuable.

In addressing the morality of aversive intervention, we borrow from the relevant work of several professions, apply that work to the disabilities profession in the issue of aversive intervention, and develop a model for analyzing the morality of interventions into the lives of persons with disabilities. We do not attempt to say whether practitioners should or should not use aversive procedures or substitute other interventions for them. In directly related work, Guess, Helmstetter, Turnbull, and Knowlton (1985) argue that aversive procedures should be replaced by other procedures, simply (but not solely) as a matter of efficacious practice.

We begin with standard policy analysis by discussing the ways in which many persons have stakes in aversive intervention. We then review what is known about aversive intervention's efficacy on the person subjected to it ("recipient") as well as on the person who administers it ("therapist"). Next, we briefly examine aversive intervention's use from the perspective of the law. Finally, we apply the dominant religious and secular doctrines of our civilization to aversive procedures.

Some will quarrel with our essentially deductive approach, in which we define doctrines, apply them, and draw conclusions about the morality of an intervention. They will argue that morality and ethics should be inductive and phenomenological, that the discovery of "right" should begin and end with the discovery of what people (in this case, therapists) do. Theirs certainly is a defensible position, but it is by no means the only defensible way to examine "right," and we chose to use another way, one grounded both in philosophy and common law traditions.

One more word of introduction: We are not antibehaviorists, probehaviorists, or members of any particular "camp," at least so far as this chapter is concerned. We have tried not to prejudge aversive intervention or to presume it to be immoral; rather, we have tried to let our conclusion emerge from our methodology. We are, however, advocates for responsible professional behavior toward persons with disabilities, and for informed and reasoned debate. We hope we have initiated such debate here about the right-wrong of our approaches to persons with disabilities. Likewise, we may be perceived as being adamantly opposed to or fearful of those who practice behavioral interventions. Again, that is hardly our intention, and we disavow any judgment to that effect.

THE STAKEHOLDERS

Human interactions often involve competing or conflicting interests. Aversive intervention is no exception; indeed, it tends to exacerbate the conflicting interests of various stakeholders. All too often, however, therapy has been justified solely on the basis of its alleged efficacious results on its recipients, without sufficient consideration of the nature of the competing interests involved. Such an approach is inadequate; too many people have too much at stake in technology's application to persons with disabilities to permit such paucity.

One method to unravel the various interests is known as interest analysis. As Turnbull (1981) noted, interest analysis carefully dissects everyone's stakes (interests) in a given situation. Interest analysis assists us (or would-be policy makers) in balancing the various interests, weighing the competing equities, and resolving conflicts among those interests. Interest analysis thus is a tool that can be used in debating, and ultimately deciding, difficult public policy issues. Such a policy issue now confronts the developmental disabilities profession. Under what conditions, if any, is the use of aversive intervention justified?

The persons most directly affected by aversive procedures are the recipient and the therapist. Both ostensibly seek to change behavior and thereby improve the recipient. The recipient has an interest in being treated with dignity and respect, being provided with as much freedom and decision making in daily activities as his or her condition allows, being provided adequate opportunities to learn and thus to become as independent as possible, and having his or her choices (decisions) respected and followed to the maximum extent appropriate.

The therapist also has several interests. First are the recipient's improvement and the amelioration of the effects of the disability on the recipient and others. Other interests, however, can conflict with the recipient's interests. For example, the therapist may be interested in being perceived as one who is capable of performing cures. He or she may also be concerned with being able to control another person's (recipient's) behavior. Such control can often make the therapist's work easier. For example, a teacher of a highly aggressive and destructive youngster is directly interested in being able to control that child's "behavioral outbursts" so that the teacher can be freed from having to watch that one child constantly. The therapist thus may be interested in the power relationship between himself or herself and a recipient. A therapist who can control a person's behavior is clearly more powerful than a therapist who has no control. Finally, the therapist may be concerned with research and experimenting with new techniques, with enlarging the boundaries of science, or with advancing his or her profession. Certainly, this latter interest has an attractive appeal for most ambitious therapists.

A third stakeholder is the recipient's family. The family may have sought treatment for their child and clearly wants therapy to succeed. The family also has a legitimate interest in its authority to make decisions for its members. This decision-making power traditionally undergirds the basic autonomy and control exercised by parents in our society. Another interest is the family's right to be able to control the member's behavior so as to ease the burden of care. A final interest may be a family's right (or desire) to keep the person at home and to not have to seek institutionalization. This concern is directly related to the family's ability to control its child's behavior.

The service system is also a stakeholder, in that it has an interest in maintaining an effective and efficient system capable of helping its clients. The system furthermore needs efficacious results so that the public will support it. Finally, when an individual therapist chooses a particular treatment method and reports successful results, other therapists in the service system, encouraged by the results, will be tempted to employ similar techniques; what one therapist reports as effective can ultimately become generally accepted practice.

The use of aversive therapy also potentially affects the interests of society, if the behavior to be modified is dangerous to others, if the behavior and/or technique are the topics of research, or if the individual's cost of care might be reduced through behavior modification. In addition, the stability of society in general depends greatly on its ability to maintain social control. Finally, what happens to one person may happen to all. The "spread effect" of aversive therapy is well known (Guess et al., 1985).

Thus, aversive intervention implicates multiple and sometimes conflicting stakeholders. For this reason, its moral dimension is not a clear-cut matter; what might be right from one person's point of view could be wrong from another's. Similarly, it could be argued that its morality should not be determined on a singular basis. What is right or wrong about it arguably could be grounded on the aggregate of moral viewpoints, that is, if it is right from more viewpoints than it is wrong, the moral prospects for aversive procedures may be favorable on that account. Conversely, if aversive intervention is wrong from more viewpoints than it is right, its moral underpinnings must be doubted. Prospects for such a combined approach are considered in a later section.

The problems with this approach—judging the morality of aversive interventions by "the aggregate of moral viewpoints"—are, first, that the approach seems to make the morality of a behavior simply a matter of majority vote, and, second, that a combined approach to its morality can be confused with a "majority-vote" approach. We do not intend to argue for the "majority-vote" approach. Rather, we attempt to combine a variety of ethical approaches, and, in doing so, we conclude that aversive interventions are not moral.

Our analysis now moves from identifying the stakeholders to inquiring about the efficacy of aversive procedures. This approach informs the conclusion by relating facts to the moral judgment. Bad facts make bad law and poor moral judgments.

EFFICACY

Problems of Defining Efficacy

When there is no consensus, actual disagreement, or ambiguity in the literature concerning the choice of an intervention or its efficacy, the task of describing its efficacy becomes extremely dangerous. It is dangerous not only because it is always risky to summarize the literature but also because any evaluation of the efficacy of a behavioral intervention, whether it is aversive or positive, depends on both the nature of the intervention as well as on the user. Here, it is often difficult to know—or agree on—whether the intervention was of sufficient quality to work and whether it was implemented consistently. There is also the difficulty of knowing whether the implementor carried out the strategy correctly. And there is a further problem of ascertaining whether the recipients of the intervention were suitable, by reason of their behaviors and etiologies, for the intervention. Thus, conclusions about efficacy should be carefully drawn.

Second, there is the problem of defining *efficacy*. Some people define it in terms of the immediate or short-term suppression of a behavior; others consider the durability and maintenance of the behavioral changes; still others look to the generalization of the behavioral change; and some use all three criteria in defining *efficacy*.

Another definitional problem concerns the term aversive. Some people would not consider a hand slap or even the administration of noxious stimuli to a person's mouth to be aversive; others would. Some would consider electric shock to be aversive, but they would not regard it as aversive in comparison to a targeted behavior (such as head banging).

Fourth, there may be multiple causes of a behavior. Some behavior may be organically or biologically caused, and some may be learned. A behavioral intervention clearly is appropriate for the learned behavior, but not necessarily for the behavior that has other causes. It may be that behavioral interventions have been applied appropriately, and their efficacy therefore can be fairly determined; that is, a behavioral intervention has been applied for a learned behavior. But behavioral interventions may also have been applied inappropriately; that is, they may have been used for conditions that are neither learned nor amenable to behavior modification. In that case, it can be wrong to assess their efficacy, since the intervention simply may not be appropriate for the manifestation (the behavior) of an "unlearned" cause.

Multiple Criteria of Efficacy

Given these considerations, the efficacy of such interventions should be considered from multiple dimensions. Such an approach takes into account these difficulties but still allows a conclusion about efficacy.

Guess et al. (1985) recently conducted a historical review and critical analysis of aversive therapy, defining *aversive therapy* as punishment, negative reinforcement, and overcorrection. They evaluated each of these aversive procedures by the following criteria: effectiveness in changing behavior, efficiency, maintenance of effects, generalization, side effects, and experimental design.

Overall, Guess et al. (1985) concluded as follows:

Published studies that used punishment or overcorrection show that these procedures can, either singly or as part of treatment packages, effectively reduce a wide range of behaviors. In addition, published studies using negative reinforcement demonstrated the effectiveness of this procedure for increasing adaptive behavior. Unfortunately, effectiveness cannot be assessed fully because research that shows weak or negative results is neither published nor submitted for review for publication.

Effects appear to be durable for short follow-up periods. Most researchers, however, fail to provide follow-up data or else do so but for only 12 months or less. In addition, follow-up conditions are described poorly.

Most researchers failed to provide data on generalization of effects. Of those reporting on generalization, over half found some degree of transfer of effects. Typically, generalization was measured in these instances in only a subset of possible conditions to which effects must transfer in applied settings.

Side effects were reported for all three aversive procedures. These effects appeared to be balanced in terms of being negative or positive.

Adequate experimental designs were present in a relatively small number of studies. While understandable in cases treating self injury or severe stereotyped behavior, this situation was evident, nonetheless, across all target behaviors. (p. 25)

Guess et al. (1985) also conducted demographic analyses of the published studies to determine what types of procedures have been used in relation to the type and severity of disabling conditions, the behaviors that were being modified, the age of the recipients, and the settings in which the investigations were conducted.

In a review of 16 journals from 1965 to 1984, they identified a total of 61 published articles that used aversive procedures with persons who had disabilities. The majority of published studies using electrical shock as a punisher were conducted in the late 1960s and early 1970s. A variety of other aversive stimuli gradually replaced the published use of electrical shock as punishers. These included water sprays to the face, substances placed in the mouth, ammonia capsules placed under the nose, ice placed to the cheeks, white noise, slaps, hair tugs, and physical restraint. Only four articles reported the use of negative reinforcement procedures with persons with disabling conditions, including a Lovaas (1965) article that used an electric shock grid as a negative reinforcer to increase social interactions. Guess et al. (1985) concluded (pp. 41–43):

1. Of the three aversive procedures, punishment has been used most extensively, followed closely by overcorrection. The number of published articles reporting the use of punishers decreased following the appearance of overcorrection procedures in 1973. Negative reinforcement procedures have been reported infrequently in the published literature.
2. All three aversive procedures have been reported to be used most frequently with persons described as profoundly/severely mentally retarded. Persons

identified as autistic/emotionally disturbed were the second most commonly identified subject population in the literature review.

3. Stereotyped/self-stimulation and self-injurious behaviors were targeted most frequently for punishment and overcorrection procedures. Punishers were used most often for self-injurious behavior, while overcorrection was used slightly more often with stereotyped/self-stimulation behavior. A variety of other behaviors, however, were targeted for aversive procedures.

4. By far the most frequent age range for the use of aversive procedures is between 7 and 21 years. The remaining two age categories, 0–6 and over 21, were almost equally divided in relation to application of aversive procedures.

5. Institutions are the most commonly identified settings for the application of aversive procedures, especially punishers. Preschool settings ranked a close second in published studies using overcorrection procedures.

It seems fair to conclude, based on the Guess et al. (1985) analyses, that the efficacy of the three types of procedures is open to question on several grounds and that their use has been most extensive (so far as the literature shows) with the most vulnerable persons with mental disabilities or other disabilities. It is appropriate now to examine these interventions from a different perspective, namely, their effects on those who use them.

EFFECTS OF AVERSIVE INTERVENTION ON THE THERAPIST

What are the effects of aversive interventions on the short- and long-term behavior of the therapist and on the relationship between the therapist and the recipient? These are largely unresearched questions. The research fails to consider whether the therapy might change the therapist's behavior in subtle and yet quite deleterious ways, immediately and over time. Since the research has focused on the recipient, this is an understandable, but not for that reason justifiable, oversight.

There are three reasons why this omission is not forgivable. First, the effects on the therapist are important human considerations, and a concern for the therapist's own welfare should evoke a study of these effects. Second, as we show in detail later, the effects are an important aspect (but not a dispositive one) of the moral analysis. Third, and most germane to our argument, the relationship between the therapist and the recipient causes deep moral concerns.

As we argue elsewhere in this chapter, the relationship is essentially a power relationship that is by its very nature imbalanced, with power strongly in favor of the therapist. Despite the efforts of the law and human rights committees and concerns to redress the imbalance (efforts that we describe later in this chapter), the relationship is inherently asymmetrical and therefore inherently poses all of the moral issues with which we are concerned in this chapter (and which are therefore paradigms for other power relationships and justify this chapter's title: "A Model . . ."). It is, moreover, precisely the asymmetry that gives moral force to our concern about the impact of aversives on the therapist: the use of power unavoidably affects the user of that power. Lord Acton's maxim is salient: Power tends to corrupt; absolute power tends to corrupt absolutely. Even more to the point is William James' observation: What is possessed comes to possess the possessor.

Potential Effects

In the short-term analysis, it is important to know whether the therapist becomes aversive to the recipient and, if so, whether the recipient's feeling transfers to other adults, including other therapists. Can the therapist interact with the person in appropriate ways outside of the treatment sessions, or does there develop a relationship based on fear? If the relationship becomes fearful, the therapist who applies aversive procedures arguably can be rendering himself or herself and other therapists impotent to work productively with the recipient.

There is another side of this problem. Does the therapist become jaundiced with respect to other recipients (just as the recipient becomes with respect to other therapists)? Could it be that the response of the therapist to one recipient might become his or her response to all recipients? Although short-term effects of aversive intervention might adversely affect the relationship of a therapist to a specific person, the more enduring effects on the therapist could well be long-term, cumulative, and resistant to change.

Let us assume, by way of example, that the same therapist applied the hand slap, Tabasco sauce, and electric shock procedure, separately, to three persons with disabling conditions. Let us further assume that, in each case, the results were "successful" in that the behavior faded or ceased, ostensibly establishing both the efficacy of the procedures and the competency of the therapist in applying them.

It is necessary to ask what may be happening to the therapist. But since research has focused on the recipient, the field has not addressed this question. Moreover, and unfortunately, the questions we should be asking are inconsistent with the very model from which the procedures are derived. These questions assume a dynamic relationship between therapist and recipient such that the procedures used, and the effects on the recipient, cannot be separated from their effects on the therapist. Reality indeed may be greater than the sum of its parts. Thus, just as the therapist is intervening on the behavior of the recipient, the recipient is intervening directly on the therapist in ways that might not be readily observed, measured, and graphed. One such long-term effect on the therapist relates to depersonalization, a phenomenon observed by Burt (1977) to occur among medical practitioners.

Depersonalization

Burt (1977) argued that a common criticism of scientific medicine is physicians' objectifying mind-set, one that focuses attention on the disease and not the patient. Describing further the implications of that paradox on the relationship between physician and patient or parent and child, Burt stated:

> I believe we are disregarding and even loosening the central psychological bonds that have kept in check some extraordinary destructive forces implicit in these relationships. The very attempt to order these relations implies an assumption that may seem self-evident—that the relationship is a transaction between two separate people. But this assumption is not necessarily self-evident to the participants. (p. 31)

The similarities between medicine and behaviorism are striking. Both are based upon a mechanistic model; both are riding the crest of an advanced technology; and both operate from a deviancy model. The question is whether the same potential for "destructive forces" identified by Burt for the medical professions operates among behavioral therapists who use intrusive intervention procedures. This is a likely but not inevitable outcome, given depersonalization (and other psychological estrangement) of the helper from the helped as well as the concerns that behaviorists themselves have voiced (American Psychological Association Commission, 1978; Association for the Advancement of Behavior Therapy, 1982; Lovaas, 1982; Wood & Braaten, 1983).

In the case of the "successful" therapist whom we have been discussing, one might argue that the results and accrued benefits for each of the three recipients are sufficient rewards in themselves. The therapist has fulfilled the professional obligation to assist other persons. The technology did work on a highly predictable schedule. Here, there is both benefit and risk. The benefit is to the recipient. The risk is that the therapist has embarked on a "slippery slope," one that seems to lead to increased use of the technology, even inappropriately. We give this slope the name "procedural decay." It is a terrain to be avoided, because a journey on it can encourage the clearly inappropriate and arguably excessive use of aversives.

Procedural Decay

The therapist has learned that aversive intervention is highly effective, possibly more so than other slower and time consuming approaches. Will this success increase the likelihood of further applications to recipients whose behavior may not be quite so problematic? Will the therapist next choose, for instance, to slap a person who exhibits high rates of stereotyped behavior? Or to shock a person who drools (Wood & Braaten, 1983)?

Guess et al. (1985) have discussed the concept of "procedural decay," what ethicists sometimes call the "slippery slope." Over time, teachers of children with severe disabilities might show an increase in the use of aversive techniques as a more expedient substitute for positive instructional programs. The concern is that aversive procedures are being used to teach new skills, not just to reduce inappropriate behavior. For these teachers, as well as for our hypothetical therapist, the unresearched question is whether the aversive intervention is seductive as an easy way out and, if so, whether the therapist will use procedures that become *even more aversive?*

Control of Goals of Therapy

This inquiry into the effects on the therapist brings us to the issue of who controls whom in the application of aversive procedures. As a safeguard against abuses of aversive procedures, a number of professional organizations have adopted previously discussed ethical codes and procedural guidelines for the protection of recipients. With the advent of behaviorism, there has also been a proliferation of human subjects research committees to monitor the use of aversive procedures. These committees have, among other functions, the responsibility of protecting the rights of recipients.

Can one assume, however, that the proper safeguards have been established? Legally, the answer is affirmative, even though a recent survey has identified some problems among the majority of human rights committees in residential settings, including role definition problems for the committees and issues of motivation among the members (Kemp, 1983). Moreover, it is doubtful that the committees will have systematically addressed the morality of the aversive procedures that they approve or reject. Given the failure of the professional codes of ethics to examine closely and to resolve the morality of aversive procedures, it seems that the committees themselves will have the same failing. In short, a purported purpose of the human rights review is not apt to be accomplished.

That is a major failure, one that suggests that both the committee and the therapist whose work is reviewed by it are seriously shortchanging their obligations to evaluate the morality of aversive procedures. But when a committee approves an aversive procedure, it sanctions—for the therapist, at least—the morality of the procedure. It thereby makes the moral judgment for the therapist; it takes the therapist off the moral hook, absolving him or her of any responsibility for inquiring into and resolving the morality of the procedure.

It might be assumed by professional standards and human rights committees that a formalized mechanism has been established to monitor the actions of the therapist who applies the aversive procedures. This itself raises some provocative questions pertaining to the issue of control.

First, the professional guidelines themselves have been established by individuals who are primarily sympathetic with both the procedures used and the theoretical underpinnings of the model from which they are derived. Thus, the guidelines that would exert control over the therapist are developed by individuals who are in agreement that behavior control is a proper method of correcting deviant behavior. This leaves the therapist in a situation where the assumptions underlying the technology are closely related to the guidelines used to regulate its use.

The therapist then applies procedures that are based upon a model that allegedly is value-free and is monitored by a code of professional ethics that is, in effect, culturally relative. This may produce no dilemma for the therapist when the procedures work. But what happens when the intervention regimen does not produce the desired change? Is the therapist now placed in a position where allegience to the procedures might well override the relativistic controls of the controllers, and what personal effect does that have on the psychological well-being of the therapist?

In raising these questions, we do not intend to argue that only absolute values can effectively counteract the professional ethical codes and their cultural relativism, although absolute values indeed may have that effect and perhaps should. Our argument instead is that procedural decay seems to have permeated some professionals' behavior, that a combination of ethical principles holds the use of aversive interventions to be wrong, and that among the combined principles are seemingly "absolute values" that likewise find the use of aversives to be wanting. Our point is that the professional codes and human rights committees are not an effective moral safeguard against the use of aversives.

A classic series of studies by Milgram (1974) has shown the willingness of therapists to deliver increasingly intense levels of shock to another person, based solely on their obedience to an authority figure, who in these studies was an experimental technician. In some cases, the subjects were willing to administer life-endangering intensities of shock.

In the case of the therapist administering aversive procedures to persons with disabilities, might we find the same obedience, in this case to the procedure, given the absence of any absolute values that regulate its use? In the final analysis, would the therapist even be capable of recognizing that the procedures were punishing? Or that there are moral issues that he or she should address but does not? Given the possibility, however remote, that the therapist has eventually reached a point where aversive intervention is justified in its own right as a proper means to the end, how and on what principles does the therapist resist its application to other people in society?

We argue, therefore, that aversive intervention has some serious undesirable potential effects on the therapist. These entail not just depersonalization and procedural decay, but also distortions in goal setting for devalued persons. It is to the issue of devaluation that we now turn, because devaluation through the establishment of dual standards of treatment raises essentially moral questions: Is there a moral code that protects some people, but not others, or condones some interventions but condemns others?

DUAL STANDARDS

Is a person with a mental disability treated differently from a person without one? Why? Why not? The crux of this inquiry is whether or not there is a dual standard and unequal treatment; whether or not that disparity can be justified; and if it cannot (or at least some of it cannot), whether or not "we" and "they" are so different that what is right or wrong for "us" is not also right or wrong for "them."

Dual Standard: A Historical Fact

It is important to inquire about the existence and rationale for a dual standard for at least two reasons. First, there is a long history of disparate treatment of persons with disabilities in comparison to that of persons without disabilities. Some of that treatment was invidious and discriminatory, as in eugenic sterilization, institutionalization, and education and in the withholding of treatment from newborns. Other treatment was intended to have, and did have, the effect of conferring a benefit. The second reason is that there has been concern that there should not be an unlimited or even a wide scope of power among therapists to determine the goals of treatment. As we have just noted, and indeed as the American Psychological Association Commission (1978) noted, the therapist faces the ethical dilemma of whether or not to use therapy as a mechanism to enforce conformity to a majoritarian norm or standard. Thus, it is appropriate to inquire into the existence of a dual standard—for example, whether or not the alcoholic is treated differently from the head banger.

A dual standard does exist. People with disabilities *are* regarded as deviant; that fact alone has justified certain interventions, including aversive ones, to correct the deviancy. But why are people with disabilities regarded as deviant, and are those reasons sufficient to justify dual standards?

Dual Standard, Therapy, and Reasons

Interventions on behalf of persons with disabilities usually are couched in terms of treatment. Usually implicit in the treatment process is the belief that the therapist, presumably acting as an agent of the recipient, his or her family, and society in general, knows and may (nearly unilaterally) determine the goal to which the treatment is directed (Friedman, 1975; President's Commission on Mental Health (PCMH), 1978; Shapiro, 1974). Upon what bases are therapeutic goals determined? Are they the same for those with and without disabilities? Should aversive intervention be used to enforce conformity to preestablished norms or standards?

In considering deviance and the therapeutic response to it, it is insightful to contemplate what is done to or for persons with disabilities and nondisabled persons alike. Consider two different people: first, a person who has mental retardation and engages in self-injurious behavior such as (at the extreme) head banging; and second, a mentally normal (nondisabled) person who engages in different self-injurious behavior, such as excessive and continuous consumption of alcohol or drugs. Assume that both behaviors are similar in their frequency, duration, intensity, and harm to the person. Assume each person's family is similarly adversely affected. Do we apply the same standards in our therapeutic interventions? Clearly, we do not.

Societal reactions to deviations from social norms vary. In fact, our society encourages a certain amount of nonconformity, provided it takes an approved direction. Alcoholism may not even be considered a deviant behavior for at least two reasons. First, some deviant acts are interpreted as attributes associated with the status the person occupies. For many people, excessive drinking is often the sign of a highly pressured and prestigious job. Such behavior is not considered necessarily deviant. Also, most Americans drink alcohol occasionally and even to excess at times. Therefore, in many situations an alcoholic would not be perceived as deviant and such behavior would be tolerated, to a certain degree. The head banger, however, almost certainly will be viewed as deviant and subject to interventions. These disparate results generally would apply even in situations where the self-injurious behavior is equally harmful to both individuals or to others. Yet, the external effects of alcoholism arguably are as wide as those of head banging.

Rhodes and Paul (1978) have identified several factors that influence whether a person or his or her behavior is labeled as deviant and thus likely to experience formal therapeutic intervention. These factors can be applied to the cases of both the head banger and the alcoholic.

One factor is the visibility of the rule-breaking behavior. It is readily apparent that a person who engages in head banging will experience greater social visibility than a person who gets drunk habitually. As a society, we are used to seeing intoxicated people; we are not used to seeing people injure themselves by head banging.

The frequency or intensity of the behavior is also a factor. Infrequent or mild aberrations from generally accepted standards of conduct cause little concern and are usually dismissed as individual idiosyncrasies. This is not true with frequent or extremely aberrant behaviors, such as head banging, which compel some sort of intervention to eliminate or decrease such shocking behavior. On the other hand, individual and societal concerns arise when a person's excessive drinking behavior increases from occasionally to almost daily.

Another factor is the individual or societal tolerance level for the rule-breaking behavior. As indicated, we are more tolerant of drunkenness (it has happened to us, etc.) than we are of head-banging behavior. Head banging is alarming to most people, and its harmful effects are much more visible than with alcoholism. Our tolerance for it is also less.

Another factor is the rule breaker's relative power in a social system. Some highly "successful" people are alcoholics; their behavior is more likely to escape social sanctions than is head-banging behavior, which is not normally associated with powerful people.

The amount of control between the rule breaker and the agents of social control is another factor. Once again we find that alcoholism does not offend most of us nearly so much as head banging. The internal strife of the alcoholic and the head banger may be similar, but it is the difference in the outward manifestations that causes us to find one behavior so clearly in conflict with our social norms and rules. And there is a significant element of social control involved. Although it is true that some alcoholics are confined voluntarily or involuntarily for their own or others' protection, not all are. By contrast, few head bangers are unrestricted.

Finally, the social distance between the rule breaker and agents of social control is a factor. Indeed, the head banger has a double barrier to overcome when we contemplate the social distance between him or her and "us." The head banger is more than likely already perceived as deviant by the mere fact of his or her disability alone; the head-banging behavior only serves to accentuate our perception of deviance. The alcoholic, however, does not have the same social distance to overcome. Unless the alcoholic engages in unusually bizarre behavior, he or she probably will be socially accepted in many situations.

Thus, society's response to the head banger is likely to be quite different than in the case of the alcoholic. The ultimate seriousness and eventual harm of the behavior may not be the overriding determinant. Instead, the determinants might be the outward manifestations of the behavior, how shocking the behavior is in light of accepted norms of behavior, and the nature of the actor (i.e., whether the person has mental retardation or not). The dual standard—intervention for the one, but not for the other—then could well rest on dichotomous views of the actor and the nature (not the consequences) of the behavior.

Dual Standard, Legal Considerations, and Interventions

In considering the nature and purpose of such regulation and its relationship to the moral rightness or wrongness of aversive interventions, it helps to note that judgments about the rightness of an aversive intervention are made in the content of the law. That is not to say that if any given intervention is legal, it is also morally right, for what the law condones other criteria might reject. It is, rather, that the law is part of the context in which we measure the correctness of intervention.

Legal challenges to the use of aversive interventions originated in cases involving residents of a state mental retardation institution (*Wyatt v. Stickney,* 1972), a psychiatric patient (*Knecht v. Gillman,* 1973), and prisoners (*Mackey v. Procunier,* 1973). In *Wyatt v. Stickney,* the judge ruled that behavior modification involving the use of aversive or noxious stimuli was allowed if approved by a human rights committee, given with the consent of the resident or guardian, and administered by a qualified mental retardation professional. In the other cases, challenges were sustained on the grounds that the administration of drugs that induced vomiting (in *Knecht v. Gillman,* involving a psychiatric maximum security hospital) and reduced breathing (in *Mackey v. Procunier,* involving convicts) violated the persons' rights of consent and rights against cruel and unusual punishment, as guaranteed by the Eighth Amendment to the U.S. Constitution.

As indicated in *Wyatt* and in *Knecht,* the first issue to be determined is whether the recipient or guardian has given legally effective consent. Such consent requires that the person giving consent be legally competent to do so, be sufficiently informed concerning the procedure, and act voluntarily in giving consent (Friedman, 1975; Michigan Law Review, 1976; Shapiro, 1974; Southern California Law Review, 1972; Turnbull, 1978). Sometimes, however, even consent that is otherwise legally effective will not render a procedure constitutional. Some procedures will be held to be inherently violative of a person's constitutional rights (*Kaimowitz v. Department of Mental Health,* 1973; *Mackey v. Procunier,* 1973). Some courts bar procedures on constitutional grounds, apparently believing that one of the three elements of consent is absent or else substituting their judgments and protective instincts for those of the person subjected to the procedure. Those rights are based on several grounds.

The First Amendment safeguards the rights of speech, worship, and association. From these explicit safeguards has been derived a right of privacy and an arguable right of "mentation" (Shapiro, 1974). The value that undergirds these explicit and derivative rights is that of personal autonomy (DuBose, 1976; Friedman, 1975; Gelman, 1984; Plotkin, 1978; Schwitzgebel, 1972; Shapiro, 1974; Smith, 1980; Zlotnik, 1981). Thus, an intervention that is likely to seriously impair a person's autonomy may well violate his or her First Amendment rights, even if he or she has given consent to it (*Knecht v. Gillman,* 1973).

The principal reason for the regulation of aversive or other procedures relates to the protection of one's autonomy. The constitutional rights of speech and privacy essentially have to do with the autonomy of the person (Friedman, 1975; Shapiro, 1974; Zlotnik, 1981). After all, the doctrines of consent and choice relate to the expression of a person's autonomy (Turnbull, 1979), and without doubt, autonomy is a fundamental legal and moral value (Shapiro, 1974). Empirically, autonomy is a value in our culture; our constitutional structures evidence this fact. Morally, it is also right that autonomy should be valued as an expression of the value of the individual. The use of behavior modification or other interventions that are intended to change one's personality or that have the potential of doing so, then, are highly suspect. This is because they also can be used to enforce a conformity of behavior; they enable someone to make someone else conform, to be less deviant, or to be more like "us" (Wexler, 1981). It does not follow that enforced conformity ipso facto is a matter of compromised autonomy. But there is a risk, against which the law guards, that enforced conformity can, at its extreme, compromise autonomy. We are all required to be vaccinated, educated, and left-side-of-the-road drivers. We are not, however, compelled to belong to only one political party, have a designated number of children, or worship only one God; indeed, we may belong to no party, have no children, and worship no gods.

It is this very potential for enforcing conformity that gives rise to two other reasons for the regulation of such therapy. It is that the controlled society—the utopia of conformity and sameness (Friedman, 1975)—is inconsistent with such democratic liberty-based values as pluralism (Shapiro, 1974; Wexler, 1981) and is fraught with the potential for abuse. The goal-setting power of the intervention and the power relationship that favors the therapist over the client, especially one who has mental disabilities, are for this reason bona fide concerns of civil libertarians and are of constitutional dimension (Friedman, 1975; President's Commission on Mental Health, 1978).

The due process guarantees of the Fifth and Fourteenth Amendments also shield a client from certain procedures, even when the client has consented to them. This is so because the Constitution prohibits a state from acting in certain ways (substantive due process) or from acting unless various safeguards have been made available (procedural due process) (Friedman, 1975; Schwitzgebel, 1972; Zlotnik, 1981). The essence of the due process objection is that certain types of behavior modification, psychotropic drugs, electroconvulsive shock therapy, and psychotherapy are so intrusive that a client's Fifth Amendment rights are violated.

The Eighth Amendment's ban on cruel and unusual punishment also has come into play as a barrier to certain procedures. If a procedure is sufficiently shocking to the court's conscience, as in the case of the administration of drugs that cause a person to regurgitate (*Knecht v. Gillman,* 1973) or to lose temporarily the capacity to breathe (*Mackey v. Procunier,* 1973), the intervention sometimes has been treated as a cruel and unusual punishment, and the fact that the person may have given consent to the procedure is disregarded under various theories, such as that the consent was not sufficiently informed or voluntary (Friedman, 1975; *Mackey v. Procunier,* 1973; Schwitzgebel, 1972; Zlotnik, 1981). The prohibition of cruel and unusual punishment reflects a concern that certain standards of humaneness (Friedman, 1975; Shapiro, 1974; Wexler, 1981; Zlotnik, 1981) must obtain in a civilized society and must therefore be enforced as a matter of constitutional (fundamental) law. Although the Eighth Amendment speaks explicitly to a deplorable type of punishment (cruel and unusual), the concern that undergirds it seems to relate to decent treatment of individuals. A person's dignity as a human being (Wexler, 1981) seems threatened by techniques developed and perfected on animals, and dehumanization seems too close at hand for both the client and the therapist (Friedman, 1975). The difficulty with applying the Eighth Amendment to aversive interventions on people who are not convicted of crime is that the amendment applies only to punishment for persons convicted of a crime and imprisoned (*Bell v. Wolfish,* 1979; *Ingraham v. Wright,* 1977; *Youngberg v. Romeo,* 1982). Thus, the setting alone—it must be a penal setting before the Eighth Amendment comes into play—seems to control whether the doctrine of cruel and unusual punishment applies as a matter of federal constitutional law. There is some possibility, however, that state constitutional prohibitions against cruel and unusual punishment may be effective.

The doctrine of the "least drastic means" or "least restrictive alternative" likewise partially restrains the state in use of some aversive procedures. Under this doctrine, a state may not act in a way that is unnecessarily restrictive of a person's freedom (assuming that it is warranted in acting at all). The doctrine has been applied to aversive procedures in at least two ways. First, it generally requires that "positive" measures be used before "negative" or "aversive" measures can be used and that, if aversive procedures are used, both positive and aversive procedures be used simultaneously. Second, it requires that the aversive procedures be used only in a descending order of restriction; for example, timeout procedures would be used before seclusion, and temporary restraints would be used before permanent ones. Under the "least drastic means" doctrine, then, the general legality of the procedures is assumed, and only their present use is at issue (Friedman, 1975; *Halderman v. Pennhurst State School and Hospital,* 1977; Shapiro, 1974; Turnbull, 1981; Zlotnik, 1981).

Finally, the doctrine of "unconstitutional conditions" may restrain the use of certain interventions. For example, if a procedure is constitutionally vulnerable and a client consents to it as a condition of acquiring certain governmental benefits, the consent is voidable because the procedure itself is unconstitutional. Thus, if release from lawful confinement in a state facility for psychopathic criminals is conditioned on the inmate's consent to brain surgery that can or likely will impair his or her intellectual processes (and thereby violate the First Amendment), the surgery will be prohibited (*Kaimowitz v. Department of Mental Health,* 1973).

In the case of persons with disabilities, the purposes of legal protection are confounded by the very fact of their disability. On the one hand, the law's regulation of aversive or other procedures is intended to conform intervention to certain constitutional precepts and common values that are expressed in constitutional doctrines. On the other hand, there is a very real claim on the person's part to treatment, rehabilitation, cure, habilitation, and the like. As Shapiro (1974) stated, the task is to ensure that "rigorous restraints are placed on any state efforts toward mental 'demolition' masquerading as 'therapy' " without jeopardizing the "plainly admirable goals of curing or arresting severe mental illness—and thereby achieving some measure of benefit to the victim/patient/prisoner, and some measure of public protection and benefit" (p. 249).

The regulation of aversive intervention therefore advances the value judgment that individuals should have conditional or qualified opportunities to develop themselves to the limits they choose. The person with disabilities, accordingly, should have a generously defined right to escape disabilities, to obtain the "liberty" of well-being (Shapiro, 1974). By insisting on consent and applying such doctrines as "least restrictive means" and "unconstitutional condition," the law enables a person with disabilities, up to a point, to acquire intervention that is designed to exorcise the disability; thus, the law does not prohibit all aversive intervention, only its use under certain conditions, namely, those that are necessary to protect the individual from the overreaching of the state or his or her own faulty judgment, folly, or impulsiveness.

In summary, substantive due process objections may stand in the way of the use of aversive procedures; procedural safeguards would obtain in any event (*Matthews v. Eldridge,* 1976; *Parham v. J.R.,* 1979; and *Secretary of Public Welfare of Pennsylvania v. Institutionalized Juveniles,* 1979). The Eighth Amendment's ban on cruel and unusual punishment used to forbid the intervention (*Kaimowitz v. Department of Mental Health,* 1973; *Mackey v. Procunier,* 1973) but may not now (*Bell v. Wolfish,* 1979). The doctrine of least restrictive alternatives may be a barrier. A concern about excessive control (state-sponsored utopianism) and about therapist-client power relationships may be at work. The decency standard also stands as a formidable interposition; shocking-to-the-conscience decisions, sometimes thinly distinguished (*O'Connor v. Donaldson,* 1975; *Youngberg v. Romeo,* 1982), have laid waste mental health "interventions" that were particularly offensive. The legal picture, then, is complex, but generally legal restraints do not absolutely forbid the use of aversive interventions. But their morality is not settled by the law, nor could it be, since the law's concerns do not necessarily relate to an inquiry into the morality of aversive procedures.

MORAL CRITERIA

There are, however, traditional precepts that can inform us about the morality of aversive procedures. They require us to focus on the value and enhancement of the individual as the ultimate end of all human activity; on religious doctrines that undergird our society; on secular doctrines that have had and continue to have widespread (but not unanimous) acceptance; on our psychological responses and inherent sense (collective and individual) of what is "decent" to do to other people; on how this rich variety of ethical precepts might be generalized; and, in the last resort, on the judgments of these doctrines.

Perils exist in applying these precepts. One is that we will not correctly describe the moral principle that we seek to apply. For example, we might misdefine *utilitarianism,* although the risk of doing that is not nearly so great as that associated with defining Judaic-Christian principles.

Second, there is the risk that we will not correctly apply the moral principle, even assuming that we define it properly. For example, we may agree on the definition of *utilitarianism,* but we may disagree on its meaning for aversive procedures.

Third, there is the risk that we will be thought to be professionally fuzzy-headed, or true believers, or something else, when we seek to apply Judaic-Christian principles to professional interventions. After all, the literature in mental retardation, other than that dealing with Baby Doe, is not replete with references to what professionals should do for or to their clients according to religious precepts.

Fourth, we may incorrectly omit some of the moral principles that we ought to apply; we may be too selective.

Fifth, what one moral principle may condone, another may condemn, and we may find that we have not finally resolved the question of whether an intervention is moral.

Finally, and perhaps most important, there are serious philosophical criticisms (MacIntyre, 1981) of the approach that we take. At its essence, the criticism is that none of the traditional philosophical perspectives are sufficient for the task of determining whether the use of aversive interventions by inherently power-imbedded therapists on persons who have mental disabilities is moral. (By extension, and hence the justification of the aversive procedures paradigm as a model, none of these perspectives is sufficient to determine the morality of any intervention between powerful and powerless people, or at least between a professional and a person who has mental disabilities.)

This last criticism rests on the argument that it is quite dubious whether Kantian or utilitarian principles ever could be relevant to the issues that we raise here, since both Kant and Mill (a utilitarian) require the exercise of reason (albeit with different focus), and, by definition, persons with mental retardation or other mental disabilities are reduced in their capacity to exercise reason. It may not be a sufficient answer to the criticism that persons with mental retardation indeed do have the ability to exercise reason, even when their disabilities are quite extreme (Grossman, 1983), but that rejoinder should be made lest those who have mental retardation be automatically and incorrectly excluded from the family of man to which Kant, Mill, and others speak. We take the other point of the criticism to be valid—that the current moral scene is "disordered" (MacIntyre, 1981). Indeed, as we note later, the social fact of pluralism has rendered a situation in which there is not only a heterogeneity of moral points of view but also one in which these points of view are conceptually immeasurable. That is, as MacIntyre shows, there is no way to assess the relative merits of each philosophical or moral perspective, choose one over the other, or assess their different claims on us. Thus, the question, "What should professionals do, as a moral matter?" is largely unanswerable by resort to any one of the traditional philosophies.

It is for this very reason that in this chapter we have adopted a different approach, one that combines the traditional philosophies, assesses the impact of an intervention by its effects on recipient and therapist, and doggedly maintains throughout a deep concern with the asymmetrical power relationship between those who on the one hand are mentally competent and entrusted by society with the habilitation of people with disabilities and those who on the other are not wholly mentally competent and are given over by society to the care of others. If we can succeed in adopting a "combined approach," where there is a high degree of relevance of concerns about efficacy and power, perhaps we can resolve the basic question: When is a professional intervention moral?

The Individual—An End, Not a Means

Let us agree that we may focus primarily on the needs of the individual recipient in deciding whether to use aversive procedures. Let us also agree that we may consider secondarily the interests of therapists and, next, the public at large. But, keeping our focus on the individual recipient, we are still faced with a troublesome question: What *is* in the best interests of the individual? This question can be answered by considering what aversive intervention means from the recipient's perspective.

First, aversive intervention is the infliction of pain upon someone by someone else, with pain being the *intended* result of the action. This definition is remarkably close to the dictionary definition of the word *cruel:* disposed to giving pain. Whether the purpose of inflicting pain is malicious or benevolent is beside the point; the *conscious awareness* by the therapist that an action will result in pain is plausible ground for considering aversive intervention to be no more than a technical term for cruelty. The question then becomes, is cruelty morally justifiable in any circumstances and, in particular, in aversive intervention?

Obviously, Judaic and Christian traditions are consistently opposed to cruelty. Equally obviously, we could carry a prohibition against cruelty absurd conclusion that a doctor is forbidden to give an injection of forbidden to spank a child who tries to run into the path of an oncoming car. A further analysis of what makes cruelty really "cruel" is therefore necessary.

Haille (1981) extensively analyzed the nature of cruelty in the Nazi death camps of World War II. He argued that cruelty does not equate solely with physical pain. Cruelty also "involves the maiming of a person's dignity, the crushing of a person's self-respect" (p. 23). An act of cruelty may or may not inflict physical pain, but it *always* inflicts humiliation. The most insidious of all, says Haille, is institutional cruelty—like slavery or Nazi extermination camps, the kind that over years instills in the victims the idea that humiliation is somehow deserved, that they are inferior. It is the kind of behavior that allows one to blame the victims for their problems and seduces the victims into believing the blame-casters are correct. At the heart of cruelty, according to Haille, is a disparity of power: "Cruelty, then . . . is a kind of power relationship, an imbalance of power wherein the stronger party becomes the victimizer and the weaker one becomes the victim" (p. 25).

According to this view of cruelty, the use of aversive procedures may not be considered cruel when employed to modify the behavior of a person who fully understands and voluntarily consents, as, for example, a smoker who consents to aversive consequences as part of a nonsmoking program.

But what about persons who are neither competent to consent nor cognizant of the purposes of the therapy? Human rights committees and substitute consent aside, from the perspective of the person with limited understanding of the world, aversive intervention is a painful assertion of power by a person who is in a position of superiority. It can be seen to be akin to Haille's institutional cruelty—an especially graphic addition to the many more subtle and cumulative cues that, in the aggregate, establish the person's inferiority.

Can aversive intervention be offset by otherwise kind treatment? Not under Haille's formulation, because kindness is not the opposite of cruelty; kindness is a patronizing maintenance of the imbalance of power. The opposite of cruelty is not kindness, but respect. Haille arrived at this conclusion after studying the village of LeChambon, a tiny French Hugeunot community near the Swiss border whose residents smuggled approximately 6,000 Jewish children out of the reach of the Nazis. They did so not out of kindness, but out of conviction that everyone "was like Jesus, had God in him f God Himself" (p. 27). We are reminded of ative: that all individuals are to be treated as eans. And we are reminded of a command to them treat us in similar circumstances.

sy answers to whether aversive intervention is he recipient does help provide an answer. For *tendent v. Saikewicz* (1977) tried to take the mining whether or not Saikewicz, a man with severe mental retardation who was dying of cancer, should be given life-prolonging chemotherapy. After noting that Saikewicz could not understand the purpose of the treatment and that it would only frighten him and cause him pain, the highest court of Massachusetts concluded that he should not be given the treatment.

> The decision in cases such as this should be that which would be made by the incompetent person, if that person were competent, but taking into account the present and future incompetency of the individual as one of the factors which would necessarily enter into the decision-making process of the competent person. (p. 431)

Such convoluted logic can be interpreted as a thinly disguised rationale for a decision already made, namely, not to treat a person with a disability solely because he or she has a disability. Nonetheless, as applied to aversive procedures, the *Saikewicz* logic would mean that we must always consider whether incompetent persons would refuse the treatment if they were competent to make that decision and could take into account the fact that they are not. Would they regard the treatment as a cruel assertion of their inferior status? If so, aversive therapy is morally unacceptable because it is cruelty.

But the *Saikewicz* case has a different aspect, too: Is it "respectful" to leave a person in a circumstance of self-injury simply because it is morally "disrespectful" for others deliberately to inflict pain? Many people would think this is another form of cruelty: injury without benefit. It seems there is a double bind. On the one hand, we are in danger of perpetuating persons in a state of self-inflicting pain, of maintaining a level of functioning below their potential, or of intruding upon them because of their behavior. On the other hand, by applying aversive procedures we are in danger of creating or exacerbating cruelty, establishing an imbalance of power, and consequently destroying the human dignity of persons both in their own eyes and in the eyes of the therapist and others. The likelihood that aversive intervention will be regarded as nothing more than cruelty seems at least as great as its being regarded as respectful (useful in effecting an improvement). Still, without it we may be doing nothing to help a person, assuming aversive intervention works. Either way, we seem to violate the tenet of respect. Is there any way out? Perhaps so, if we are able to apply various doctrines to our problem.

Religious Doctrines

Christian Doctrine   The Christian ideal is to enable persons to be or act more like God. This ideal is best thought of in terms of love between persons. Thus we have such Christian precepts as "Love your neighbor as yourself" and "Do unto others as you would have them do unto you" (Luke, 6:31; Matthew, 7:12). These are the linchpins of the doctrine of reciprocity. Applying these precepts to the issue of aversive intervention requires that we empathize with the recipient, assessing whether in similar circumstances this is how we ourselves would wish to be treated and whether this is an act that enhances our likeness to God, our ability to be more loving.

What does it mean to be more like God? If it means to be more loving (as traditional doctrine suggests), the question must be whether any intervention increases a person's capacity for giving and receiving love. No research data or commentary address the power of aversive procedures to affect this capacity. Accordingly, no ground exists for assessing the rightness of aversive intervention by this standard.

The Christian doctrine of reciprocity is not unlike a contemporary doctrine formulated by Allen and Allen (1979), called the doctrine of empathetic reciprocity. That doctrine teaches that we should see in others the same needs to be loved, fulfilled, and respected as we see in ourselves. This emphasizes the humanness of the individual as reflected in the basic needs of human beings. Aversive procedures, therefore, must be examined in terms of their reflection of humanness and in terms of their fulfilling human needs. Does aversive intervention advance our capacities—as its recipients *and* as its administrators—for love, fulfillment, and respect? If the data were more informative, we might know. Unknowing, we can only guess. Empathetic reciprocity carries us no farther along in finding an answer, at this point, than Christian reciprocity.

Judaism Traditional Judaism requires that we provide treatment that fulfills the humanness of the individual and that, in the teachings of Rabbi Hillel, we shall not do to others anything we would resist their doing to us (the reciprocity doctrine in the negative). It also requires consideration of one's enjoyment of life as well as how much one learns. It prohibits treating individuals like animals. Arguably, it forbids techniques that are based solely on animal research. It also prohibits intrusive interventions (e.g., electric shock) unless direct and sustained results can be achieved.

What does "humanness" mean? If humanness means we should seek the enhancement of one's and others' lives by increasing our and their capacities for enjoying life and for learning, then aversive intervention is right only if it has results that advance these goals. But if humanness means being more like the "normal" person than not, then an intervention that eliminates severely self-injurious behavior (head banging) is permissible, because such behavior clearly is aberrant. But what about behavior that is only moderately or mildly self-injurious (pica or nail biting)? For it, aversive intervention becomes increasingly debatable; "normal" behavior has so many characteristics that defining the norm is nearly impossible as well as abuse-prone. Of course, Judaism would approve of aversive intervention only if it produces direct and sustained benefits. Does aversive intervention do that? The efficacy data, as we have seen, are not convincing that the long-term effects are durable, generalizable, and free of debilitating side effects.

Religious or related tenets may not satisfactorily solve the problems raised by interventions with people who already are vulnerable. But they may show us where our actions overstep the boundaries of acceptability. The use of shock for head banging may conform to doctrines of reciprocity and humanness; shock for nail biting may not. The doctrine of reciprocity may permit some aversive procedures for some behaviors, but not for all. Or, it may be intolerant of all such procedures, because no one would want to administer them or be subjected to them, even when they are administered with good motive. Such results seem more instinctively grounded than rationally derived or data-based. They are, nonetheless, defensible. Reciprocity does not rule out instinct. Judaism seems less tolerant of aversive intervention than Christian doctrine: A technique developed from animal research that is of dubious efficacy hardly tends to promote a person's humanness or enjoyment of life or to be sustainable (i.e., generalizable and durable).

Secular Doctrines

Categorical Imperative   Among the secular doctrines that we might apply is Kant's Categorical Imperative. Kant describes the Categorical Imperative as the supreme principle or law of morality that a good person must follow. A moral principle is valid only if it is rational, that is, if it can be applied to all rational beings without contradiction (Albert, Denise, & Peterfreund, 1953). Thus, nondichotomous and equal treatment of "rational" people must be the rule. Would we want for ourselves the same action we would want for persons with disabilities? Or do we escape answering the question by regarding these persons as nonrational? If self-injurious behavior is not the result of rational processes, we need not overly concern ourselves with the Categorical Imperative and Kant.

If, however, self-injurious behavior is the result of a rational process, as learning theory teaches, then we must confront the Categorical Imperative. In doing so, we must ask about the validity of a moral principle that says that all self-injurious behavior in all people may be corrected by aversive means, with or without the consent of the recipient. In applying the Categorical Imperative, our decisions must be so consistent that a rational person wo~~ upon and approve our action for *all* persons. The ~~~ persons with disabilities thus must be se including, for example, the alcoholic.

Utilitarianism   By contrast, utilitaria greatest happiness of the maximum numb 1957). To do this, we must know what rep happiness, in society. Applied utilitarianism political, and personal impact of our actions society. Does aversive intervention produce n people than fewer? If so, it is right under u

intervention may well benefit some people if it enables them to protect themselves from self-harm or to control others who might harm them. Do more people benefit according to these criteria?

Leaving aside for the moment the data on benefit from aversive procedures, consider the competent person (i.e., one who does not have mental disabilities but who effectively objects to the therapy). Assume that the person not only has mental competency to consent or object, but also displays behavior that is self-injurious (substance abuse) and potentially damaging to others (e.g., family or the public).

Shapiro (1974) pointed out that, from the perspective of classical utilitarian ethics, it may be preferable to override a competent person's objection to aversive procedures so that the person can be made well (or better). There is a short-term denial of autonomy in order to achieve a long-term increase in autonomy; the person thus becomes more functional and, in a sense, freer. The utilitarian principle would favor treatment and freedom from disability because the result would be greater functionality, greater autonomy, and greater happiness, with resulting increased productivity. These are the positive externalities that justify the intervention. That result benefits not only the previously disabled person but also those who otherwise would be charged for his care. Thus, the state's parens patriae interests are well served, and there is benefit to family and others, including the public, who are charged with care of the person. Finally, certain negative externalities are avoided by intervention, such as harm to self and others and the cost of care.

Yet Shapiro disagrees with reaching this result on utilitarian grounds alone, because it may be "unjust" to require a person, concededly competent to make decisions on his or her own behalf, to submit to changes in his or her mental functions or behaviors when there are not serious "negative externalities" other than the cost of care (and possibly support of the person's dependents) that result from not treating the person (Shapiro, 1974).

The rule-utilitarian view requires that the rightness of an act is not to be judged by its own consequences but by the consequences of adopting the rule under which the particular act falls (Shapiro, 1974). Rule-utilitarianism seeks to maximize benefits: Right actions are those that are optimal for the society of which the person performing the act is a member, where "optimal" refers to maximizing net benefit or utility (Brandt, 1983). The focus is on net benefit: The act is right if, on balance, it does more good than not for the person on whom it is performed as well as for all others. Although Shapiro ῭es not seem to make it clear that the net benefit test of an action should take ῭account the interests of people other than the person with disabilities, it is ῭t that everyone's interests are to be considered in determining net ῭randt, 1983).

῭under the rule-utilitarian approach, the issue is not whether a ῭on, given a particular intervention, improves or is cured as a ῭res to which he or she objected. Instead, it is whether enforced procedures always should be imposed over the objection of all people who are competent to give or withhold consent because intervention will improve them and help others (''positive externalities'') without causing too much harm to them or others (''negative externalities''). In a sense, says Shapiro, ''justice'' may require intervention because of the likelihood that the procedures will have net benefit.

Shapiro's objection to a treatment-in-spite-of-objection rule is that it would be hard to verify that intervention over objection will produce more ''good'' than ''evil.'' This very objection implicates the efficacy studies. For him, the decisive factor is whether a policy of societally institutionalized coerced intervention in spite of an objection would ''tend to erode values of personal autonomy, and to generate over-reaching by the state in forcing therapies over competent protest'' (p. 287). Granting that there may not be such adverse consequences, however, Shapiro distinguishes between ''effective'' and ''effective but not intrusive'' procedures. He clearly favors effective but relatively unintrusive procedures, if intervention is to be imposed over a competent person's objection. The utilitarian rule, then, is qualified by the ''least drastic means'' test; the power of the state to coerce is limited by the constitutional principle of ''least restrictive alternative.'' Thus, for Shapiro the legal concerns with therapy are posited on utilitarian grounds, as qualified by the ''least restrictive alternative'' rule.

Another form of utilitarianism is apposite. Act-utilitarianism holds that a particular act is right if and only if the actor could have performed no other act at that time that definitely or probably would have had better consequences than the one he or she performed, given what the actor knew at that time about the acts he or she could have performed (Brandt, 1983). Act-utilitarianism thus assesses the rightness of aversive procedures by measuring their efficacy against the efficacy of any other intervention or of no intervention, where ''better consequences'' refers to consequences for the person with a disability and for others that flow from the act as well as from other possible acts of intervention or nonintervention. If aversive intervention would be ''better'' for the person (in terms of preventing an undesirable behavior without creating new ones equally or more undesirable) and for others than any other intervention (e.g., restraint, seclusion, or DRO), then aversive intervention would be right under act-utilitarianism. As is true of rule-utilitarianism, then, act-utilitarianism implicates the efficacy of aversive procedures compared to other procedures' efficacy.

Utilitarianism therefore does not unconditionally sanction all aversive intervention. Indeed, if aversive intervention does more harm to the recipient, to the therapist, or to others than it does good, it does not pass muster under utilitarianism.

Aristotelianism   A third secular doctrine is the Aristotelian notion that everyone acts for some purpose (all behavior is purposeful) and that one achieves proper excellence when one's purpose—one's activity—is perfectly done. Under Aristotelian doctrines, happiness depends on the actualization of our distinctively human function of reasoning, that is, our rationality (Albert et al., 1953). In appraising the use of aversive procedures, the increase of the recipient's rational capacities should be the guide. Does aversive intervention increase the capacities of recipients to attain higher intellectual functioning? Does it decrease the obstacles to higher intellectual functioning? Does it increase a person's autonomy? If so, it is moral under Aristotelian principles.

Appeal to General Formulations of Morality

Up to now we have focused on the establishment *by individuals* of standards of morality as applied to aversive procedures and persons with disabilities. How might society as a whole establish such standards? One approach is to determine the standards that would be established by a "reasonable person." This requires, first, that we identify the characteristics that indicate reasonableness in a person. Our task, then, would be to discover why a community of such reasonable persons establishes its particular standard of decency.

A second approach to developing a standard of decency would be to survey a cross section of society as to what constitutes moral treatment. Moral decisions about the treatment of persons with disabilites would be based on the decisions' congruence with the standards that are established thereby.

A third approach would be to have professional organizations—such as the American Association on Mental Deficiency (AAMD), The Association for Persons with Severe Handicaps (TASH), and the Council for Exceptional Children (CEC)—and advocacy organizations such as the Association for Retarded Citizens/United States (ARC/US), collaborate on establishing standards of morality for the treatment of persons with handicaps. The AAMD position paper, "Use of Physical, Psychological, and Psycho-Pharmacological Procedures to Behaviors of Mentally Retarded Persons" (1973–1975) condones the use of aversive intervention only in connection with behavior-building therapies, only with careful monitoring, and only subject to elaborate procedural safeguards. AAMD also asks the practitioner to consider the doctrine of empathy: whether one would agree to identical treatment for oneself. This seems to be a secular formulation (Allen & Allen, 1979) of the Christian doctrine of reciprocity. TASH's (1984) position is wholly opposed to such therapies. CEC does not deal with the matter directly. The American Psychological Association Commission (1978) is not opposed to such therapy provided certain preconditions are met. The recent ARC/US position paper on "Behavior Management" (1984) imposes limits on the use of aversive therapy, similar to the AAMD stance, and posits that aversive therapy, along with all other behavioral therapies, must be grounded on "humanistic" and "caring" applications that seek the "ultimate goal of growth and habilitation." A resolution of delegates to the 1985 ARC national convention, however, called for a halt to those aversive practices that, among other things, inflict pain, and required a revision of its 1984 position. In brief, the use of aversive intervention is not regarded as wrong in the views of some of these organizations.

Generalizability of Moral Precepts

A question exists whether ethics are or should be role-differentiated. Various commentators have argued in favor of each position (Ryan, 1975). These arguments have interesting implications when applied to aversive intervention. It would bode ill to overlook the implications; by the same token, it is prudent to look critically at the generalizability of these precepts as they apply to such intervention.

Ethical Pluralism If ethics are role-differentiated, the behavior of clinicians who use aversive intervention should be judged, so the argument goes, only by the discipline of the clinicians themselves. Thus, the same type of intervention could be morally right in one setting and simultaneously wrong in another. Likewise, what one professional may do could be morally wrong for a person in a different profession. What the clinical psychologist working with convicted psychopaths may do, the clinical psychologist working with voluntarily admitted mental patients perhaps might not; what the clinical psychologist working with institutional residents who have severe retardation may do, the community-based special educator working with students who have severe retardation may not. The results—morality and practices that vary according to the setting in which the clinician works or according to the clinician's profession—make it difficult to conclude that aversive procedures are moral or not in any nearly absolute sense. Situational ethics prevail. How a person is treated morally depends only on where the person is and by whom he or she is served. This, of course, is the situation that now exists, as Guess et al. (1985) have shown.

This is not an unexpected result. The cultural, ethnic, and political pluralism that characterizes our society is reflected in ethical pluralism, which was implicitly demonstrated in our previous discussion of moral criteria. In such a milieu, it is difficult to generalize moral precepts, to apply a consistent standard of right or wrong to aversive procedures.

Causalism The equivocation that results from such pluralism seems exacerbated by the application of "causalism" to aversive procedures. As Ryan (1975) indicates, causalism asks a simple question in determining whether any behavior is morally right or wrong. The question is: "What harm does the behavior cause?" Ryan contends that such a question promotes the general welfare but also forbids any attempt to set absolute boundaries on what society may demand of its members. Its connection with the sovereignty of the individual, he states, is one of simple hostility; thus, abortion may or may not be allowed, depending on whether the mother is pregnant with a defective, normal, or gifted child—if with a defective or normal child, abortion is allowable, but if with a genius, abortion is forbidden. One may act consistently with causalism only if the result of the action will not impinge on general welfare interests. Since it is in the general interest to have a Bach born but not especially in the general interest to have a defective or ordinary child born, the mother is free to abort in some but not all cases. By the same token, causalism does not indicate the equal distribution of medical treatment to all people; the "defective newborn" may be allowed to die because no general societal welfare is promoted by its life. Causalism thus is highly nonpermissive, states Ryan; the individual becomes a means, not an end, of public policy and the rightness or wrongness of public and private action must, it seems, be judged on the sole basis of its contribution to the general welfare. Therefore, aversive intervention is moral or not only in light of its potential to contribute to the general welfare, not primarily or even necessarily to the welfare of the individual on whom it is practiced. If more people are helped than hurt by aversive intervention, and if among those people we include all those who have any stake in aversive therapy, then aversive therapy is morally permissible as a coercive treatment.

But what does it mean to be helped or hurt, to advance the general welfare, when data show that aversive procedures are of questionable efficacy? As to the recipient, the procedures may change some behaviors without creating new objectionable ones. But they will not always and inevitably do so. Nor will their effects necessarily be widespread or long-lasting. What about the therapists and those who actively condone the procedures (e.g., the therapists' supervisors) or tolerate them (e.g., policy makers)? What are the effects on them? There is reason to believe that the effects not only may well be adverse, but also may show that power-relationships rest not solely on respect but on less altruistic instincts. The ethics of aversive procedures are very doubtful under causalism.

"Rights" Perspective The strongly utilitarian result of causalism poses difficult problems if the morality of aversive procedures is judged from a rights perspective. Is it the right of the person with disabilities to be free from compulsory aversive intervention, even granted that constitutional safeguards have been satisfied? Or is it the right of the person to be free of the disability, the Constitution notwithstanding? The answer is by no means clear.

Nor is the answer any less opaque when the rights of the individual to be treated in particular ways conflict with the rights of other individuals to be free from danger caused by the individual's disability and its behavioral manifestations. What is the general welfare in such a case: to protect the public and the person; to rehabilitate the person; or to both protect and rehabilitate? When rights collide, are there any satisfactory criteria for determining which rights prevail? Is this truly a world without trumps, as Luban (1981) argues? If so, there apparently is no way of defining the rightness or wrongness of aversive intervention according to generalized ethical precepts. The intervention will be right or wrong only as determined by ethical criteria that have little in common with each other. In short, there could be no generalizable ethical precepts, no common denominators by which to tolerate or proscribe aversive procedures.

This conclusion seems highly unsatisfactory. Rights collide all the time; if anything, the rights arguments are escalating and, withal, the inevitability of collision is greater. Yet a constant state of rights warfare is of little profit to most people. There must be superior rights, and their identification perhaps should not rest on the moral views of any given profession, the setting in which aversive intervention is used, or the nature of the recipient or therapist. Without superior rights, all that is assured is a constant cacophony, a permanent inconsistency of practice, unpredictability of law, and, for some of us, the sense that our professions are either misguided or adrift.

The Use of Minima

Several attempts to establish superior rights and, inferentially, moral claims take a "minimalist" approach. To say that John Rawls's (1971) theories of distributive justice are grounded in part on a "minimalist" theory is a vast oversimplification. But Rawls does argue that the minimum wants or needs of every person establish the rightness or wrongness of government policy. By the same token, the most thoughtful legal theory derived from Rawls rests not on an equal-protection basis but on a "minimum protection" basis; Frank Michelman's (1969) interpretation of Rawls and his application of Rawls to constitutional positivism regards the Constitution as establishing minimum rights that government must satisfy. Finally, Caws (1978) approaches the solution of ethical dilemmas from the minimalist perspective, asking us to answer these questions: What would we least like to lose if we had to sacrifice some aspects of our lives; what would we most want to have if we could enforce a claim to those desiderata; what would our "ideal" world be if we could design it; and what would we do if we lived in it?

Some may object to applying Rawls to people who have retardation, on the grounds that Rawls apparently does not include such persons in his universe of people who should determine the minimum needs of us all, since retardation disqualifies a person from determining those needs (incompetence disqualifies). This objection can be answered in two ways. First, people who have mental retardation are, by and large, not so intellectually different from people who are not to be automatically excluded from the decision-making population (Grossman, 1983). Second, excluding people with retardation from the decision-making populace simply reinforces their second-class status and assumes that their views on minimal values will only indirectly be taken into account, if at all (by nonretarded people applying the doctrines of reciprocity).

More to the point is the question of whether we would accept aversive intervention as a means to accomplish our goals of having certain minima. Would we tolerate hand slapping, noxious stimuli, or shock therapy as techniques that are morally legitimate for achieving our minima? To answer this question, it may be helpful to revisit the ethical doctrines discussed earlier.

The Role of Efficacy and Moral Principles The reciprocity test, expressed in Christian and Judaic teachings, also is inherent in Kant's Categorical Imperative and contemporary doctrines of empathy. One way of formulating the reciprocity/empathy doctrines is this: What is right is what we want for ourselves and therefore want for others. Indeed, the minimalists tend to take the same approach; if one sets such a high value by certain characteristics of life and living, it may be assumed that one also would equally value those in the lives of other people.

There is yet another way to answer the question of whether we would tolerate aversive intervention as a means to accomplish given ends. It is to base one's decision on the efficacy of aversive procedures. After all, the efficacy test subsumes Judaism (prohibiting intrusive interventions unless direct and sustained results can be achieved thereby), utilitarianism (justifying aversive intervention by whether it advances the greater good of the greater number of people), Aristotelean rationalism (justifying aversive intervention by whether it enhances the rational capacities of people), and causalism (justifying aversive intervention by "no-harm" or "low-harm" criteria). One way of formulating the efficacy/effectiveness standard is this: What is right is what works, for the individual would not want that which does not work.

A combination of these approaches yields interesting results. Under a combined approach, what is right is what we want for ourselves and for others; we want only that which works; and we do not want that which does not work, particularly if the procedure is deliberately painful and imposed on especially vulnerable people. By extension, we do not want to harm others because we ourselves would not want to be harmed; thus, we do not want to harm either the person who administers or the person who receives aversive procedures.

In this formulation of right and wrong, the efficacy of aversive intervention has a major role in determining its rightness, but only as we are willing to apply aversive intervention to ourselves and to others. By this standard, we would conclude that most aversive procedures for most behaviors do not work. Thus they are desirable neither for ourselves nor others. Accordingly they are morally wrong, especially when they are compulsory. Similarly, we also would conclude that aversive procedures for some behaviors do actual harm to the recipient and possibly to the administrator and thus are not what we want for ourselves or others; accordingly they are morally wrong, especially when they are compulsory.

By revisiting the "rights" approach—the person with a disability has two potentially conflicting rights, namely the right to be cured of the disability and the right to be treated with respect—one reaches the same result as is reached under the efficacy-reciprocity test. The intervention that both cures (or improves) and treats with respect (i.e., does not unnecessarily maim the person's behavior or psyche) is morally right, and any other intervention is wrong.

These three approaches seem to oblige one to conclude that only some aversive intervention is right, namely that which is: 1) maximally efficacious on balance (does more good than harm in that it has more benefit than not in direct and collateral effects), 2) minimally harmful to the recipient, therapist, and others, and 3) maximally related to both of the two rights, weighted together. By this standard, very little, if any, aversive intervention is morally right, particularly when it is coerced.

Even this result, however, is tentative because it does not yet take into account the minimalist approach, which is directly implicated by the rights approach. One must recognize that the minimalist approach is highly subjective; it gives great leeway to individual preferences. To be a basis for an ethic, it seems that it must generalize, that is, be acceptable across a broad range of people. This suggests that the views of professional and advocacy organizations are relevant; those views generally do not absolutely condone aversive therapy. The impetus to generalization in minimalism in turn further suggests not only that general public opinion should determine what minima undergird rights and fix the moral rightness or wrongness of aversive intervention, but also that the determination of public opinion should be informed concerning aversive procedures.

For public opinion to be informed, it must be educated concerning the techniques of aversive intervention, the efficacy of such intervention for the recipient, its impact on the therapist, and personal experience. That is, both abstract knowledge (concerning its nature, efficacy, and impact) and concrete knowledge are requisite to informed opinion. Accordingly, those who determine the morality of aversive intervention should directly experience it themselves; they should put themselves in the position of the recipient and, having experienced aversive therapy, then judge its rightness or wrongness on the basis of personal experience as well as on the basis of abstract knowledge.

One way to secure such an informed public opinion is to allow someone else to set goals for us and, because people with disabilities are different from nondisabled people, require that the goal setters be of the same as well as of different cultures, have different values, and be of different socioeconomic, ethnic, or other backgrounds than us. Next, it requires that those people—those who are like and unlike us—set goals for us that we do not choose as well as goals that we do choose for ourselves. It also allows others to enforce those goals by means of aversive procedures, that is, by deliberately painful means.

Accordingly, other people should be allowed to determine for us where we shall live, with whom, how, and for how long; whether we shall work, for how much time and money, when, where, at what, and for how long; whether we may eat, drink, smoke, wear, or say certain things, and so forth. Then others should be allowed to slap us, spray us with noxious sauces, or shock us with electricity if we do what we choose but what others forbid. Finally, we should allow others to treat us this way persistently, that is, for as long as we do not behave in the ways they specify, and we should also arrange it that those who hit, spray, and shock us shall also be our caregivers, teachers, counselors, therapists, and advocates.

We should experience, directly and vicariously, a hand slap for biting our nails, laughing too loudly, cursing, or engaging in such mildly self-injurious behavior as drinking socially, smoking, or not exercising. We should experience Tobasco sauce cocktails for overeating, crash diets, or unbalanced nutrition. We should experience the electric shock on our arms, backs, abdomen, or necks for such potentially serious self-injurious behavior as speeding or driving under the influence of alcohol or drugs, using heroin or other addictive nonprescription drugs, alcoholism, or masochism as a sexual preference. Only then will we begin to answer for ourselves, and thus for others, whether aversive therapy is right or wrong.

We also should be obliged to administer these procedures to those people for whom we have volunteered to provide care (our patients, clients, or even our children), for the same behaviors that would subject us to aversive procedures at others' hands. As we experience the giving and receiving of these procedures, we also should be constantly reminded there is no assurance that they will be efficacious, or that they will have a long-term effect (be durable), or help us in other ways (be generalizable). And we should bear in mind that the procedures may cause undesirable direct and collateral side effects and turn our therapists into even more insensitive people, apt to use aversive procedures on us to a greater extent than at present and for other behaviors than those targeted for extinction.

And we should experience and know all of this because this is what therapists do to, for, or with persons who have disabilities: They determine what they should do, and they correct noncompliance accordingly, often by painful means.

CONCLUSION

Does aversive intervention habilitate persons who have disabilities? Its short-term effects sometimes are powerful, but its long-term ones are not convincingly durable, generalizable, or free of debilitating collateral effects. Nor were they intended to be.

Does aversive intervention dehumanize the person? Arguably, it does. Surely the behavioral model depicts the human being as a set of component parts or behaviors. The parts, in a sense, may be regarded as greater than the whole. Does scientific objectivity—the trained detachment and uninvolved relationship with the person—outweigh a client-therapist bond that can ameliorate dehumanizing treatment? There is that likelihood, and it is great. Does aversive intervention have adverse effects on the therapist? There is that possibility, too.

Are definitions of deviancy—are the behaviors that intervention seeks to change—sufficiently equalized that "normal" and "disabled" persons are treated equally? There seems to be some doubt about this and thus concern that a double standard exists ("morality for you, but not for me").

Have persons with disabilities been treated respectfully in that legal concerns do not present themselves and the interests of the person in being helped without being victimized are satisfied? Again, there is doubt about this.

Does the doctrine of reciprocity (both the Christian and the secular versions, i.e., the Categorical Imperative and the doctrines of empathetic reciprocity) tolerate aversive intervention? With the exception of a limited number of procedures targeted for only a few behaviors, it does not. Does the efficacy test, which subsumes a variety of definitions of morality (particularly Judaism, Aristotelianism, utilitarianism, and causalism), justify aversive intervention? The answer generally is negative, but it is not always so for all behaviors. Do the "rights" and "minimalist" doctrines tolerate aversive intervention? They might, but just minimally, and then only for some procedures for some behaviors. Would a majority of nondisabled people tolerate goal setting by others different from or like themselves and the enforcement of goals, related to everyday behaviors, that can be self-injurious, by aversive means, that is, by the deliberate infliction of pain? That is most debatable.

Is aversive intervention moral? Applying the principles to our paradigm and relying on our knowledge of efficacy of aversive procedures, we conclude that, for the largest number of procedures (e.g., those similar to the first and second in our paradigm, viz., slapping and administering a noxious drink) and most behaviors (e.g., those similar to mild to moderate self-injury, viz., nail biting and pica), aversive intervention, as we defined it, is not moral, particularly when it is coerced. Indeed, even for severe behavior (head banging), aversive intervention (particularly in its more extreme forms) also is not moral under some, but not all, of the principles we applied, although we regard it as immoral under our "combined approach."

Our arguments have depended mightily on what is known about the efficacy of aversive intervention. The research teaches that much of aversive intervention's efficacy is doubtful. We have applied principles to facts, believing that solid facts will defensibly undergird conclusions.

But let us change the basis for the conclusions by assuming a different factual context. What if the research showed that aversive intervention had unquestionable and widespread benefits for the person who has disabilities in that it produced durable and generalizable behaviors, without substantial negative side effects on the client? And what if there were no doubts about any negative effects it might have on therapists, or about its dichotomous use? Would we then be willing to say that aversive intervention is morally right? It is possible, but not desirable, as we will argue. Just because something works, it does not necessarily follow that its use is moral.

Assume that one can satisfy the traditional legal concerns (equal protection, due process, least restriction, etc.). An issue then is whether the *non*use of efficacious aversion intervention is respectful: Does its *non*use leave a person in a worse condition than its use? A possible answer, at least in the case of serious self-injury, is "yes." Conversely, does its use leave a person in a better condition than its nonuse? Only in some respects, but not generally or for a long time. Thus, its use may be viewed as short-term moral and long-term not moral. But the intervention must be efficacious, as we have defined efficacy. Again, the interventions have difficulty passing moral muster.

Another issue is whether various doctrines of reciprocity (Christian, Kantian, or more modern ones) morally justify efficacious aversive intervention. They may very well do just that: Many of us might be willing to undergo specific, time-limited pain for long-term gain.

Do rights and minimalist doctrines tolerate efficacious aversive intervention? It may well be that they do: The "right" to "development" (or "cure") coincides with many and powerful psychological forces, and minimalist approaches may impel us to accept treatment and cure in exchange for aversive procedures.

Would most of us allow others to set goals for us and to enforce those goals by aversive intervention? That is debatable, although some of us allow some of it as a matter of course (in our children's education, and in our employment and social lives).

If aversive intervention worked, or at least worked much better than it does, would it be moral? Most likely, for all of the above reasons.

There is yet another reason one might conclude that efficacious aversive intervention would be right. Almost no one familiar with gross aberrations in persons with disabilities—fecal eating, head banging, and the like—is content to tolerate them. Our very instincts are to protect the person from the consequences of his or her disability and to "re-form" the person so he or she will have less of a disability, be less offensive to our sense of what a human being should be, and be less deviant. These instincts may impel us to intervene by nearly any *useful* means at our disposal. If aversive intervention is even temporarily or minimally efficacious, we are sorely tempted to use it for these beneficent (as well as for other less altruistic) reasons. And we do that both out of a complex psychological sense about what we want to do to help others as well as to be relieved, for our own sakes, of the effects of such disquieting behavior.

Where we oftentimes have fallen short is when we do those things that are not generally useful, such as using most aversive procedures, because of our frustration with the failure of other procedures to bring about the results we want. Nothing is so apt to make us behave in wrong ways in attempting to do right things for persons with disabilities as our realization that we have not yet cured a problem. The conspiracy of success (Haring, 1975), coupled with our own altruism, paradoxically can make us act sometimes in wrong ways, to use procedures that, according to what we know about them and judged by several moral criteria, are wrong. The good person can act in wrong ways, for good reasons.

There is no easy antidote. It is supremely unhelpful to say that the behavior of some human beings is so imperfectly understood that, in some cases, we will fail to correct it and cure them. That kind of advice does not comfort us in the sense of strengthening our resolve to understand or in the sense of giving us solace when we reach the bottom of our bag of teaching procedures.

And it also is unprofitable to say that we should stop trying because we have not yet succeeded. To say that we will continue to fail because we have always failed in the past would justify inaction. Perhaps, and this is indeed paradoxical, we feel we must continue to do research that is based on arguably immoral actions (e.g., aversive procedures) so that some time hence we will know more and be able to do better, to be able to act more morally. If today's immoral behavior might lead to tomorrow's cure, we may think we are morally obliged, by every moral tenet we have examined here, to act immorally.

Yet are we truly obliged to proceed in immoral ways to obtain moral results? Have the ends so justified the means? If so, would it not be preferable to do nothing? Has not the pursuit of moral ends too often excused means that are too immoral to tolerate? We think so, and we believe that the discomfort we experience in recognizing our own limitations—in acknowledging that we have failed, in coming to an uneasy truce with the conspiracy of success and our own frustrated altruism—is the very capacity that will rein us in and prevent us from becoming immoral beings. If intelligence is the capacity simultaneously to tolerate two opposing points of view, perhaps morality includes the capacity to tolerate our own and others' limitations and to restrain, because we have that tolerance, from immoral behavior for moral purposes.

One final observation is warranted. It might be thought that, on balance, we find a very limited use of aversive intervention for a very few behaviors to be moral from some perspectives. That is a conclusion that we resist, for two reasons.

First, other interventions are in therapists' arsenals. They include less intrusive and less morally objectionable aversive interventions (such as seclusion, time out, physical restraint), as well as positive therapies (such as differential reinforcement). If one recalls that it is disrespectful for a professional to do nothing for a person with a disability (i.e., it is wrong for professionals not to intervene at all) and that it is equally wrong for a professional to use aversive interventions (many of which just barely pass moral muster as we have described them and none of which passes muster under our combined approach); and if one further recognizes the possibility that other aversive interventions (seclusion, timeout, physical restraint, or chemical restraint) are also apt to be regarded as immoral, then one must conclude that the only right action is that which uses positive interventions, or, at worst, a combination of positive interventions and those aversive ones that are the most efficacious and the least intended and likely to produce pain. Of course, even this approach tolerates some aversive procedures on moral grounds. But it hedges the tolerance with other requirements.

There is yet a second reason for us to resist the conclusion that aversive intervention is even partially moral. It is that the moral principles we have applied to aversive intervention each result in a minimum passing grade for some types of aversive intervention for some types of behavior, and a failing grade for others. Some people might infer that we therefore would approve all aversive procedures on moral grounds. We ourselves do not accept that inference, and we resist it. Our reason is quite simple. It is that it is not sufficient, we believe, for aversive intervention to receive minimum passing grades. In order to justify the purposeful infliction of pain, the known effects of aversive intervention on the person who has a disability, and the reasonably predictable effects of aversive intervention on therapists and society as a whole, it is necessary for there to be compelling reasons for using aversive procedures in all cases.

Given the inadequate efficacy of aversive interventions, the potential results of aversive intervention for the person with a disability and for others, and the availability of efficacious positive interventions, it is more wrong than right on moral grounds to use aversive procedures. Moral action requires us to use means that are more moral than others, when we can choose to do so. If we elect to use the means that are less moral than others, we ourselves act in less than moral ways. When we elect to use means that are more moral than others, we ourselves act in ways that are more moral than not. We are obliged to persons with disabilities, ourselves, and each other to do just that.

REFERENCES

Albert, E.M., Denise, T.C., & Peterfreund, S.P. (1953). *Great traditions in ethics.* New York: American Book Company.

Allen, D.F., & Allen, V.S. (1979). *Ethical issues in mental retardation.* Nashville, TN: Abingdon Press.

American Association on Mental Deficiency. (1973–1975). *Use of physical, psychological, and psycho-pharmocological procedures to behaviors of mentally retarded persons.* Washington, DC: Author.

American Psychological Association Commission. (1978). *Ethical issues in behavioral modification.* San Francisco: Jossey-Bass.

Association for the Advancement of Behavior Therapy. (1982). The treatment of self-injurious behavior. *Behavior Therapy, 13*(4), 529–554.

Association for Retarded Citizens/United States. (1984). *Position statements on programmatic issues.* Arlington, TX: Author.

Bell v. Wolfish, 441, U.S. 520 (1979).

Brandt, R. (1983). The real and alleged problems of utilitarianism. *The Hastings Center Report, 13*(2), 37–43.

Burt, R.A. (1977). The limits of law in regulating health care decisions. *Hastings Center Report,* December, 29–32.

Caws, P. (1978). On the teaching of ethics in a pluralistic society. *Hastings Center Report, 8*(5), 32–39.

Council for Exceptional Children. (1983). Code of ethics and standards for professional practice. *Exceptional Children, 50*(3), 205–218.

DuBose, E. (1976). Of the parens patriae commitment power and drug treatment of schizophrenia: Do the benefits to the patient justify involuntary treatment. *Minnesota Law Review, 60*(6), 1149–1219.

Friedman, P.R. (1975). Legal regulation of applied behavior analysis in mental institutions and prisons. *Arizona Law Review, 17,* 39–104.

Gelman, S. (1984). Mental hospital drugs, professionalism, and the Constitution. *Georgetown Law Review, 72*(6), 1725–1784.

Goldiamond, I. (1974). Toward a constructional approach to social problems: Ethical and constitutional issues raised by applied behavior analysis. *Behaviorism, 2*(1), 1–84.

Grossman, H. (Ed.). (1983). *Classification in mental retardation.* Washington, DC: American Association on Mental Deficiency.

Guess, D., Helmstetter, E., Turnbull, H., & Knowlton, S. (1985). *Use of aversive procedures with persons who are disabled: An historical review and critical analysis.* Lawrence: University of Kansas, Department of Special Education.

Haille, P. (1981). From cruelty to goodness—The personal voyage of a student of ethics. *The Hastings Center Report, 11*(3), 23–28.

Halderman v. Pennhurst State School and Hospital, 446 F. Supp. 1295 (E.D. Pa. 1977), *aff'd. in part, rev'd. in part,* 612 F. 2d 84 (3d Cir. 1979), *rev'd. and remanded.* 451 U.S. 1 (1981).

Haring, B. (1975). *Manipulation: Ethical boundaries of medical behavioral and genetic manipulation.* Slough, England: St. Paul Publications.

Ingraham v. Wright, 430 U.S. 651 (1977).

Kaimowitz v. Department of Mental Health, No. 73-19434-AW (Cir. Ct. Mich., filed July 10, 1973, *Prison Law Reporter, 2,* 433).

Kemp, D.R. (1983). Assessing human rights committees: A mechanism for protecting the rights of institutionalized mentally retarded persons. *Mental Retardation, 21*(1), 13–16.

Knecht v. Gillman, 488 F. 2d 1136 (8th Cir. 1973).

London, P. (1969). *Behavioral control.* New York: Harper & Row.

Lovaas, O.I. (1965). Building social behavior in autistic children. *Journal of Experimental Research in Personality, 1,* 99–109.

Lovaas, O.I. (1982). Comments on self-destructive behaviors. *Analysis and Intervention in Developmental Disabilities, 2,* 115–124.

Luban, D. (1981). Professional ethics in a world without trumps. *The Hastings Center Report, 11*(3), 38–40.

MacIntyre, A. (1981). *After virtue: A study in study theory.* Notre Dame, IN: University of Notre Dame Press.

Mackey v. Procunier, 477 F. 2d 877 (9th Cir. 1973).

Matson, J., & DiLorenzo, T. (1984). *Punishment and its alternatives: A new perspective for behavior modification.* New York: Springer Publishing Co.

Matthews v. Eldridge, 424 U.S. 319 (1976).

Michelman, F. (1969). Foreword: On protecting the poor through the Fourteenth Amendment. *Harvard Law Review, 83,* 7–59.

Michigan Law Review. (1976). Note: Regulation of electroconvulsive therapy. *Michigan Law Review, 75*(2), 363–412.

Milgram, S. (1974). *Obedience to authority.* New York: Harper & Row.

Mill, J.S. (1957). *Utilitarianism.* New York: Bobbs-Merrill Library of Liberal Arts.

O'Connor v. Donaldson, 422 U.S. 563 (1975).

Parham v. J.R., 442 U.S. 584 (1979).

Plotkin, R. (1978). Limiting the therapeutic orgy: Mental patients' right to refuse treatment. *Northwestern Law Review, 72,* 461–525.

President's Commission on Mental Health. (1978). *Report to the President.* Washington, DC: Author.

Rawls, J. (1971). *A theory of justice.* Cambridge, MA: Harvard University Press.

Rhodes, W.C., & Paul, J.L. (1978). *Emotionally disturbed and deviant children: New views and approaches.* Englewood Cliffs, NJ: Prentice-Hall.

Ryan, A. (1975). Two kinds of morality—causalism or taboo. *The Hastings Center Report, 5,* 5–6.

Schwitzgebel, R. (1972). Limitations on the coercive treatment of offenders. *Criminal Law Bulletin, 4,* 267–320.

Secretary of Public Welfare of Pennsylvania v. Institutionalized Juveniles, 442 U.S. 640 (1979).

Shapiro, M. (1974). Legislating the control of behavior control: Autonomy and the coercive use of organic therapies. *Southern California Law Review, 47,* 237–338.

Smith, S. (1980). Constitutional privacy in psychotherapy. *George Washington Law Review, 49*(1), 1–60.

Southern California Law Review. (1972). Note: Prisoners and mental patients. *Southern California Law Review, 45,* 616–684.

Superintendent v. Saikewicz, 370 N.E. 2d 417 (Mass. 1977).

The Association for Persons with Severe Handicaps. (1984). *Resolution and intrusive interventions.* Seattle: Author.

Turnbull, H.R. (Ed.). (1978). *The consent handbook.* Washington, DC: American Association on Mental Deficiency.

Turnbull, H.R. (1979). Law and the mentally retarded citizen. *Syracuse Law Review, 30,* 1093–1143.

Turnbull, H. (1981). Two legal analysis techniques and public policy analysis. In R. Haskins & J. Gallagher (Eds.), *Models for social policy analysis* (pp. 153–173). Norwood, NJ: Ablex Press.

Wexler, D. (1981). *Mental health law: Major issues.* New York: Plenum Publishing Corp.

Wood, F., & Braaten, S. (1983). Developing guidelines for the use of punishing interventions in the schools. *Exceptional Education Quarterly, 3*(4), 68–75.

Wyatt v. Stickney, 344 F. Supp. 387 (M.D. Ala. 1972), *aff'd. in part, rev'd. in part, sub nom.,* Wyatt v. Aderholt, 503 F. 2d 1305 (5th Cir. 1974).

Youngberg v. Romeo, 457 U.S. 307 (1982).

Zlotnik, D. (1981). First do no harm: Least restrictive alternative analysis and the right of mental patients to refuse treatment. *West Virginia Law Review, 83*(3), 376–448.

Response

AVERSIVE INTERVENTION
GUILTY UNTIL
PROVEN OTHERWISE

William E. MacLean, Jr.

THROUGH THE EFFORTS of influential social scientists in the late 1950s and early 1960s, a number of behavior modification procedures were demonstrated to be effective intervention methods for persons with mental retardation (Thompson, 1977). Programs based on operant conditioning principles offered a way to teach persons with mental retardation fundamental adaptational skills through positive reinforcement. At the same time, operant techniques such as withdrawal of reinforcement and punishment procedures proved effective in altering maladaptive behavior. Despite being heralded as nearly revolutionary in the habilitation of persons with mental retardation, not all behavior modification techniques were greeted with the same level of enthusiasm. Punishment procedures have been the most controversial. Indeed, those punishments that have been described as aversive and typically produce physical pain are considered the most suspect. The concerns raised by Turnbull and his colleagues in the previous chapter are not unique to mental retardation. There was considerable outcry during the early 1970s about the use of aversive procedures with prison populations (Stolz & Associates, 1978). Professional groups such as the American Psychological Association and the Association for Advancement of Behavior Therapy formed special committees to examine the use of aversive procedures with clients, partially in response to the fear that behavior modification methods were being employed for illicit purposes.

It is noteworthy that while Turnbull et al. acknowledge that aversive procedures instigate a great deal of intense discussion, the authors appear to have gotten caught up in that reaction. Their choice of nail biting, pica, and self-injury as potential target behaviors was an attempt, I presume, to provide some continuum for comparison, but the tone of the discussion is such that aversive procedures are presumed guilty until proven otherwise. In that sense, the chapter seems to be more of a treatise against aversive procedures than an essay on a model for analyzing the moral aspects of behavioral and educational interventions.

My comments here focus on three aspects of Turnbull et al.'s discussion. First, I wish to emphasize further the role of society in intervention. Second, I address the importance of efficacy in assessing the ethical status of an intervention. Finally, I consider Turnbull et al.'s discussion of various legal and moral criteria.

INTERVENTION

Any discussion of a particular intervention technique begs the question of why there is a need for intervention. I would ask Turnbull et al. to assume the role of an intervention agent confronted with a self-injurious boy with severe retardation whose self-injury has resulted in several concussions, numerous hospitalizations, and significant visual impairment. While the agent is afraid of what this boy might do to himself, the agent is also mindful of what the child is depriving himself of. That is, the boy's self-injurious behavior interferes with his participation in habilitative programming that might lead to a move from a highly restrictive institutional environment to a community-based group home. Moreover, the agent is aware that intervention professionals are supported by society as legitimators, universe maintainers, and deviance preventers and controllers. Here I am borrowing terms used by Berger and Luckmann (1966) in *The Social Construction of Reality* to point out that just as deviance is defined by society so is the need to intervene. This societal interface is further illustrated by Krasner (1976), who wrote, "The social responsibility of behavior modification includes the placing of one's own contributions in the social context of the times. The behavior modifier is an influencer and is continually influenced" (p. 631). In the case of self-injurious behavior, the societal response is overwhelming and in favor of quick and decisive intervention. It is no small wonder that these forces would lead intervention professionals to utilize powerful techniques such as aversive procedures without first attempting less restrictive alternatives. Such decisions probably occurred in the past, before human rights committees (Griffith, 1983; Griffith & Henning, 1981) and the guidelines proposed by professional organizations (Association for Advancement of Behavior Therapy, 1977; Stolz & Associates, 1978). In my view, the development of these procedural considerations was an important step in bringing society into the decision to intervene with very restrictive methods. In a sense, the burden or tension is moved from the intervention professional back to society, albeit a subset of the population.

EFFICACY

I agree with Turnbull et al. that a central issue in determining whether intervention procedures are ethical relates to the efficacy of an intervention in producing a desired effect. What I want to argue for is the rigorous testing of interventions based on clear theoretical underpinnings. In my opinion we get into considerable trouble as intervention agents by considering too narrow a set of intervention techniques and ignoring the limitations of our methods. In a sense what I am describing is the situation where if the only tool that you have is a hammer then everything begins to look like a nail. There are other examples. One has only to wonder about the dramatic increases in the rate of diagnoses of affective disorders and schizophrenia at a time when pharmacological interventions had been proven effective in ameliorating these disorders (Blum, 1978).

More central to the discussion of Turnbull and his colleagues is our understanding of self-injurious behavior. A fundamental assumption of their position is that self-injurious behavior is a learned phenomenon. While Lovaas and his colleagues (Edelson, Taubman, & Lovaas, 1983) provide data suggesting that self-injurious behavior varies with particular environmental events, this is a far cry from saying that it was learned originally. Moreover, if behavioral interventions based on learning principles are effective in suppressing the behavior, this in no way demonstrates that the behavior was learned to begin with. It could simply be that the intervention overrides the naturally occurring factors that maintain the behavior (Baumeister, 1978). Indeed, there are data that demonstrate an association between pathological neurological conditions and the occurrence of self-injurious behavior (Baumeister, Frye, & Schroeder, 1984). Perhaps two of the best examples of this relationship are seen in people with Lesch-Nyhan and Cornelia de Lange syndromes. It would appear more efficacious for the intervention agent to address these physiological variables directly rather than shock a person or make them inhale ammonia. What I am arguing is that the ethics of intervening are inextricably tied to our understanding of what maintains the behavior that we choose to intervene upon. So one answer to the question "When are intervention decisions for people with severe handicaps ethical?" would be when an intervention agent applies an intervention that has established efficacy in altering the targeted problem.

Obviously, efficacy rests on our determination of what should be. In the case of self-injury, is a little okay? Is suppression satisfactory, or do we require complete elimination of the behavior? How do you determine that the behavior will not recur? What if you merely alter the expression of the behavior? Which collateral effects are tolerable, which are not?

There are no absolute answers to these questions. Each is answered on a case by case basis by those working with a particular person. The answers usually depend upon the nature of the self-injury. The typographies exhibited by persons with mental retardation vary across several important dimensions. Potential lethality is clearly paramount in that our society spurns self-destruction, but we also believe that persons with mental retardation have a right to habilitation. In that case, self-injury that decreases a person's opportunity for habilitation is equally destructive.

COMMENTS ON THE MODEL

Turnbull et al. have proposed a variety of legal and moral criteria for analyzing whether education and behavioral interventions are ethical. In examining the lawfulness of an intervention, consent is obviously an issue, but so are constitutional safeguards such as personal autonomy, guarantees of life, liberty, and property, and bans on cruel and unusual punishment. A further criterion is the doctrine of "least drastic means" or "least restrictive alternative." At issue is the right to treatment or intervention. Turnbull et al. conclude that the law does not prohibit all aversive therapy, only its use under certain conditions. I agree with Turnbull et al. that the lawfulness of an intervention must be considered first, but that additional moral criteria should also be a factor in the decision.

One criterion is the doctrine of reciprocity—what is right is what we want for ourselves and, therefore, want for others. Turnbull et al. discuss this from both religious and secular perspectives. It makes sense that such a doctrine would be important in determining the morality of an intervention. My previous comments regarding the role of society in determining the need to intervene appear consistent with this view.

Another criterion is the efficacy test—what is right is what works. Turnbull et al. argue from several moral perspectives that the efficacy standard is of considerable importance in determining the morality of a particular intervention method.

Up to this point in the model, I agree that these are essential criteria. Where I have difficulty is in the discussion of the minimalist approach. Turnbull et al. maintain that public opinion must be formed and that the best way to do this is to inform the public-at-large about the therapeutic intervention. I have some trouble with this approach, since it sounds like the task is impossible and may not be worth attempting. I do not think this is the case. I believe one of the roles of professional organizations such as the American Association on Mental Deficiency is to provide the societal response to intervention methods. I feel that such decisions must be made on the basis of an intimate understanding of the problem—something that simply will not happen in society as a whole. This is not to say that I think that society is incapable—it is merely a practical matter.

CONCLUDING REMARKS

In summary, Turnbull and his colleagues raise interesting ethical questions regarding intervention generally and especially in the case of aversive procedures. I agree with the authors that we have a tendency to ignore the morality of intervention decisions because we get caught up in fixing things. While there are probably some professionals who view people as a means rather than an end, I do not feel that this is necessarily the case with aversive therapies. I support the view that society is ultimately responsible for defining the need to intervene, given its role in defining deviance.

Turnbull et al.'s discussion of various legal and moral perspectives on intervention is both interesting and enlightening. I wish that the authors had remained at the level of interventions in general and spent less time dealing with aversive therapies per se. The tone of their argument, their concerns, and their conclusions are dated. They are, in a sense, revisiting a previous time with regard to aversive therapies. Most informed, responsible interventionists openly acknowledge the limitations of aversive therapies, the ethical difficulties encountered in their utilization, and that other less aversive methods provide comparable or superior results.

REFERENCES

Association for Advancement of Behavior Therapy. (1977). Ethical issues for human service. *Behavior Therapy, 8,* 763–764.

Baumeister, A.A. (1978). Origins and control of stereotyped movements. In C.E. Meyers (Ed.), *Quality of life in severely and profoundly mentally retarded people: Research foundations for improvement,* pp. 353–384. Washington, DC: American Association on Mental Deficiency.

Baumeister, A.A., Frye, G.D., & Schroeder, S.R. (1984). Neurochemical correlates of self-injurious behavior. In J.A. Mulick & B.L. Mallory (Eds.), *Transitions in mental retardation: Advocacy, technology, and science.* New York: Ablex.

Berger, P.L., & Luckmann, T. (1966). *The social construction of reality. A treatise in the sociology of knowledge.* Garden City, NY: Doubleday & Co.

Blum, J.D. (1978). On changes in psychiatric diagnosis over time. *American Psychologist, 33,* 1017–1031.

Edelson, S.M., Taubman, M.T., & Lovaas, O.I. (1983). Some social contexts of self-destructive behavior. *Journal of Abnormal Child Psychology, 11,* 299–312.

Griffith, R.G. (1983). The administrative issues: An ethical and legal perspective. In S. Axelrod & J. Apsche (Eds.), *The effects of punishment on human behavior* (pp. 317–338). New York: Academic Press.

Griffith, R.G., & Henning, D.B. (1981). What is a human rights committee? *Mental Retardation, 19,* 61–63.

Krasner, L. (1976). Behavior modification: Ethical issues and future trends. In H. Leitenberg (Ed.), *Handbook of behavior modification and behavior therapy* (pp. 627–649). Englewood Cliffs, NJ: Prentice-Hall.

Stolz, S.B., & Associates. (1978). *Ethical issues in behavior modification.* San Francisco: Jossey-Bass.

Thompson, T. (1977). History of treatment and misconceptions concerning the mentally retarded. In T. Thompson & J. Grabowski (Eds.), *Behavior modifications of the mentally retarded* (2d ed.) (pp. 3–15). New York: Oxford University Press.

Chapter 10

FAMILY CARE

TOWARD A
RESPONSIVE SOCIETY

Robert M. Moroney

ABRAMOWICZ AND RICHARDSON (1970), in reviewing 20 of the "more reliable" epidemiological surveys, have concluded that the prevalence of severe mental retardation is somewhere between 3 and 5 per 1,000 population. (Severe mental retardation is defined as persons with IQs of 50 and under.) Conley (1973) has offered age-specific prevalence rates that show slightly higher rates for children than adults. Tizard (1974) and Kushlick (1964) estimated the peak prevalence rate at 3.6 per 1,000 persons aged 15–19. Tizard (1974) suggests that this rate is the best estimate for all persons below 15 years of age, in that severe retardation is almost always present from birth or early infancy. While these rates are more conservative than those proposed by Conley, they have the advantage of being replicated a number of times. Given these rates, we estimate that there are over 560,000 persons with severe retardation in the United States and that over 180,000 of these are children.

Severe retardation usually brings with it a range of physical disorders such as epilepsy, visual, hearing, and speech defects. Abramowicz and Richardson (1970) found that approximately one-half of all persons with severe retardation have at least one additional handicap and that one in four have multiple associated handicaps. Their findings are supported by other studies (Bayley, 1973; Conroy & Derr, 1971; Moncreiff, 1966; Tizard & Grad de Alarcon, 1961).

Based on Kushlick's (1964) surveys, we estimate that 1 in 5 of all persons with severe retardation needs assistance in personal care functions; 1 in 8 has severe behavioral problems; and 1 in 14 is incontinent. With the exception of behavior problems, those under 15 years of age are more likely to have associated handicaps. Children are twice as likely to be incontinent and to need assistance in personal care and four times more likely to be nonambulant. Eighty percent of children with severe retardation are likely to have a physical or behavioral problem, compared to 40% of adults with severe handicaps.

Based on the prevalence rate of 3.6 per 1,000 for this age group, over 44,000 children with severe retardation are nonambulant; 52,000 need assistance in feeding, washing, and dressing; 23,000 are severely incontinent; and almost 26,000 have severe behavioral problems. (It should be noted that these are duplicated counts).

THE REALITY OF FAMILY CARE

Severe mental retardation is not, then, just a measurement of the intelligence level of an individual. For children, it means that someone has to provide care and supervision beyond what "normal" children require. The decision to maintain the child in the family setting seriously affects the family life of the other members.

One of the more critical areas affected is the physical health of the primary caregiver. In their studies, Hewett (1972) and Tizard and Grad de Alacron (1961) found that 14% of the mothers with children with severe retardation were in poor health, 12% were run down, and 60% experienced periods of depression. Holt (1958) found almost one in five mothers exhausted at the time of her study. The presence of a child with severe retardation also means additional household chores. Aldrich, Holliday, Colwell, Johnson, Smith, & Sharpley (1971) reported that 44% of mothers interviewed felt these additional chores were excessive.

These physical demands, coupled with other sources of stress, often resulted in high degrees of social isolation. Holt (1958) found that 66% of families were noticeably isolated. Furthermore, 74% of parents felt that their neighbors objected to the child with handicaps associating with their children. What is even more telling is that in 40% of these families, the parents were never able to go out together. These findings have been supported by other researchers who reported that normal social contacts were extremely limited (Aldrich et al. 1971; Gottleib, 1975; Justice, Bradley, & O'Connor, 1971; Kershaw, 1965; Peck & Stephens, 1960; Tizard & Grad de Alacron, 1961).

A third area of stress is financial. Children with handicaps obviously cost more to raise and care for than nonhandicapped children. The amount of the additional cost, however, remains unknown. Aldrich et al. (1971) found in 44% of families that financial problems associated with the care of a child with retardation adversely affected the family's life-style. In some instances, this meant that parents turned down promotions because it required their leaving communities in which they had support systems and services. In their studies, Dunlap (1976) and Holt (1958) reported that 29% and 27% of parents, respectively, were faced with additional expenses. It was also found that the severity of the retardation is correlated with the amount of the additional expenses.

Finally, the presence of a child with handicaps creates stress in family relationships. Wolfensberger (1967) suggested that the family of a child with retardation is typically faced with three types of crises. The first occurs when the diagnosis is made.

> At a point of great vulnerability, an unexpected event disorganizes the parent's adjustment. . . . The parents realize that the event is rare and that their expectations have to be radically revised, but they know virtually nothing about what the realistic expectations now are. The crucial element here is not retardation at all; it is the demolition of expectations. (p. 34)

The second crisis is described as a value crisis: "Retardation and its manifestations are unacceptable to many persons for a number of reasons. . . . Fear of social [stigma] and abhorrence of physical stigma, censure by in-laws, feelings of guilt or failure, and other essentially subjectively determined anguish may contribute to the value crisis" (p. 35). The third is the reality crisis: "Forces external to and only partially controllable by the parents result in situations that make it impossible, exceedingly difficult, or inadvisable for the retardate to remain integrated in the family or the community" (p. 35).

Researchers have reported that parents of a child with handicaps experience severe strain, often resulting in marital breakdown (Bone, Spain, & Martin, 1972; Farber, 1959, 1960, 1975; Farber & Ryckman, 1965). Parents have been described as both angry and guilty; angry that it has happened to them and guilty that they might be responsible (Cohen, 1962; Reid, 1958). Another researcher speaks of the "chronic sorrow" in parents' lives (Olshansky, 1962). The trauma that brings on bitterness, guilt, and shame, in turn, may contribute to serious emotional problems, such as quarreling, and, in a number of instances, disintegration of family relationships.

These strains are experienced by more than the parents. A number of parents felt that their normal children were experiencing problems (Fowle, 1968; Tew & Laurence, 1973). Some siblings resent their parents paying too much attention to the child with handicaps, and often they are embarrassed when interacting with their peers.

INSTITUTIONAL OR FAMILY CARE?

It is a gross understatement, then, to say that these families are "at risk." The problems and demands that they are experiencing are staggering. For two distinct sets of reasons it would be reasonable to expect that most families with children with severe retardation would seek to institutionalize them.

First, throughout this century, especially the first 60 years, official policy and professional practice have supported institutionalization as the most desirable alternative. Families who did decide on institutionalization were not likely to be stigmatized. In fact, the evidence seems to suggest the opposite. Families who decided to care for their child with retardation felt isolated from the rest of the community.

The second reason relates to the changing expectations and aspirations of women, and an economy that requires women to join the labor force. Caring for a child with retardation runs counter to these shifts. Extrafamilial activities, whether social or recreational, are curtailed, and individual life-styles and self-fulfillment are difficult, if not impossible, to achieve since so much time and attention are given to the family member with handicaps. The wife and mother is especially penalized since it is she who most often becomes the caregiver.

Given these reasons for not maintaining a child with severe retardation in the home and for seeking institutionalization instead, what have been the rates of institutionalization? While the absolute number of persons with retardation living in institutions increased by 50% during the 20-year period 1950–1970, the rates per 100,000 population increased by only 11% (from 89 to 99). Available data (both census and institutional) show that most institutionalized persons below the age of 15 are those with the most severe retardation (California Department of Mental Hygiene, 1975; Scheerenberger, 1976; Tarjan, 1958).

When examined from another perspective, however, these statistics show that 8 of 10 children with severe retardation and slightly more than 2 of 3 persons of all ages with severe retardation are *not* in institutions for persons with mental retardation. These ratios have remained fairly constant from 1950 to 1980. Not all of these persons, of course, are being cared for by their families. A number are in foster care, nursing homes, boarding homes, hostels, or other facilities. Although it is not possible to determine the numbers involved, it is fair to estimate that, at least for children, most live with their families if they are not institutional residents. This suggests that, as of 1980, more than 165,000 children with severe retardation were living with their parents or other relatives.

Most families today either do not seek, or they delay, institutionalization, and those children who are institutionalized are likely to have the most severe handicaps. Comparison studies of families who decided on institutionalization versus families who kept their children at home have revealed significant differences. Hobbs (1964) reported that the institutionalized group of children had a higher incidence of antisocial behavior and were more likely to be from broken homes. Graliker, Koch, & Handerson (1965) found that the institutionalized children had more severe and multiple handicaps and that 68% of their parents showed significant emotional problems requiring professional help. In yet another survey, Wolf and Whitehead (1975) found that 92% of the families choosing institutional care mentioned major disruption of family life as the most important contributing factor. Unfortunately, none of these studies identified how long these families provided care before the decision was made. Still, long-term or permanent institutionalization does not seem to be the norm. When a child is placed, he or she is likely to have severe handicaps, causing problems with behavior or management, leading one researcher to conclude that despite the numerous hardships faced by many families caring for children with retardation at home, the proportion choosing institutional care is small (Tizard, 1974). To what extent are families helped when they are caring for these children?

THE SOCIAL WELFARE RESPONSE TO FAMILY NEED

The response to families has been, at best, mixed; at worst, counterproductive. If policies and programs are categorized by purpose and function, the states have emphasized those that in essence substitute for the family, an emphasis that is expressed in both the scale of social welfare expenditures and the type of services or benefits developed. The reasons are complex, and while the rationale may have changed over time, the net effect has been the same. Social services that are organized to support the family have received lower priority than those that replace the family (Moroney, 1980).

Most policies and programs are "neutral" toward the family. Neutral in this context does not mean that they neither benefit nor harm families, for such is not the case. These policies and programs are neutral in that the family (with the exception of those receiving assistance from Aid to Families with Dependent Children [AFDC]) is ignored. The explicit beneficiary in almost all instances is the individual with handicaps. Existing policies recognize that a person with severe handicaps is not likely to be active in the work force. These individuals are also likely to require medical care and other health-related services, and policies do exist to pay for these for some persons with handicaps. Finally, a network of support services has been developed, in recognition that these persons need social support if the quality of their lives is to be protected. There is little recognition, however, that when family members provide care to the person with handicaps, the *family* is at risk financially, physically, socially, and emotionally.

A second social policy theme is that the preferred way (in terms of scale of expenditures) to meet the needs of persons with handicaps is through financial support. This choice of strategy seems to be based on several assumptions. There is an implicit belief that by providing money to dependent persons, most of their needs will be met; they either have no need for social services, or they will be able to obtain them in the market. Given the level of expenditures for social services, it would appear that the state, through its social policies, anticipates that a percentage, albeit small, of dependent persons will require more than financial assistance, and that services will be provided directly to them.

These conclusions related to social services are supported when the intended beneficiaries of these services are identified. By intent, most social services are targeted for the poor or near poor. Even in the case of Title XX (PL 93-647), a program that allows for services to be provided to the general population through fee schedules, most users are recipients of public assistance or are financially eligible for public assistance. Fundamental to these policies is the affirmation of a dual approach to social welfare, which approves the notion of a private system for the nonpoor and a public system for the poor. Although most critics of separate systems emphasize the negative and even harmful effects experienced by the poor (e.g., the arbitrariness of the system and its accompanying stigmatization), few critics argue that this dual approach has penalized the nonpoor in a number of ways. A separate system for this group assumes that since they have financial resources, the market will respond and their needs will be met. The private sector's response, however, has been uneven. Some communities have few private services, and others have limited services, resulting in high fees. Furthermore, in its evolution and implementation, Title XX has emerged as the major social service program throughout the country. By purchasing services from social agencies, the state agency guarantees them financial stability. The providers, in turn, tend to gear their services to Title XX clients, thereby excluding many families whose income is too high although their need is great.

Ideological Underpinnings of Social Policy

Why is it that our social policies and programs deemphasize services that would support families with members who have handicaps? Why is it that these policies and programs, even when they do provide supportive services, restrict their availability to one category of families, the poor? The usual response is that, with limited resources, we have to establish priorities. Services should be given to those with the greatest need, and the poor have the greatest need. Although this argument may seem reasonable, it is not the only reason, nor is it even the major reason.

For over a decade, our social welfare system has been under serious attack. Both the Carter and Reagan administrations have charged that this system has harmed rather than helped people; has weakened families rather than strengthened them; has made families dependent rather than independent. They have been critical of the welfare state's expansion that began in the 1930s—a period that can be characterized as proactive. The mood today is for a reactive state—intervention only when absolutely necessary. If this were to occur, the Reagan administration has argued, families would be restored to their earlier position of strength.

This position assumes that families, at some time, were self-sufficient, presumably during a period that preceded the modern welfare state. Furthermore, this conception is tied to historical and contemporary assumptions about community. Before modernization and urbanization, some believe that families were the basic institution of social life—producing their own food, making their own clothing, socializing their children, and providing social and physical care for dependent members, including those with handicaps. During this earlier period, presumably, there was a strong belief in mutual support and community responsibility. If an individual family experienced a problem, other families stepped in. Families willingly gave of their time and resources to help one another. They did so, of course, with the understanding that if they, in turn, needed help, they would receive it.

Critics of the welfare state thus have such conceptions in mind when they speak of the family reassuming its functions. A strong family is synonymous with a self-sufficient family; a strong community is synonymous with interdependent families who cared for each other.

The Reality of Self-Sufficient Families

The strong community of interdependent families was not the norm, however, for all communities. When such communities existed, they were agrarian. Family life in urban areas was quite different. As far back as 17th century England, we find the state establishing in law, with accompanying sanctions, the principle of filial and parental responsibility. The common perception of that time was that families were divesting themselves of their "natural responsibility" to care for their dependent members. By the 19th century, the state decided that even harsher measures were necessary to coerce the family to care for its vulnerable members.

The American colonies adopted the Elizabethan Poor Law, including the family responsibility clauses. By 1836, all states on the Atlantic seaboard, with the exception of New York, expanded family responsibility to include the legal responsibility of grandchildren to care for their grandparents and for siblings to care for each other (Coll, 1973).

The first colonial almshouses and workhouses were established during the middle of the 18th century in urban areas such as Boston, New York, and Philadelphia. By the middle of the 19th century, all major seaboard cities had almshouses. And yet, even with the proliferation of these institutions, it has been estimated that only 9% of families unable to care for themselves were in the almshouses and workhouses. The majority receiving assistance were either: 1) contracted out to another family for a lump sum fixed as low as possible, 2) auctioned or sold to another family, or 3) in some instances provided "out-door relief" in their own homes. Even this latter description is misleading in that most families did everything in their power to stay outside the welfare system with its degrading Benthamite underpinning of personal moral pathology and the notion of less eligibility.

The image of the self-sufficient family living in a supportive community had disappeared in the urban areas by the middle of the 19th century. How realistic are recent administration proposals that families should become more self-sufficient, and that the care of dependents should be an intrafamily or, if necessary, interfamily responsibility? Furthermore, how accurate is the charge that the welfare state brought about these changes in family responsibility and the willingness of families to develop and maintain supportive networks?

The weight of historical evidence runs counter to this charge. "Deteriorating" or "weakened" families existed long before the introduction of the modern welfare state. The situation was endemic during the Poor Law era of the 18th and 19th centuries—an era that attempted through repressive policies to coerce family responsibility. Even then, the pattern that emerged appears to have been a cycle of major or minor economic depressions followed by more and more families seeking help, followed by greater expenditures for social welfare, and not the reverse.

Social Welfare and Dependency

We still face the charge that social welfare measures (especially the social services) foster dependency. If the welfare state is a necessary intervention because of urbanization, modernization, and a more complex society, can its proponents develop mechanisms that will "provide contexts in which people can help each other" (Featherstone, 1979)? Is it possible to establish artificial means (in the sense that the social services are artifacts of the welfare state) to augment rather than harm natural social arrangements? More specifically, what types of social arrangements would emerge if we focus on families with children with severe retardation? To deal with these questions we need to reformulate the rationale for state intervention; and we need to identify a different set of principles upon which to build such a system. The next section attempts to identify what some of these principles might be.

ETHICAL CONSIDERATIONS OF FAMILY CARE

In *A Theory of Justice,* Rawls (1971) introduces us to the notion of a "veil of ignorance," behind which people attempt to devise the rules and principles of society under which they will live. He assumes that people have limited information about the environment beyond that veil: their place in that society, their class or status, and whether their unique characteristics will be assets or liabilities. Given this lack of knowledge, no one is in a position to tailor these principles to his or her advantage. Still, Rawls argues that each person will act rationally, that is, will attempt to maximize his or her own interest. In so doing, each person searches for those principles that are to his or her advantage. The problem is, of course, that each person cannot act rationally in the classical sense of the term. This would require that the person have sufficient information to articulate preferences or utilities, rank order these preferences, analyze options, and then choose a course of action. Rawls, drawing on the work of decision theorists, suggests that, lacking this, the rational person will resort to a different calculus and will analyze alternative principles in terms of how they might negatively affect him or her as an individual, and then choose the alternative that will harm him or her the least. Rawls's rational person will support the "best of the worst scenarios."

While this strategy sounds defensive, Rawls argues that such an approach to deciding upon the rules, procedures, and priorities that will shape a society would result in a just and fair society. Each person would begin with the assumption that he or she might be one of the "unfortunate" when the veil is lifted and would want to have mechanisms in place that would protect the individual. These principles would become the basis for determining what is ethical, that is, what is appropriate behavior or conduct governing social behavior. Furthermore, if that social policy can be viewed as a "statement of social goals and strategy . . . dealing with the relations of people to each other and to their government" (Schottland, 1967), these principles will shape those policies.

If we had incorporated Rawls's formulation in deciding upon social policies for families with children with severe handicaps, our current mix of social institutions, social programs, and social services would be dramatically different. Each of us, standing behind the veil of ignorance, would approach the issue defensively. With our limited knowledge (incidence, prevalence, etiology, etc.), we would assume that our chance for having a child with handicaps would be equal to every other person's chance (the "accident of birth" notion). Faced with this "lottery," we would want to protect ourselves and would probably do so by supporting policies that would guarantee an array of services that would help us care for our child if we became the "unfortunate" when the veil was lifted.

Ethics and Choice

This Rawlsian world would allow for an array of choices, which would, in theory, include the parental decision to abort during pregnancy or to carry to term; to provide care at home or to institutionalize the child; or to provide care for only a limited time.

But what choice do parents have when they are told that their unborn child has severe handicaps, and further, that if they decide to carry to term, few supportive services will be available to help them care for the child?

Recently, during hearings on the abortion issue, the U.S. Senate debated when human life begins. A number of senators, supported by vocal factions from the New Right and the Moral Majority, argued that life begins at conception and that the state had an obligation to protect the rights of the unborn if parents seek an abortion. In effect, they were arguing that parents have no choice during pregnancy. They would be required to carry the child to term, even if the unborn child had severe handicaps. The state, presumably acting in the best interest of society and, when necessary, using sanctions, would identify its concern for the child and, by default, its lack of concern for the parents.

What in fact happens when the child is born? Are options available? Do parents have choices? The same senators who argued that parents have no choice have fought against expenditures for the social programs that would support these parents. In theory, they argue the protection of the handicapped child, but in action, this protection would be withdrawn with the child's birth.

One can argue that parents have the choice to care for or to institutionalize the child. But do parents really have a choice if they find that there are no community resources to call upon when the stress becomes unbearable even if institutional care is available? Conversely, do the parents really have a choice if the institution is known to be lacking resources, if care is sporadic, and if their child with handicaps will be left alone? Maybe parents do have a choice in principle, but is the choice meaningful?

Tizard (1966) dealt with this issue 20 years ago:

> In principle, at least, parents of the mentally handicapped have the choice whether to keep a grossly handicapped child at home or to place him in institutional care. It is right that they have this choice, even though it is one which they must find difficult to exercise. . . . Now some experts on mental subnormality believe that parents should always strive to keep a handicapped child at home, irrespective of the family's circumstances. There are others who usually advise hospital care. . . . It is only when both the domiciliary services and the institutional services are as good as we can make them that the choice can remain open. . . . What prevents parents from being able to make a rational choice between the alternatives, is the inadequacy of the services. (p. 6)

Meaningful choice, then, implies choice from a range of appropriate alternatives. If the choice is home care, adequate support services should be available for the person with handicaps and other family members. If the choice is institutional care, these facilities should be as good as they possibly can be. Choice also implies that the family and the individual concerned (when possible) are viewed as carrying major responsibility for the decision and that professionals should not impose a course of action even if they believe it to be more appropriate.

Reciprocity and Social Exchange

To what extent can family members interact with social service providers in complementary roles? Can parents of children with mental retardation interact as equals with physicians, teachers, social workers, and others? Even though professionals, by definition, bring expertise that family members do not have, is the idea of partnership possible in the vital function of social care, or will the transactions always create unwarranted dependency?

Pinker (1973) has provided a systematic and extremely useful analysis of this issue. Building on the tradition of Mauss (1954), Titmuss (1971), and Fox and Swazey (1978), he begins with the position that social services are social exchanges in which it is possible to distinguish between categories of givers and receivers. These exchanges, however, tend to be unequal.

In theory, if someone gives us something, we can never make up for it completely, even if we return the equivalent. While the giver gave voluntarily, the receiver returns under a sense of moral or psychological duress. The initial giver experiences a sense of generosity—the receiver a sense of gratitude accompanied by a sense of obligation. While most people prefer a measure of equivalence in social exchanges, instability and inequality always characterize giver-receiver relationships.

Pinker (1973) extends the argument by distinguishing between non–social service and social service transactions. Using the example of borrowing money, he suggests that the borrower experiences dependency toward the lender, but that the dependency is temporary and ends with the payment of the principal and interest on the loan. When one receives social services, however, the dependency is permanent, in that it cannot be repaid with interest.

Moreover, argues Pinker, in attempting to be responsive to individual family differences and needs by providing highly personalized support, the exchange may make the receiver acutely feel his or her dependency. The dilemma is that while more generalized and anonymous support might reduce this perceived dependency, it does so at the risk of being unresponsive to need.

In reviewing the works of anthropologists studying preindustrial or "simple" societies, Pinker concludes that a sense of obligation and reciprocity along kinship lines and among neighbors appeared to permeate these relationships. The issue of dependency, however, did not seem to be as critical, in that interdependency was then more a way of life. Systems of exchange were more likely to have been based on norms of reciprocity between equals.

Pinker continues his argument that in industrial, modern societies, kinship obligations begin and stop within the nuclear family, or at times and under certain conditions, within the modified extended family unit. Moreover, while simpler societies tended to be more egalitarian in that resources were usually not concentrated in a small number of families, more complex societies are characterized by social inequalities and class distinctions.

Where does this argument take us? First, the issue does not seem to be one of dependency, which has existed in all societies, simple preindustrial and complex industrial. Within the former, family members were dependent upon each other and families were dependent upon other families. This interdependency operated at times along kinship lines and at other times among neighbors. Within more complex societies, families no longer functioned within extensive kinship networks and found that mutual aid among neighbors was limited.

If the issue is not dependency, what is it? Pinker (1973) suggests that it is the nature of the dependency—the extent to which the exchange is among people who perceive themselves to be equal or unequal; the degree to which receivers are able to reciprocate. In simple societies, receivers were more likely to believe that they would be able to reciprocate if necessary, and givers gave with this understanding. In complex societies, this reciprocity appears to be more elusive. While neighboring continues to exist (as documented by researchers such as Litwak, 1965, and Litwak & Szeleny, 1969), neighbors do not have the requisite resources, including goods, services, specialized knowledge, and time that most families caring for children with severe retardation require. Given this, modern societies, in theory, created social institutions (e.g., the school to share the education of children with the family, the hospital to share in the care of the sick, the social services to share in meeting the social and economic needs of family members).

In practice, however, modern societies have not developed mechanisms to share these caring functions for all who might benefit. Supportive services are withheld from families when they themselves provide care and are given when the families are unable or unwilling to provide care. This assumes an either/or system—either family care or care by the welfare state.

The evidence clearly demonstrates that families with children with severe retardation benefit society when they themselves provide care. Institutionalization is thus averted or delayed. The amount of social care provided by families far exceeds that undertaken by the state. While it is impossible to assign a monetary value to this care, the public cost involved if the state were to become the primary caring institution would undoubtedly be of staggering proportions.

If the evidence demonstrated that families are actually institutionalizing their children with severe retardation at higher rates, that they are unwilling to provide care because supportive services are unavailable at the required scale, it is likely that the state would intervene and increase the level of expenditures for support services. This shift would be defended on grounds of economic rationality. In preventing more costly institutional care, savings would be effected.

If families are to be supported and are to continue as capable caregivers, principles other than economic rationality are called for. These principles, however, would not entail retrenchment, which would only compound the issue by suggesting that reduced support is in the best interest of the family. The state needs to enter into a partnership with families caring for children with severe retardation—a relationship that begins with the recognition that families are providing extraordinary amounts of care. If this were to occur, exchanges would be more egalitarian between families and professionals— and interdependency rather than dependency would be the organizing principle.

CONCLUSION

I suggested earlier that Rawls's notion of the "veil of ignorance" was a useful way to rethink the principles necessary to organize a responsive and supportive social welfare system for parents with children who have handicaps. It is useful because it helps create an environment in which each of us would anticipate the worst and would therefore support principles that would benefit us if we were to have a child with severe handicaps. These needed principles include meaningful choice, reciprocity, and interdependency.

The use of Rawls's formulation, however, may have limitations in that the idea is grounded in the notion of a social contract. Moreover, contractual thinking is a part of our history. Beginning with the American Revolution, we have emphasized the *rights* of people. This response was articulated initially in the Constitution and the Bill of Rights and has become the major emphasis in our approach to social policy. Recent examples of this include:

The landmark 1954 Supreme Court decision (*Brown v. Board of Education*) guaranteeing blacks and other minorities educational rights;

Civil rights legislation beginning in the 1960s, guaranteeing voting rights, nondiscriminatory hiring practices, and so forth;

The rights of persons with mental illness to treatment *if* they are patients in institutions; and

PL 94-142, which guarantees the person with retardation access to the public school system.

Given our history, a contract-and-rights emphasis is understandable. The Revolution was sparked, in part, because of oppressive measures introduced by the British government—measures that infringed on the rights of citizens. Rothman (1978) points out that most of the "rights" expressed in the Bill of Rights are written as negative statements (e.g., "Congress shall make no law . . . .", "No person . . . shall be compelled . . . .") and suggests that this preoccupation with rights grew out of a profound mistrust of government.

The contract-and-rights approach, however, assumes an adversarial society, one in which people are in competition. Lowi (1969) describes this as "interest group liberalism." Furthermore, in emphasizing rights, one begins with the position that some groups are being treated unfairly or unequally by others, whether these "others" are institutions, such as government or educational systems, or individuals, such as employers or landlords. Policy instruments, then, include laws, regulations, and sanctions intended to coerce compliance. The results, however, more often than not end up being divisive, and the sense of community is weakened.

Rothman (1978) argues that an expansion of rights only responds to a part of any problem, in that it does not address the equally important issue of needs: "imbalances in economic and social power, in inherited physical constitutions, that demand redress. . . . To this end advocates of the liberty model (rights) are far more comfortable with an adversarial approach, an open admission of conflict of interest, than with equality with its presumption of harmony of interests'' (p. 92). Can we as a society continue to recognize and respect rights and ignore needs? What is the value of granting people rights to inadequate or nonexistent resources?

The principles of meaningful choice, reciprocity, and interdependence are better served by balancing our preoccupation with contract and rights with an emphasis on need. Concern with need is in the tradition of Tawney (1964), who argued for justice, of Marshall (1967), who suggested that citizenship be the basis for social policy, and of Titmuss (1971), who argued for and demonstrated the societal value of altruism with its basis in shared common need and responsibility. Exploration and development of these principles and traditions should be at the top of the research agenda for ethics and mental retardation.

REFERENCES

Abramowicz, H., & Richardson, S. (1970). Epidemiology of severe mental retardation in children: Community studies. *American Journal of Mental Deficiency, 80,* 18–39.

Aldrich, F., Holliday, A., Colwell, D., Johnson, B., Smith, E., & Sharpley, R. (1971). The Mental Retardation Service Delivery System Project: A survey of mental retardation service usage and needs among families with retarded children in selected areas of Washington State. *Research Report* (Vol. 1). Olympia, WA: Office of Research.

Bayley, M. (1973). *Mental handicap and community care.* London: Routledge & Kegan Paul.

Bone, M., Spain, B., & Martin, F. (1972). *Plans and provisions for the mentally handicapped.* London: Allen & Unwin.

California Department of Mental Hygiene. (1975). *Annual mental retardation census tabulations: 1970–1974.* Sacramento: Author.

Cohen, P. (1962). The impact of the handicapped child in the family. *Social Casework, 43,* 137–142.

Coll, B. (1973). *Perspectives in public welfare.* Washington, DC: U.S. Department of Health, Education & Welfare.

Conley, R. (1973). *The economics of mental retardation.* Baltimore: Johns Hopkins University Press.

Conroy, J., & Derr, K. (1971). *Survey and analysis of the habilitation and rehabilitation status of the mentally retarded with associated handicapping conditions.* Washington, DC: U.S. Department of Health, Education & Welfare.

Dunlap, W. (1976). Services for families of the severely disabled. *Social Work, 21,* 220–223.

Farber, B. (1959). Effects of a severely mentally retarded child on family integration. *Monographs of the Society for Research in Child Development, 19.*

Farber, B. (1960). Family organization and Crisis: Maintenance of integration in the family with a severely mentally retarded child. *Monographs of the Society for Research in Child Development, 25.*

Farber, B. (1975). Family adaptations to severely mentally retarded children. In M. Begab and S. Richardson (Eds.), *The mentally retarded and society: A social science perspective.* Baltimore: University Park Press.

Farber, B., & Ryckman, J. (1965). Effects of severely mentally retarded children on family relations, *Mental Retardation Abstracts, 2,* 1–17.

Featherstone, J. (1979). Family matters. *Harvard Educational Review, 49,* 20–52.

Fowle, C. (1968). The effects of the severely mentally retarded child on his family. *American Journal of Mental Deficiency, 73,* 468–473.

Fox, R., & Swazey, J. (1978). *The courage to fail.* Chicago: University of Chicago Press.

Gottleib, J. (1975). Public, peer, and professional attitudes towards mentally retarded persons. In M. Begab and S. Richardson (Eds.), *The mentally retarded and society: A social science perspective.* Baltimore: University Park Press.

Graliker, B., Koch, R., & Handerson, R. (1965). A study of factors influencing placement of retarded children in a state residential institution." *American Journal of Mental Deficiency, 69,* 553–559.

Hewett, S. (1972). *The family and the handicapped child.* London: Allen & Unwin.

Hobbs, N. (1964). A comparison of institutionalized and noninstitutionalized mentally retarded. *American Journal of Mental Deficiency, 69,* 206–210.

Holt, K. (1958). The home care of the severely retarded child. *Pediatrics, 22,* 746–755.

Justice, R., Bradley, J., & O'Connor, G. (1971). Foster family care for the retarded: Management concerns of the caretaker. *Mental Retardation, 9,* 12–15.

Kershaw, J. (1965). The handicapped child and his family. *Public Health, 80,* 18–26.

Kushlick, A. (1964). The prevalence of recognized mental subnormality of IQ under 50 among children in the south of England with reference to the demand for places for residential care. *Proceedings of the International Copenhagen Congress on the Scientific Study of Mental Retardation.*

Litwak, E. (1965). Extended kin relations in an industrial democratic society. In E. Shanas and G. Streib (Eds.), *Social structure and the family.* Englewood Cliffs, NJ: Prentice-Hall.

Litwak, E., & Szeleny, I. (1969). Primary group structures and their families: Kin, neighbors, and friends. *American Sociological Review, 34,* 465–481.

Lowi, T. (1969). *The end of liberalism: Ideology, policy, and the crisis of public authority.* New York: W. W. Norton & Co.

Marshall, T.H. (1967). *Social policy.* London: Hutchison University Library.

Mauss, M. (1954). *The gift.* London: Allen & Unwin.

Moncreiff, J. (1966). *Mental subnormality in London: A survey of community care.* London: Political and Economic Planning.

Moroney, R. (1980). *Families, social services and social policy* (DHHS Publication No. ADM80-846). Washington, DC: U.S. Government Printing Office.

Olshansky, S. (1962). Chronic sorrow: A response to having a mentally defective child. *Social Casework, 43,* 191–194.

Peck, J., & Stephens, W. (1960). A study of the relationships between the attitudes and behaviors of parents and that of their mentally defective child. *American Journal of Mental Deficiency, 839.*

Pinker, R. (1973). *Social theory and social policy.* London: Heinemann Educational Books.

Rawls, J. (1971). *A theory of justice.* Cambridge, MA: Harvard University Press.

Reid, E. (1958). Helping children of handicapped children. *Children, 1,* 15–19.

Rothman, D. (1978). The state as parent. In W. Gaylin (Ed.), *Doing good: The limits of benevolence*. New York: Pantheon Books.

Scheerenberger, R. (1976). *Public residential services for the mentally retarded*. Washington, DC: National Association of Superintendents of Public Residential Facilities for the Mentally Retarded.

Schottland, C. (1967). *The social security program in the United States*. New York: Appleton-Century-Crofts.

Tarjan, G. (1958). The natural history of mental deficiency in a state hospital. 1: Probabilities of release and death by age, intelligence quotients, and diagnosis. *Journal of Diseases of Children, 96,* 64–70.

Tawney, R. (1964). *Equality*. London: Allen & Unwin.

Tew, B., & Laurence, K. (1973). Mothers, brothers, and sisters of patients with spina bifida. *Developmental Medicine and Child Neurology, 15,* 69–76.

Titmuss, R. (1971). *The gift relationship*. London: Allen & Unwin.

Tizard, J. (1966). The integration of the handicapped in society. *Occasional Papers in Social and Economic Administration, No. 1.* London: Edutext Publications.

Tizard, J. (1974). The epidemiology of mental retardation: Implications for research on malnutrition. In L. Hambraeus and B. Vahlquist (Eds.), *Early malnutrition and mental development*. Symposia of the Swedish Nutrition Foundation, No. 12. Uppsala: Almquist & Wiksell.

Tizard, J., & Grad de Alarcon, J. (1961). *The mentally handicapped and their families: A social survey*. Cambridge, England: Oxford University.

Wolf, L., & Whitehead, P. (1975). The decision to institutionalize retarded children: Comparison of individually matched groups. *Mental Retardation, 13,* 3–7.

Wolfensberger, W. (1967). Counselling the parents of the retarded. In A. Baumeister (Ed.), *Mental Retardation: Appraisal, education and rehabilitation*. Chicago: Aldine.

Response

FAMILY-RESPONSIVE POLICY AND MENTAL RETARDATION

Kathleen V. Hoover-Dempsey

MORONEY HAS DONE A characteristically fine job of bringing data to bear on the analysis of policy development in a critical area of family life. He has outlined clearly our society's persistently paradoxical view of families. This historical course has found us simultaneously valuing families as re-positories of individualism and self-sufficiency, while at the same time pressing in on many of them in ways that deny their ability to be self-sufficient. As he accurately notes, we have tended to substitute for, rather than complement, families. When we have not overtly substituted, we have tended to ignore families. Now, psychologists know that to ignore behavior is often to extinguish it. It is a compliment to the families of many children with severe retardation that societal ignorance of their efforts and contributions has not extinguished their capacity or willingness to care. But our collective ignorance of their efforts—manifested in lack of support, failure to acknowl-edge their contribution to the social good, failure to care about the costs that our ignorance or misunderstanding inflict on self-esteem and spirit—may certainly work to diminish the quality of care that is possible. Insofar as our policy responses to the needs of dependent individuals have ignored their families, we have likely increased, rather than diminished, the stress that attends all parents' efforts to care well for their children.

CRITICAL ISSUES

In working toward the derivation of responsive policies, Moroney suggests several issues of critical importance to the topic. These points of tension have long characterized efforts to craft policies in areas touching on family life. Among the most important are the following:

1. A focus on individual and group *rights,* with the possibilities of adversarial jockeying for advantage that the notion implies, rather than human *needs,* an idea that conveys both concern and vulnerability;
2. A focus on monetary solutions rather than services, trusting—as is our historical tendency—in the ability and propensity of the free market to meet the demands (or "real needs") of individuals and families;
3. A tendency to believe that policy responses involving services, when we permit them, ought to be limited in access to the genuinely dependent and should be held to the minimum time frame necessary to restore the individual's self-sufficient functioning; and
4. A tendency to idealize a collective memory of the family, hazed over with nostalgia and wishes to recreate a more positive day than we have now.

The cumulative effect of these tendencies has been to deny that families often need long-term access to publicly accepted supportive services if they are to care adequately and well for their chronically dependent members.

Over a period of years, several of us at Vanderbilt University's Institute for Public Policy Studies worked to build a framework for analysis and action through which we might develop more responsive public policies for families with young children (Hobbs et al., 1984). We posited the need to work toward the development of a competent and caring society—competent in the skills and abilities brought by each new generation to the tasks of working, problem solving, and evolving in a changing world; and caring in the sense of individual and collective concern for the rights and needs of each citizen to feel worthy and valued. We set these goals for competence and caring within the framework of responsive communities—large communities such as the nation and small communities such as the neighborhood, one's friends, one's town. I suggest that the goals of competence, caring, and community are pertinent also as we consider the needs of families with members who have severe mental retardation.

MEETING NEEDS

I suggest further that the development of ethical and responsive public policy concerning citizens with severe mental retardation is grounded at least in part in efforts to meet the developmental needs of the children, parents, and families involved, and in part in efforts to expand communities' sense of purpose and success in supporting the development of their members. Of course, there may be deep conflicts between the needs of individuals or systems within this cast of characters and, in fact, there usually are. My purpose is not to imply that everyone's needs can be maximized and met; it is rather to suggest that we begin to craft responsive public policy by examining and understanding the needs of all participants and then work with the greatest wisdom we can muster to balance the needs that are critical to the well-being of the individuals and systems involved.

The Needs of the Person with Severe Mental Retardation

Beginning with the needs of the person with severe mental retardation—infant, child, adolescent, adult—we can derive observations from the literature on children's development that I believe apply across the developmental span (see, for example, Bronfenbrenner, 1979; Clarke-Stewart, 1977; Erikson, 1963; Maslow, 1970). Fundamentally, children need to know that they are loved and are a source of joy and satisfaction to those who love them. They need to live in an environment peopled with those who love them—parents, siblings, grandparents, friends, other caregivers. They need access to a store of unconditional positive regard: being loved because they are. And they need caregivers—in or outside the family—who are responsive to them, who come to know their individual capacities, preferences, frustrations, temperament, and delights, and who are able to affirm them as they are and lead them in the development and use of skills. They need, further, an environment that nourishes the growth of trust, a deeply rooted knowledge that their needs will be met. They also need a sense of safety: safety from physical and emotional harm, safety in a predictable and orderly world, which, through its basic order, enables explorations of which they become capable. They need opportunities and support, too, for their autonomy as it develops—support for their ability to create a concept of self. And they need to be treated as individuals; whatever labels they have acquired, even for helpful purposes, need to be taken as information, not as definitions.

Parents' Needs

Parents, I suggest, have at least two dimensions of need, one along which they perform their parenting role and one along which they live their lives as individual adults. Hobbs et al. (1984) postulated that adults need several resources in order to be good parents: time, energy, resources, skill, and knowledge. Parents need *time* to be with their children—time to play, explore, meditate, learn about each other, and come to know each other. They need the *energy* requisite to loving their children, caring for them, and meeting the ever-changing demands of growing people. They need the *resources* to back up their efforts—resources to meet multiple needs, such as money for necessities, trusted others to give care when they cannot, supportive friends to give comfort and advice when needed. They need *skills,* so that the efforts they undertake with their children will meet at least sometimes with success, and will be effective as well as loving. Finally, they need *knowledge,* so that responses to the multiplicity of intense demands and minor needs characterizing all parent-child relationships are laced with the capacity to solve problems, examine needs in perspective, find meanings beneath the surface of behavior, and respond (at least at times) with wisdom. Hobbs et al. suggested in 1984 that *all* parents need these resources. We could assert further that parents of children with mental retardation, who experience extraordinary demands and intensified stresses in the course of raising their children (e.g., Gallagher, Beckman, & Cross, 1983; Lavelle & Keogh, 1980; Paul & Porter, 1981), are especially in need of these resources.

Parents as individual adults need to develop life work that has meaning beyond the meeting of their children's immediate needs. In the usual course of family development, it has been estimated that over half of two parents' life together will be lived without children in the household (Duvall, 1977). This estimate varies across families, of course, but it speaks to the fact that parents' lives are not wholly defined by their children's needs (e.g., Erikson, 1959; Levinson, 1978). Some have suggested, in fact, that the ability to be a good parent is contingent in part upon an individual's ability to be involved in meaningful activity that extends beyond the immediate parenting role (e.g., Knox, 1981). Finally, parents, as is true of children, need to be treated as individuals. One cannot read the Turnbulls' 1978 volume, *Parents Speak Out,* without gaining a deep appreciation for the uniqueness of each writer's experience of parenting and for the uniqueness of their children and families.

The Family's Needs

The family, as a system, has a paramount need to pursue its developmental course. Family development theorists have outlined basic tasks of families and family systems (e.g., Carter & McGoldrick, 1980; Minuchin, 1985). These are defined in part by the presence or absence of children and, during child-present stages, by the changing needs implicit in children's development. The lives of families with children with severe handicaps challenge the bounds of "normal" family development, insofar as such development is seen as resting in part on the movement of child members from dependence to independence. But all families have a need to be treated as normally as possible. Many families—some would argue all—have a need for access to support that will enable their full development through the various stages mandated by the emerging needs of their members.

Family-Society Reciprocity in Meeting Needs

Moroney speaks of reciprocity and obligation between a society, or community, and its members who are the beneficiaries of public support. Reciprocation between society and its families who care for members with severe retardation would seem to occur at several levels. If we can articulate and implement policy that is responsive to the needs of families of children with severe mental retardation, we will likely gain as a society an enriched awareness of the fullness and diversity of human life. We are also likely to gain an experientially based opportunity to conceptualize human development as embracing a continuum of possibilities rather than a dichotomy separating "normal" from "abnormal." We may well acquire also, as individuals and as a community, an awareness of the reality of Rawls's "veil of ignorance" (Rawls, 1971). If there is wisdom to be gained from participating in community, surely it lies, in part, in a deepening awareness of the limits to an individual's ability to control the course of events that impinge on his or her life. It must lie, too, in an intensified sense of the vitality and constancy of the struggle (and I use the word *struggle* positively) to create caring and competent responses to unanticipated people and events in the life of a community.

Moroney points to principles central in the creation of policy that responds more adequately to the needs of families with children with severe mental retardation. His introduction of the idea of universal vulnerability to events that strain self-sufficiency; his emphasis on the importance of an array of services leading to choice; his examination of the notion of reciprocity—all are important. As a nation, we seem to be fixed on the substance and size of the public contribution, inadequate though it may be, to the well-being of individuals with severe handicaps. Moroney's ideas lead us in the direction of articulating and integrating into public consciousness the private contributions to the public good made by families whose everyday life is characterized by the struggles and satisfactions of meeting the chronic, changing, and immediate needs of members with severe handicaps. If we refuse to accept as a matter of social value and public policy that community members with severe handicaps should be disallowed in the first place, or hidden away in the corners of warehouses, it seems incumbent upon us to acknowledge and value their presence among us. Equally, it would seem incumbent upon us to acknowledge and value the contributions and extraordinary efforts of their families who work to meet simultaneously the often disparate needs of their children, themselves, and their society.

REFERENCES

Bronfenbrenner, U. (1979). *The ecology of human development.* Cambridge, MA: Harvard University Press.

Carter, B., & McGoldrick, M. (Eds.). (1980). *The family life cycle.* New York: Cardner.

Clarke-Stewart, A. (1977). *Child care in the family: A review of research and some propositions for policy.* New York: Academic Press.

Duvall, E.M. (1977). *Marriage and family development.* New York: Harper & Row.

Erikson, E.H. (1959). *Identity and the life cycle.* New York: W. W. Norton & Co.

Erikson, E.H. (1963). *Childhood and society.* New York: W. W. Norton & Co.

Gallagher, J.J., Beckman, P., & Cross, A.H. (1983). Families of handicapped children: Sources of stress and its amelioration. *Exceptional Children, 50,* 10–19.

Hobbs, N., Dokecki, P.R., Hoover-Dempsey, K.V., Moroney, R.N., Shayne, M.W., & Weeks, K.H. (1984). *Strengthening families*. San Francisco: Jossey-Bass.

Knox, L.L. (1981). *Parents are people too*. New York: Prentice-Hall.

Lavelle, N., & Keogh, B.K. (1980). Expectations and attributions of parents of handicapped children. In J.J. Gallagher (Ed.), *New directions for exceptional children: Parents and families of handicapped children* (pp. 1–27). San Francisco: Jossey-Bass.

Levinson, D.J. (1978). *The seasons of a man's life*. New York: Alfred A. Knopf.

Maslow, A.H. (1970). *Motivation and personality*. New York: Harper & Row.

Minuchin, P. (1985). Families and individual development: Provocations from the field of family therapy. *Child Development, 56*, 289–302.

Paul, J.L., & Porter, P.B. (1981). Parents of handicapped children. In J.L. Paul (Ed.), *Understanding and working with parents of children with special needs* (pp. 1–22). New York: Holt, Rinehart & Winston.

Rawls, J. (1971). *A theory of justice*. Cambridge, MA: Harvard University Press.

Turnbull, A.P., & Turnbull, H.R. (Eds.). (1978). *Parents speak out: Views from the other side of the two-way mirror*. Columbus, OH: Charles E. Merrill Publishing Co.

Chapter 11

PERSONS WITH SEVERE MENTAL RETARDATION AND THE LIMITS OF GUARDIAN DECISION MAKING

Robert M. Veatch

IN 1971, THE KENNEDY FOUNDATION sponsored a conference in Washington, D.C., at which the first Baby Doe–type case was presented. Since that time it has been apparent that the single most complex ethical case involving life-or-death decisions involves a group of patients that includes many who have severe retardation. Among the most difficult patients to gain ethical clarity about are those who need major medical interventions, interventions that, if provided, save the patient's life but which, if omitted, result in the patient's death. Of these patients the special group that presents the *most* perplexing problems includes those in which the patient has never been competent to express any wishes about such care. Thus it is not surprising that the Baby Doe cases finally have emerged as the most controversial of medical treatment decisions. They all involve patients who obviously cannot participate in their own treatment decisions, and they involve life-threatening conditions: duodenal atresias, tracheo-esophogeal fistulas, spina bifida, extremely low birth weights, and the like. Without the treatments the babies will die; with them they will live, but live lives that some people apparently consider not worth living.

In order to establish a research agenda for coping with the questions raised by such cases, it is critical to understand exactly what the ethical problems are and, in particular, what role, if any, the guardians of these patients ought to play in the choices. I shall attempt to construct a research agenda for dealing with these problems by starting with three assumptions.

The first assumption is that infants with severe retardation are not competent to make their own treatment choices, so someone else must make them for them. The position that no one should have the authority to make any choices is obscurantist confusion. It would lead to the babies' inevitable death. It would mean no babies would ever be treated. The only questions that apply are what standard should be used in making the choices and who should be vested with that authority. Thus my second assumption is that the presumed standard for the decision maker is that the infant with severe retardation is a human being with moral standing exactly the same as any other human being. Just as for any other human being, we can assume that the patient's best interest must be served. That is the standard for decisions for persons with retardation, just as it is for any other incompetent patient.

Finally, my third assumption is that the family is such an important institution in our society that the parents must be the presumed decision maker for the child with severe retardation, just as they are for any other children. Although surely there are cases where the parents eventually will have to be removed from that responsibility, the presumption of parental decision making is the only way to begin without radically disrupting the family unit. Moreover, while there may be extreme cases when concerns other than the best interest of the patient must be taken into account, patient interest is the only reasonable way to begin.

It is crucial to distinguish the decision-making responsibilities of two different types of guardians or agents for incompetent patients. One group—including parents, other family members, and those designated by adult patients while competent—can be referred to as "bonded guardians." They have some preexisting bond with the patient that establishes responsibility that is quite different from an ordinary stranger. Bonded guardians may be contrasted with "nonbonded" or "stranger" guardians, such as those who might be appointed by a court when no bonded guardian is available.

Essential to creating a research agenda for establishing limits on guardian decisions for persons with severe retardation is the recognition that these two types of guardians have different responsibilities. In particular, while both types must strive to promote the best interest of the patient, the bonded guardian must have a broader range of discretion in determining what the best interest is. The most important issues for research, I shall argue, stem from a recognition that these bonded guardians must be given limited discretion in choosing the best interest of their wards, while nonbonded guardians should have virtually no discretion.

WHAT WE CAN LEARN FROM
COMPETENT AND FORMERLY COMPETENT PATIENTS

Before we could do serious ethical work on the most difficult cases, our society required a period of debate and clarification pertaining to simpler cases involving competent patients and formerly competent patients who expressed their wishes while competent.

Competent Patients

In the early 1970s many of the most critical cases involved adult patients with no manifest signs of incompetency—for example, adult Jehovah's Witnesses trying to refuse lifesaving blood transfusions. Some people argued that both as a matter of law and a matter of ethics, treatment should be forced upon such patients. It was so argued because life was precious, even sacred, or because there was a duty to live that generated a professional duty to save life even in the face of expressed wishes grounded in religious or ethical objections to treatment.

During that period a substantial consensus emerged that, at least as a matter of law, the competent patient's right of refusal took precedence over any alleged state interest in forcing lifesaving treatment (Cantor, 1973). Further consensus emerged, at least among most groups, that there was also an ethical duty to respect such wishes (even if others considered the refusal motivated by ethically unacceptable concerns). The moral foundation for respecting this refusal usually stems from the ethical principle of autonomy. A right of self-determination flows from the principle that persons are autonomous agents whose considered judgments deserve respect. The Catholic church, for example, has generally acknowledged the right of competent patients to refuse treatment even in cases where the refusal itself is not ethically justifiable (United States Catholic Conference, 1971).

More important for our task of establishing a research agenda for the limits of guardian decision making for the case of the person with severe retardation, there has also been substantial consensus on the criteria for making an ethically justifiable refusal. Ethicists (Ramsey, 1970; Veatch, 1976), medical professional groups (Ad Hoc Committee on Medical Ethics, 1984; American Medical Association, 1984), and public policy bodies (President's Commission, 1983) all now agree (although the professional bodies are not nearly so precise in their language as the other groups) that certain criteria justify nontreatment. While at one time, especially among medical professionals, it was sometimes held that treatments were determined to be expendable on the basis of how complex or how unusual the proposed treatment was, those criteria are now largely rejected (but cf. Ad Hoc Committee on Medical Ethics, 1984, p. 27, where treatments are determined to be expendable on the basis of how unusual they are). Instead, two more patient-centered criteria are used independent of the complexity or unusualness of the intervention. Treatments are justifiably refused by competent patients if the treatments are useless or if they are gravely burdensome.

It is important to realize that both criteria are inherently nonmedical. Determining that a treatment is useless is a judgment that it serves no useful or fitting purpose. That, in turn, requires a set of beliefs and values that cannot be derived from the science of medicine. These beliefs and values must be based on religious, philosophical, and ethical commitments of the individual patient. What is useful for an Orthodox Jewish patient—because it preserves comatose life indefinitely, which is considered a worthwhile purpose—can be useless for the Roman Catholic patient, who considers preserving comatose life of no worthwhile purpose.

Likewise, determining that treatments are gravely burdensome requires ethical, philosophical, or religious judgment. A burden that is bearable for one patient may be excruciating for another, and it is considered ethically supererogatory (or even ethically wrong) to impose grave burden on a human being.

This discussion of the competent patient, of course, only informs us of how patients should choose for themselves. It does, however, make clear that treatments can be justifiably refused and what the criteria are for that refusal.

Formerly Competent Patients

The next step of the analysis is to extend it to formerly competent patients. If the ethical principle of autonomy means anything at all for critically ill patients, it must mean that patients' wishes must be respected. If respect for patient autonomy ceased when the patient lapsed into incompetency, treatment refusal would be meaningless (since virtually every treatment refuser would become incompetent before dying and would then be resuscitated only to be destined to an endless round of karmic treatment refusal and resuscitation cycles.

Most people have similarly concluded that if competent patients have the right of refusal based on uselessness and grave burden, then a formerly competent patient's wishes should similarly be respected. In the case of the formerly competent patient, however, it is important that some agent for the patient be identified who can assure that the patient's wishes will be carried out. This person may be designated by the use of a durable power of attorney (President's Commission, 1983; Veatch, 1976) or in several states now (Arkansas, Florida, Louisiana, New Mexico, North Carolina, Oregon, Virginia) state law designates agents for the formerly competent patient, normally the next of kin if the patient has not designated an agent for this purpose (Society for the Right to Die, 1984).

Often certain questions of the specifics of treatment may arise when the patient is no longer able to comment. Even if a patient has refused all "heroic" or "artificial" or "extraordinary" means or has signed a statement specifying that no "life support machines" are to be used, questions are likely to arise requiring interpretation. Is a feeding tube or an intravenous (IV) tube heroic or artificial or extraordinary? Is it a "life support machine"? These questions have actually arisen in the care of formerly competent patients. If the principle of autonomy applies, then the task should be to determine what the patient would have wanted based on the patient's own beliefs and values. The agent for the patient—the person the patient designated, or the next of kin or, if necessary, a stranger designated by the court or by a hospital—is plausibly given the task of determining what the patient would have wanted. The criterion is now commonly referred to as the substituted judgment test. The agent substitutes his or her judgment while trying to use the patient's own beliefs and values to determine what would have been desired.

There is the problem of a possible difference between bonded and non-bonded guardians. Suppose the agent faces a difficult choice. He or she cannot determine, for example, whether the patient would really have wanted an IV removed, and the patient is in no condition to say. If the guardian is a stranger to the patient, surely he or she must reach the most reasonable conclusion about what the patient would have wanted—based on the patient's own expressed wishes. There is no room for agent discretion to choose anything less than the most reasonable interpretation of the patient's wishes.

Suppose, however, that the patient had designated a close friend for this role—a long-term trusted companion. Suppose further that the friend so designated adopts what does not seem to most objective observers to be the most reasonable interpretation of the patient's wishes? Should bonded agents be given any discretion in interpreting the patient's wishes? Probably they should. If they are given no discretion, they really have no role at all. They can choose, but they must choose the best interpretation. They know the patient better than anyone else, and, in any case, the patient designated them for the decision-making role. Clearly, however, they cannot choose any imaginable interpretation of what the patient would have wanted. Some interpretations are "off the wall," too implausible to be tolerated and to still show respect for the patient. If the patient's wishes, for example, were to continue treatment unless recovery "seemed hopeless" and a designated agent concluded that a 50–50 chance for recovery was "hopeless," such a conclusion would be beyond reason and intervention would be necessary to have the agent removed. Whether 1 chance in 100 is hopeless is debatable, however, and surely the agent should be permitted to make that determination.

But what if the agent for the formerly competent patient is not someone he or she designated, but a family member who assumes the agent role by default as next of kin? If there is any reason to believe that the next of kin had views contrary to the patient, surely he or she should be disqualified, but unless there is such evidence, the person should be given the guardian role as one previously bonded to the patient. He or she, likewise, knows the patient's history, knows what the patient would have wanted. Moreover—and here is the most critical step—as a family member he or she has responsibility to be a special agent for the patient by trying to serve the patient *even if not so designated by the patient*. It is part of what we mean by being a responsible family that we have responsibility one for another. When the now incompetent family member has developed a set of beliefs and values that are his or her own, then the bonded guardian is not only in the best position to know those views, but also has a special responsibility to determine what they are.

But just as the designated agent bonded guardian has a range of discretion for making the critical choices so long as the choice is not beyond reason, so, likewise, the family member bonded guardian who has not been so specially designated has a similar responsibility (so long as he or she in no way violates the views of the patient). The bonded guardian's job is to determine what the patient would have wanted. So long as the bonded guardian makes a decision that is within reason, society should not step in to override the decision. Bonded guardians for formerly competent patients should try to do what the patient would have wanted, but they have considerably more latitude than a nonbonded guardian in deciding what those wishes would be.

THE PERSON WITH SEVERE RETARDATION AND OTHER NEVER-COMPETENT PATIENTS

Persons with severe retardation differ significantly from competent and formerly competent patients, but, in my view, are in no way morally different from any other patients who have never been competent to participate in their own medical decisions. Thus, in order to know how guardian decision making for persons with severe retardation is structured, all we need to know is what the limits of decision making are for any patients who have never been competent.

Although for competent and formerly competent patients the ethical principle governing guardian decisions is the principle of autonomy, that clearly cannot apply to persons with retardation and other never-competent patients. When autonomy is out of the question, the only reasonable thing to do is to substitute the standard of best interest of the patient. For all patients who have never been competent—regardless of whether they have retardation—the moral mandate is to promote the patient's best interest.

Although the standard is different for the never-competent patient, there is no reason to believe that the criteria are any different. As with the competent patient, the proposed treatment intervention is expendable if it is useless or involves grave burden for the patient. To inflict treatment in either of these cases on a person with retardation would be pointless or inhumane. Just as competent patients view useless and gravely burdensome treatments as supererogatory or morally wrong, so, likewise, the decision maker for the incompetent should serve the patient's interest by insisting on treatment unless it is useless or gravely burdensome.

The corollary of that conclusion is that some treatments for persons with severe retardation and other never-competent patients are morally expendable. The uselessness criterion has been recognized in recent Baby Doe policy debate. U.S. Department of Health and Human Services (DHHS) regulations have acknowledged that an infant born with the extreme of mental retardation—the chronically and irreversibly comatose—need not have treatment (DHHS, 1985). It is reasonable to conclude that the treatment is useless. Just as useless treatment extends to the competent patient, so also it is for the incompetent. To inflict treatment in such a case could only be for the benefit of others—for research purposes or for practice by health professionals. The infant with retardation should no more be used as a tool to benefit others than should any other patient. Providing useless treatment is ethically unacceptable.

By the same token, it is reasonable to conclude that treatment that is gravely burdensome to the patient should be withheld because one should not ask a person with severe retardation or an otherwise incompetent patient to bear what competent patients would not bear. The only real problem in both useless and burdensome treatment is deciding on behalf of the incompetent when a treatment is so useless or burdensome that it is expendable.

For persons with severe retardation and other never-competent individuals, someone else must step into the guardian role to attempt to promote the patient's best interest. There is no possibility of deciding on the patient's formerly expressed wishes. It seems reasonable that the logic of guardian decisions should be exactly parallel to that developed in the case of the formerly competent patient, only now instead of asking the guardian to try to determine what the patient would have wanted, one asks the guardian to determine what is in the patient's interest. In fact, when one knows nothing of any idiosyncratic views held by a patient or when none have been developed, it is reasonable to conclude that the patient's best interest is, in fact, what the patient would have wanted. Thus the best interest test for the never-competent person is simply a limiting case of the substituted judgment test.

Just as with the case of the formerly competent patient, if the patient with severe retardation is unfortunate enough to have no family available to play the guardian role, then a nonbonded guardian must be appointed. That nonbonded guardian will have to make the best possible choice based on the best available, objective evidence. If, for example, a court appointed a guardian, that guardian should not automatically assume that continued treatment is in the patient's best interest. On the other hand, if the court-appointed stranger-guardian were to refuse the treatment based on some idiosyncratic beliefs and values of his or her own, surely the society should insist that the guardian be removed in favor of someone who would make the best possible choice about best interest.

The most difficult case arises when parents are available to step into the guardian role. Surely they must try to choose what is best, but just as surely there will be some range of opinions about what is best. The most critical question in the ethics of decision making for the person with severe retardation is whether society should insist that the parents acting as guardians make the best possible decision about what is in their ward's best interest. Should the parent be treated the way the stranger-guardian was, such that any reliance on familial religious or cultural values that leads to anything less than the most reasonable choice will disqualify them?

At first it would appear that the parents should meet this same rigorous standard. To permit anything less is to acknowledge that society is willing to tolerate something slightly less than the best for its citizens with retardation. Yet insisting on the single best course may be unwise. In the case of the stranger-guardian, the courts are already involved, and there is no possible reason why the idiosyncratic views of the guardian should influence the decision. In the case of the bonded guardian, however, there are, as has been shown, good reasons why we might hesitate to get the courts involved when they are not already so involved.

If society insists that the parent as bonded guardian make the best possible choice (as the nonbonded guardian must), then there will have to be some formal review process for every parental decision. Since any parental medical treatment choice has potential life-threatening consequences, if society really insisted on the best choice, the courts would have to review every parental treatment decision. That clearly is unworkable. No one wants that.

There is an even more basic reason why bonded guardians should have some discretion. Families are a fundamental unit of our society. We rely on the family to socialize young ones into a set of beliefs and values. We permit parents a range of discretion in choosing among alternative values—for example, we permit them to choose from alternative schools systems and from among religious groups even though some of those groups hold unusual views on matters such as treatment refusal. No one insists the parents choose the best possible school or religious group. We would be offended at such an intrusion into familial functioning in spite of the fact that the choice can have profound effects on the youngster's development, to the point of being literally a life-or-death choice. Just as the individual has autonomy in choosing the values upon which medical treatment decisions are based, so, by analogy, the family has its own autonomy, which can be called family autonomy.

At the same time, there is a crucial difference. While the individual autonomy of the competent patient is unlimited in medical choices, familial autonomy cannot be. Parents have discretion to choose among competing school systems, but they cannot go too far. In other words, they can choose military or experimental or parochial schools, but they cannot choose no schooling at all. If they do, the state steps in because the parents have exceeded what I shall call the limits of reason. In the case of bonded guardians, there is limited familial autonomy.

This means that parents and other bonded guardians should be permitted to choose among reasonable answers to the question of what treatments are too useless or too burdensome to the patient to be required. They must try to give the best answer, but some range of variation is to be expected. Unless the choice varies beyond reason, the parental choice should be and normally is honored. The alternative is to impose a heavy-handed state and squash the family as an important unit in our society for socializing the child into a set of beliefs and values.

THE BECKER CASE AS AN ILLUSTRATION

This theory of the limits of reasonableness on guardian discretion gives us some room to maneuver in those instances where some discretion is called for, and holds us to the single best course when there is no one involved who has a legitimate claim to deviate from that course. The ultimate test of a theory of guardian responsibility within the limits of reasonableness in the contemporary legal situation is probably whether it can give a plausible account of what has happened in the tragic case of Phillip Becker. In 1978, at the time his case first emerged, Phillip Becker was a 12-year-old boy with Down syndrome and a serious cardiac defect (a ventricular septal defect). When a cardiac catherization to explore the feasibility of surgery for his heart problem was proposed, his parents refused, thus precipitating a court hearing that led to a decision upholding the parental refusal (*Bothman v. Warren B.*, 1980; *In re Phillip B.*, 1979).

In early 1981, an additional judicial procedure led to the appointing of another couple, the Heaths, as Phillip's guardians. They were known to favor diagnostic preparation for surgery. It was argued that they were his "psychological parents" (*Guardianship of Phillip Becker*, 1983).

This case has been interpreted widely by laypersons, some lawyers, philosophers, and physicians as one in which a youngster was originally prohibited by his parents from having potentially lifesaving surgery deemed to be the most reasonable course for one in his condition. The more recent shift of custody from the natural parents to the Heaths, who made clear their commitment to the surgery, is taken as a rejection of the Beckers' position about the surgery refusal.

The case is, however, much more complex than this. The theory of guardian refusal of treatment within the limits of the standard of reasonableness would interpret this case as follows. Since the Beckers were Phillip's natural parents, they would be presumed to be the proper authority to make medical decisions for or against treatment of Phillip until such time as they were shown to be foolish, malicious, or otherwise failing in their responsibility to Phillip.

In the original judicial proceeding, consideration was given to the question of whether the Beckers were negligent in their parental duty by the fact of their decision to refuse surgery, but little attention was devoted to the broader question of whether they were, in fact, the most appropriate ones to function generally as Phillip's parents. Instead, the critical question dealt with the acceptability of the parental decision to refuse intervention.

The Beckers' position was based on complex considerations including expert opinion that the proposed surgery itself had a 5% to 10% mortality rate and that Down syndrome children "face a higher than average risk of postoperative complications" (*In re Phillip B.*, 1979). Without the operation, Phillip's pulmonary function would deteriorate gradually and he could live "20 or more years," while if the surgery were successful he would at best have the life expectancy of a child with Down syndrome, which is estimated to be somewhat less than a normal life expectancy. Other reports surrounding the case, not all of which appeared in the court records, indicated that among the considerations of the Beckers was the fact that they feared that if Phillip outlived them, they would not be able to guarantee that there would be someone to take care of him should the state abandon its present institutional commitment.

According to the notion of guardian refusal within the limits of reasonableness, the critical question facing the original court was not what is the single best possible course for Phillip, but, rather, whether the course chosen by the parents—presuming they were acting in good faith and presuming for the moment they were the most appropriate ones to play the guardian role—was one among possibly several reasonable courses.

While, of course, the court did not use precisely these terms, it did show evidence that it was using such logic. The California Court of Appeals (*In re Phillip B.*, 1979), upholding the trial court, referred to the principle of "parental autonomy," a notion very close to the "limited familial autonomy" developed here. The court said, "Inherent in the preference for parental autonomy is a commitment to diverse lifestyles, including the right of parents to raise their children as they think best." The court did acknowledge that "under the doctrine of *parens patriae,* the state has a right, indeed, a duty to protect children," but went on to state that "it has a serious burden of justification before abridging parental autonomy by substituting its judgment for that of the parents."

A reasonable restating of the court's position is as follows: Assuming the parents are acting in good faith as Phillip's appropriate guardian, their conclusion (that the risks as described to the court were on balance too grave) is a judgment within the realm of reason. The parents' position was that the high mortality risk and the pain of the surgery made the operation "extraordinary," that is, gravely burdensome for Phillip when compared to the benefits. Given the assumptions about the high mortality rate of the procedure, the high complication rate, and the relatively small difference in life expectancy with and without the procedure, the critical question becomes: Is that conclusion tolerable even if it is not the conclusion others would have reached? Certainly the court never said it was the best choice. Apparently, however, the court concluded that Phillip's parents were within reason, and it considered that to be its only task.

How, then, are we to interpret the more recent court decision designating the Heaths as guardians of Phillip? One interpretation is that the court found the Heaths' position in favor of Phillip's surgery a more appropriate position, but there is no evidence to that effect. An alternative is to consider the later deliberations more akin to a straight custody determination with the recognition that whoever appropriately has custody should decide for or against the surgery.

Although it was not emphasized at the time, the Beckers had institutionalized Phillip soon after birth and had had relatively little contact with him since, apparently on the advice of psychologists who recommended against bonding with Phillip. Phillip had for many years resided in a facility in which Mrs. Heath served as a volunteer. Gradually, a close bond emerged between Phillip and the Heath family, so that eventually he spent weekends and holidays with them and began to view them as his parents. Using the novel concept of psychological parent, the court ruled that the Heaths were the appropriate guardians.

Although it is possible to view the custody judgment as one based on the conclusion that the Heaths' judgment in favor of the surgery was more appropriate than the Beckers' against, there is no evidence that that was the basis. There were good independent grounds in favor of the guardianship decision for the Heaths (albeit in part possibly rooted in the tragic and now outdated advice the Beckers received against bonding with Phillip). It is impossible to know if that is the correct interpretation of the court decisions. If, however, it is the correct interpretation, it is impossible to conclude that the first court endorsed the decision against the surgery made by the Beckers as the most appropriate choice or that the second court endorsed the decision in favor of surgery made by the Heaths as the most appropriate choice. One could conclude that the first court found that parents presumed to be functioning appropriately in the role of guardian acting in good faith could, on the basis of the fact presented, decide against the treatment. The first court, not examining in detail the question of the appropriateness of the guardianship, reluctantly acknowledged the Beckers' decision as being within the realm of reason. The second court, closely scrutinizing the guardianship question, reluctantly concluded that the Heaths more appropriately served as guardians. They, by implication, accepted that the decision for surgery was within the realm of reason, just as the decision against it was earlier.

We can, at most, conclude that if the burden of the intervention were as great as presented, then those presumed to be functioning appropriately as guardians are within the realm of reason in refusing it. Some other person established by careful scrutiny to be functioning appropriately as guardian may also reasonably decide in favor of the surgery even in circumstances where, due to the passage of time, the risks of the procedure are even greater and the potential benefits less.

One might legitimately second-guess the 1978 California court for its failure to examine more closely the question of appropriateness of the guardianship. It seems clear, however, that courts should not routinely review the appropriateness of the presumption of parental guardianship in all cases before them. One might also second-guess the 1978 court's conclusion that the Beckers had not exceeded the limits of reasonableness in their original decision. On the other hand, one might argue that the Heaths, given the new facts in which the surgery in 1981 had become much riskier, exceeded the limits of reasonableness by authorizing the surgery. One cannot conclude, however, that either guardian decision was endorsed by the court as the most reasonable action or that anything was resolved other than the matter of guardianship.

MOVING BEYOND THE PATIENT'S BEST INTEREST

Everything that has been said thus far is premised on the assumption that the proper standard to be used in the decision is the best interest of the person with retardation. It is probably best if that assumption is left intact for the normal case. Lurking in the background, however, is serious doubt about that exclusive patient-centered perspective. Pope Pius XII (1958), for example, said that treatments are expendable if they involve a grave burden for oneself *or another*. At some point, one must ask when, if ever, the person with retardation, as a member of the human community, should have his or her interests interwoven with the interests of others.

The question arises in two different ways for guardians. First, guardians may feel a pressure to take into account the burdens on others in society generally—the costs of the care of the person with retardation, the social and economic costs of treatment. For the most part, there are good reasons to exclude this perspective entirely. At least for the parent as bonded-guardian decision maker, it is inhumane both to the person with retardation and to the parents to even hint that the parents should have the welfare of the society on their agenda. Parents have a special duty to serve their wards. If this question ever must arise, and normally it should not, the care-limiting decision must be the responsibility of someone other than those whose first responsibility is the welfare of their children.

Similarly, the question normally should not even arise in the minds of others because, insofar as justice is a criterion for allocating health care, the most needy deserve the highest priority. It is hard to imagine anyone having a higher priority claim than the infant with severe retardation whose health is compromised by having a physical anomaly needing medical attention. Justice might be based on priority to those having special mental or physical needs; the physically compromised infant with severe retardation qualifies on both accounts. Justice might also be based on priority for those who have not yet had the benefits of living their lives; the physically compromised infant with severe retardation qualifies on that account as well.

A subtler problem arises when parents perceive that the welfare of their other children competes with the welfare of the child with retardation. Since the parent is simultaneously the agent responsible for the welfare of both parties, benefiting one might necessarily compromise the other. Often these forced choices are brought about because society has failed to do its part in providing the resources needed to care for the person with retardation. Even then, however, the compromise might have to be made. Little work has been done on the ethics of parental trade-offs of the interests of one child for the welfare of another. Once it has been determined that an intervention would benefit the physically compromised infant with severe retardation, the principle of egalitarian justice would give the infant priority as the one who is the least well off, but we do not yet have a clearly thought-out rationale for when, if ever, exceptions might have to be made.

THE RESEARCH AGENDA

The foregoing model provides a systematic theory of the normative justification for the use of guardians as decision makers for persons with severe retardation and other never-competent patients. It acknowledges the guardian's central role, but at the same time sets limits. In this model the guardian is the presumed decision maker and, as such, should strive for the best interest of the incompetent one. Only in those rare instances where it is suspected that the guardian has exceeded the limits of reason would one turn to the courts to determine whether custody should be taken of the person with retardation in order to avoid serious infringements on the patient's welfare. The model holds open the hypothetical possiblity that parents also might have to compromise the welfare of one of their children for that of another and the possibility that society may someday have to decide that justice requires diverting some resources from persons with retardation to those in greater need. For the most part, however, for critical decisions in the care of persons with severe retardation, the guardians will be the presumed decision makers and will make that decision on the basis of what they take to be the best interest of the person with retardation.

This model of the limits of guardian decision making, if accepted as an approximation of the correct decision-making structure, poses a range of researchable questions that will need attention before much further progress can be made. These questions fall into several disciplines. Most important is the distinction between normative philosophical research and empirical research. In many cases it will not even be clear what the correct empirical questions are until some critical normative questions are answered. For example, if one concludes at the normative level that the goal should be to sacrifice the welfare of the person with retardation whenever the aggregate benefits that could come from other uses of the money on more "normal" people are greater, then it would be very important to do the empirical work comparing the benefits of expending resources on persons with retardation and on others. If, however, one concludes that a principle of justice demands that resources go first to the most needy (a position increasingly being selected by those committed to the welfare of the persons with retardation, as well as by virtually all religious ethicists and most secular philosophers), then it would make no difference for policy purposes whether the benefits of expending resources on the more "normal" are greater, and that empirical study would be pointless.

Questions for Normative Research

The first group of normative philosophical questions raised by the model for guardian decision making presented here centers most critically on the concept of the "limits of reasonableness." If it is true that for bonded guardians the critical line is not between the best course and all other courses but between several reasonable courses (some of which may be slightly better than others) and some courses that are beyond reason, then we need to know how to determine where that line is drawn.

The concept is an old one in legal and public policy analysis. It is suggested by the "reasonable person" concept in the informed consent debate and a number of other areas. We need legal and philosophical scholars to review that literature and attempt to determine the implications for using the reasonable person standard for deciding when guardians of persons with retardation have "gone too far."

Closely related is the question of why families should be given a range of limited familial autonomy. Although familial discretion is widely honored in our society, the reasons for granting such discretion vary. Some argue that children are almost like parental property, to be used as parents see fit. Others argue that parental discretion is a prudential policy viewed as a necessary evil in order to give parents an incentive to fulfill their nurturing functions. Still others hold that the family, as a fundamental institution, has a right, even a duty, to transmit familial values and beliefs to offspring. We need to know why families have limited autonomy before we can decide what the reasonable limits are.

A third closely related normative question is whether other bonded guardians—extended family, foster parents, and (in the case of the formerly competent patient) designated agents—have the same basis for discretion, and, if not, what the limits on their discretion might be.

Fourth, we need further normative analysis of the concept of nonbonded guardians and the discretion, if any, that they have.

Another set of questions relates to the notion of "best interest." This analysis has made extensive use of the idea of a *best* choice as contrasted with other reasonable choices. At least in the nonbonded guardian, I have suggested that there is no reason to deviate from the best choice, if we can figure out what that might be. Normative research is needed on that concept. Is the best choice necessarily what a judge or jury determines? If not, on what grounds can we determine what is best? One of the great advantages of the "limits of reasonableness" approach to bonded guardian decision making is that we can finesse the "best-choice" question. We still have to face it, however, when dealing with nonbonded guardians. Moreover, if we are in the role of advising bonded guardians or of being bonded-guardian decision makers ourselves, we will want to know how to get to the best choice, not simply one of the reasonable ones.

Presumably these decisions will rest on the now established criteria of uselessness and grave burden. Each of those criteria in turn generates important researchable problems in normative ethics. For example, if a respirator can be considered useless for preserving the life of a comatose baby even though it would preserve comatose life indefinitely, then uselessness must mean something other than simply "incapable of extending life." We need to know what useless means.

Even more complex is the question of when something becomes a grave burden. There are at least two dimensions to the problem. First we need to know when a burden becomes grave. Second, and more complicated, we need to know if it makes any difference why the intervention leads to a grave burden. Consider three different possibilities. In one case the treatment itself may be burdensome, as, for example, in the case of an infant with a cardiac septal defect that required repeated painful operations. In another case the treatment process may not be painful, but the treatment could lead to a very painful future existence. A child with retardation and with incurable osteoblastic sarcoma may have chemotherapy omitted, not because of the pain of the drug treatment but because of the fact that the pain of the underlying condition will simply be prolonged with the therapy. Does it make any difference whether the grave burden emanates from the treatment or from the underlying condition? Still a third child with retardation may be headed for an unbearably burdensome existence not because of the treatment or the underlying disease. What should happen if it is known with certainty that a child with retardation is destined for gravely burdensome custodial care if treated, but will die peacefully without treatment? This may have been a realistic description of the situation of a child of a poor Staten Island family born in about 1965 who was destined to live in the old Willowbrook.

Some would argue that the child should be treated so that society is forced to face the responsibility of improving its facilities to care for persons with severe retardation and so that at least future children will not have to suffer in archaic institutions. While that is an attractive out, it involves the unattractive moral position that it is appropriate to use a child with retardation for the benefit of others, to make him or her suffer gravely in order to prevent the suffering of others. Does socially caused burden differ from burden caused by either the treatment itself or the underlying disease process?

Finally, there are cases where the retardation itself can cause the calculation of grave burden or uselessness to change. What do we do in light of the emerging Baby Doe principle that underlying handicap cannot be taken into account in deciding treatment? Consider the situation in which a mentally normal child might justifiably have a painful oft-repeated treatment omitted on the grounds that the anticipation of the treatment was unbearable. If it is the anticipation of the treatment rather than the pain of the treatment itself that is burdensome, the child with severe retardation would be in a totally different position with regard to the oft-repeated intervention. If the retardation were severe enough, he or she would be unable to anticipate the treatment, and it would, therefore, be much less burdensome. In such a case, if grave burden is the criterion, two children with medically identical problems would be treated differently; the mentally normal child would be allowed to die because the burden was grave, while the child with severe retardation could be treated because the burden was not as severe. Only by taking handicap into account could one conclude that the child with retardation should be treated while the mentally normal child should not.

In other cases the reverse might be found. The severe retardation might make an intervention burdensome that otherwise would not be. The Saikewicz case in Massachusetts is an example. Although blood transfusions and chemotherapy for a normal 65-year-old leukemia victim would not be gravely burdensome, they would be for a similarly afflicted individual with severe retardation who cannot understand why his friends and longtime caregivers are repeatedly forcing painful needles into him. Much more work is needed on the ways, if any, in which mental handicap can be taken into account in deciding treatment. We want to avoid saying that the child should die simply because he or she is handicapped, but we also want to avoid saying that handicap can never be taken into account.

Questions for Empirical Research

Depending on how the normative questions are answered, some important empirical questions may have to be addressed. For example, we may need to know how the population as a whole, or certain groups within the population, perceive the treatment decisions in a number of classical syndromes such as spina bifida, the gastrointestinal atresias, and low birth weight—all of which are associated with retardation. If a reasonable person standard is adopted for determining which treatment decisions are beyond reason, then empirical research could help clarify what reasonable people would find acceptable.

Such research would face extremely difficult questions about who reasonable people are, but empirical findings could help clarify the situation.

Closely related, it may be important to know how groups differ in their perceptions of which treatment decisions are within reason. For example, we might choose to use hospital ethics committees (or Infant Care Review Committees) as the "gatekeepers" to decide which parental decisions are so unreasonable that the cases should go to court. If we adopted that strategy, it would be important to know what the patterns of opinion were among committee members.

Two problems could emerge. First, if we could establish that committees vary tremendously from one hospital to another, then, at a minimum, cases would go to court from one institution while identical cases would not from another institution. If referring pediatricians began to learn of these patterns, they could control whether nontreatment decisions would be reviewed simply by recommending which hospitals are used.

Second, if we discovered that committee members *on average* differed from other reasonable people about treatment decisions, then the very idea that committees provide appropriate protection for patients with retardation may be challenged. If the committee members on average were more conservative than other reasonable people, then too many cases would be taken to court, to the great detriment of parents, caregivers, and patients. If, on the other hand, they were much more liberal, then too few cases would be taken to court. The committee, which is now often viewed as a protection for the patient with retardation, would, in fact, be a pseudoprotection. There are no data to support the assumption that ethics committee members are typical in their views and no reason to assume that they are.

One final piece of empirical information could be extremely important. Right now we know little about the patterns of parental decision making. We are informed primarily by a small number of cases that reach the courts usually because of some whistle-blower on the professional staff or some outsider who insists on publicizing the issue. It would be valuable to know what the typical patterns of guardian decision making are when persons with retardation are involved. How often do parents make decisions that are suspect? How often do they make choices that would fall outside the "limits of reasonableness"?

It would be even more valuable to know why parental decisions are made that fall outside these bounds. Three radically different kinds of deviant parental choices can be made. One group of parents may be unreasonably malicious—wanting to let a baby die to punish it for the inconvenience it has caused. Another group may be well motivated, but misguided or confused. These cases would include parents who are convinced unreasonably that faith healing will cure the baby, that the proposed treatment will kill the baby, or that what will really be a minor burden is one they consider grave. Finally, some guardians may make unreasonable decisions because of other obligations (such as to other children) that they believe will conflict with responsibilities for the child with retardation. It would be very valuable to know how often each of these types of guardian-decision problems arise.

These empirical questions for a research agenda related to establishing limits of guardian decision making for persons with severe retardation are closely interconnected with the basic questions on the normative research agenda. It seems clear that the guardians—normally the parents—of persons with severe retardation have a crucial roll as the presumed primary decision makers until such time that they are proved to have exceeded the limits of reasonableness. Only by completing the normative and the empirical research agendas will we as a society be able to know when those limits of reasonableness have been exceeded.

REFERENCES

Ad Hoc Committee on Medical Ethics. (1984). *American College of Physicians ethics manual.* Philadelphia: American College of Physicians.

American Medical Association. (1984). *Current opinions of the judicial council of the American Medical Association.* Chicago: Author.

Cantor, Norman L. (1973, Winter). A patient's decision to decline life-saving medical treatment: Bodily integrity versus the preservation of life. Reprinted from *Rutgers Law Review, 26*(2), 228–264.

Guardianship of Phillip Becker, No. 101-981, at 4 (Cal. Super. Ct., Aug. 7, 1981), aff'd 139 Cal. App. 3d 407, 420, 188 Cal. Rptr. 781, 789 (1983).

In re Phillip B., 92 Cal. App. 3d 796, 156 Cal. Rtpr. 48 (1979), *cert. denied sub. nom.* Bothman v. Warren B., 445, U.S. 949 (1980).

Pope Pius XII. (1958). The prolongation of life: An address of Pope Pius XII to an International Congress of Anesthesiologists. *The Pope Speaks, 4,* 393–398.

President's Commission for the Study of Ethical Problems in Medicine and Biomedical and Behavioral Research. (1983). *Deciding to forego life-sustaining treatment: Ethical, medical, and legal issues in treatment decisions.* Washington, DC: U.S. Government Printing Office.

Ramsey, P. (1970). *The patient as person.* New Haven, CT: Yale University Press.

Society for the Right to Die. (1984). Checklist chart of 23 living will laws. New York: Author.

United States Catholic Conference, Department of Health Affairs. (1971). *Ethical and religious directives for Catholic health facilities.* Washington, DC: Author.

U.S. Department of Health and Human Services. (1985, April 15). Child abuse and neglect prevention and treatment program: Final rule: 45 CFR 1340. *Federal Register: Rules and Regulations, 50,* 14888.

Veatch, R.M. (1976). *Death, dying, and the biological revolution.* New Haven, CT: Yale University Press.

Response

DETERMINING THE LIMITS OF REASONABLENESS

Charles E. Scott

VEATCH'S WORK IN THE area of medical treatment for incompetent persons is intended to encourage change in the processes and procedures by which decisions are made in one group of life-threatening situations. He distinguishes among patients according to mental alertness, physical state, and the nature of the patient's social relations. He does not make his distinctions by reference to natural laws, religious beliefs, or metaphysical principles. He defines "best interest," for example, without theological or metaphysical appeal. The term *best interest,* is used by him to refer to a broad range of options that will encourage what is most desirable for a patient under specific circumstances.

Moreover, Veatch's idea of autonomy is designed to allow for many different religions, ideologies, and social differences with regard to the issue of refusing treatment. A person's right to be reasonably different from other persons regarding life and death issues is part of a person's autonomy. A broad social consensus allows both your and my values in relation to continuing or refusing treatment. Both of our perspectives, even though they differ radically, may be taken as reasonable. What is reasonable involves not only how we think and articulate our values but also our feelings and intuitions as well as the bodies of laws, statutes, and social practices that characterize our environment. *Reasonable* as Veatch uses the word names a domain open for argument—legal and professional argument as well as ethical and religious argument. The term *reasonable* does not refer to a transcendental domain of universal truths. For example, one will find reasonable those decisions that one thinks are right on target, or those that could be improved but are allowable, or those that are not too good but are tolerable. Decisions are also reasonable even though they are not tolerable in my group but are in your group, if our society has accepted as allowable both your and my group's way of life. Even a decision that I consider to be wrong by right standards but one that our society will tolerate is reasonable.

So one can say that *reasonable* means arguably plausible, tolerable within a broad social context. A decision is reasonable if it fits in a broad, shifting confederation of laws, legal precedence, professional practices, intuitions, feelings, and beliefs that vaguely define what is minimally tolerable. When one affirms the right of individual autonomy, one is thus accepting, in Veatch's discourse, a broad, loosely defined consensus and a willingness to give up demands for tightly drawn sets of rules and principles. Our society can tolerate a variety of rules and principles even in relation to medical treatment and its refusal.

I wish to emphasize that for Veatch individual autonomy is a social reality and does not indicate an isolated individual. In his discussion of the rights and autonomy of an individual, he consequently underscores the importance of family relations or their absence, as well as of financial situations and familial ties. The move for Veatch from individual decision to familial decision regarding questions of living and dying is thus a natural one within the authority of the principle of autonomy.

A key word for Veatch in relation to decisions regarding incompetent patients is *guardian*. The guardian is one who acts officially for the patient with the life history and the autonomy of the patient uppermost in his or her criteria for decisions. The guardian seeks the patient's "best interests." The guardian is thus a protector of the patient's autonomy in relation to institutional interests expressed by the medical profession and the judiciary. Veatch argues for increased guardian advocacy for patients within the processes that function around incompetent patients. Instead of institutional mediation, at best the *bonds* between the patient and the guardian will function toward making life-death decisions regarding the patient. Veatch, in other words, wants to maximize the importance of positive affection and personal affirmation in the difficult decisions regarding incompetent patients. Such positive bonds will tend to respect the patient's autonomy and will make more likely decisions that are based on affirmation of the individual's autonomy. To the extent that such bonds become functional, we may expect a declining importance in the role played by medical professionals in such situations. Medical professionals increasingly will become advisers to guardians on a par with friends, other advisers, and, perhaps—do we want this?—medical ethicists.

Like Veatch, I believe that research in this area will have to determine the limits of reasonableness in our society. What are the live options, the limits of toleration, the strongly opposed but socially tolerated differences? *The* issue for Veatch's work is how to discover the functioning norms in the absence of a universal, normative idea of human being. For example, what is tolerable within and among the relevant institutional structures? We do not find adequate answers to that kind of question by asking for opinions, and in many cases we will not find relevant information by statistical reports. What norms are built into the various *functions* of different institutions? What role do institutions play regardless of what their participating individuals think? How do the different values of different institutions mix and clash in their social interplays? Such issues have not dominated thought about institutions and social reasonableness in this country. We probably need to examine the work of such people as Michel Foucault, Giles Deluse, and Jacques Derrida, as well as many others who are working now on formulations that will allow us to approach institutions and practices and unearth their values in their structures, functions, and histories. Our task is to learn how to ask the questions necessary for us to answer what constitutes the reasonableness of our society concerning the treatment of incompetent patients.

INDEX